Merry Christmas
2015
Gary & Bonnie

THE GREAT AMERICAN WEST

PURSUING THE AMERICAN DREAM

KENNETH W. RENDELL

Whitman Publishing, LLC
PUBLISHING SINCE 1934
www.whitman.com

The Great American West

www.whitman.com

© 2013 Whitman Publishing, LLC
3101 Clairmont Rd. • Suite G • Atlanta, GA 30329

Correspondence concerning this book may be directed to the publisher, Attn: Great American West, at the address above.

ISBN: 0794833594
Printed in the United States of America

About the cover: The wonderful allegorical scene on the cover embodies for me the Spirit of the West, the Pursuit of the Promised Land. Led by Manifest Destiny, this archetypal American with his family is heading west to new opportunities, to new lives, to the American Dream.

I first saw this scene engraved as the centerpiece of a stock certificate of one of the first transcontinental railroads. This was many decades ago, but like my own American Dream, its image has never faded.

If you enjoy the fascinating history and images in *The Great American West*, you will also enjoy *America's Money, America's Story* (Doty), *Pictures From a Distant Country: Seeing America Through Old Paper Money* (Doty), *World War II: Saving the Reality* (Rendell), *America's Heroes Collector's Vault*, and *The Great War: A World War I Historical Collection* (Dalessandro and Mahan). For a complete catalog of numismatic and historical reference books, supplies, and storage products, visit Whitman Publishing online at www.Whitman.com.

Scan this QR code to browse
Whitman Publishing's full catalog of books.

CONTENTS

FOREWORD

Pursuing the American Dream is an idea and concept unique to America. It has been the guiding hope and inspiration for Americans since the first settlements on the Atlantic Coast. Generations of Americans have believed that they could make their lives better— the American Dream—and the West has always been in people's thoughts as the special place to find new opportunities. The frontier, from the Appalachian Mountains to the Rocky Mountains and the Pacific Coast, offered new chances to realize their dreams. Whether people went west to follow their dreams or just knew that they could, it has been a powerful influence throughout American history. The Promised Land was to the west of wherever you were.

Ken Rendell's concept of history is to open windows into the lives and times of people and see them as they were, along with the events in their period of history as they experienced them. His goal is to make available the thoughts and feelings of the people who were actually there so that today we can have some sense of their experiences. We can never experience their anxieties, but their original letters and diaries bring us as close as possible to them and their lives.

In this book, the pioneers of every generation, pursuing their many different American Dreams, are personally experienced in their own words— writing not retrospectively but in their present about their hopes and realizations. Their words haven't been distilled by historians, and their experiences haven't been copied from one book to another, so the reader isn't separated from them—in fact, the reader is directly linked to them by the reproductions of original letters and documents found here. From the earliest explorers writing about their hopes of riches to Davy Crockett defending his backwoods manners to Jesse James writing about buying a farm and retiring, this book illustrates in its unique way the intimacy of the daily life and dreams of those who over hundreds of years have defined America. Ken Rendell's collection is their story, and this book puts their letters in the reader's hands, their lives in the reader's mind, and their dreams in the reader's heart.

Alan K. Simpson
U.S. Senate minority leader from Wyoming
Co-chair of the Simpson-Bowles Commission on Debt Reduction

INTRODUCTION

The American Dream is the freedom to change your life from the bonds of your birth and upbringing to the opportunity to be who you can be. It is about self-realization. It is the freedom to make your own destiny, independent of who your ancestors were.

It is about entrepreneurship in all senses—being responsible for yourself and making the most of your abilities and opportunities.

The Western pursuit of the American Dream manifested itself in many ways beginning with the first settlers seeking religious freedom—the Pilgrims and the Quakers—alongside those seeking economic opportunities—the colonists who founded Jamestown in Virginia, and the Spanish in Florida and elsewhere.The pursuit of new economic opportunities drove Western expansion from the Appalachians to the Pacific. New towns on the frontier provided opportunities for everyone, from blacksmiths to merchants to clergymen. The American Dream could be pursued in places where the past was forgotten, previous failures didn't count, and frontiersmen had to prove themselves using individual skills that frequently blended Indian ways with those of the settled areas, which were becoming more distant to the east.

As the rocky soil of New England wore out and crops withered (before crop rotation was understood), the lands of the Ohio and Mississippi river valleys beckoned. As these farmlands in turn produced less, the rich soil of the Willamette Valley in Oregon and many areas of California drew settlers in the 1840s.

The American Dream of the Mormons was to be left alone to pursue their religious beliefs, and their journey to the Valley of the Great Salt Lake is one of the great Western epics.

Gold wasn't just an American dream—but where to find it and how to get there was. Thousands of people went to California in 1849 and the early 1850s and a great many found a new dream—to go back home to their families.

Many dreamed of uniting America, east and west, and the transcontinental railroad was the means to accomplish this. In 1869 its completion united the Atlantic and Pacific oceans, and it rapidly became the way for thousands to emigrate west.

The American Dream was fundamentally about hope: the hope that a better life awaits your initiative, your perseverance, your cleverness, your hard work. If you were born in a tenement in a crowded city, the great expanse of the West awaited you and your ambition. From the days of the Erie Canal and the Ohio River to the railroad, which in the late 1800s could take you to your own 160-acre homestead free for your hard work and enterprise, the American Dream was about having a future.

That's what the American Dream is—hope for the future, and the knowledge that it's yours for your initiative. That is what America is all about.

■ Washington Irving, July 13, 1831. "One of the most striking characteristics of an American is his self dependence. Born to no fortune he knows, from his earliest years, that he has nothing but his own mental and bodily exertions to rely on in the great struggle of existence. This self dependence produces a remarkable quickness and versatility of talent. He turns his mother wit, as the Indian does his knife, to all purposes, and is seldom at a loss. At his first outset in life the world lies before him, like the wilderness of his own country, a trackless waste, through which he must cut his own path; but what would be a region of doubt and despondency to another mind appears to him a land of promise, a region of glorious enterprize tinted with golden hope."

1 EARLY EXPLORATION

Christopher Columbus's discovery of the New World was followed by the arrival of conquistadors—generally former soldiers in the wars that ended in Spain in 1492—whose dreams about America were of a land of gold and, to a much lesser degree, silver. The islands of the Caribbean were soon passed over, and their exploration of Florida (and later the Southwest) was in vain. Central and South America, however, did provide vast mineral wealth, and Mexico City by the mid-16th century became the principal city of New Spain. Beginning during the early 1500s, the conquistadors hastily melted native silver and gold artifacts, and then shipped the resulting crude ingots to Spain, where they were then re-melted and divided into smaller ingots.

1492, October 12..........Christopher Columbus goes ashore in the Bahamas.
1499...............................John Cabot discovers Newfoundland.
1513...............................Ponce de Leon discovers Florida.
1541...............................Hernando de Soto discovers the Mississippi River.
1609...............................Henry Hudson explores the river that now bears his name.

■ This bar was cast from silver artifacts taken from the natives during the conquest of Mexico. It was recovered from a Spanish shipwreck off Grand Bahama Island. The name of the ship taking the treasure to Spain is unknown, but the stamps on the ingot show it to have been cast between 1521 and 1558; we can assume it is most likely from the earlier period because of the crudeness of the bar, which has signs of metals other than silver, and indeed of the source objects themselves, still visible. This ingot weighs 6.9 pounds, measures 9 by 27 by 2 centimeters, and contains two partial tax stamps of King Charles I of Spain (Charles V, the Holy Roman Emperor).

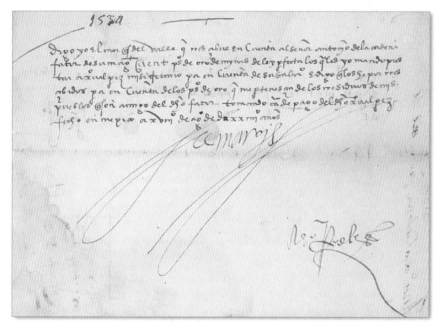

■ Hernando Cortéz, August 18, 1534. The conqueror of the Aztecs and Mexico signed this document—a receipt and payment order for 100 gold pesos—in Mexico City.

William Prescott, in his *History of the Conquest of Mexico*, remarked that

the history of the Conquest . . . is necessarily that of [Hernando] Cortez, who is . . . not merely the soul, but the body, of the

enterprise, present everywhere in person, in the thick of the fight, or in the building of the works, with his sword or with his musket, sometimes leading his soldiers, and sometimes directing his little navy. The negotiations, intrigues, correspondence, are all conducted by him; and like Caesar, he wrote his own Commentaries in the heat of the stirring scenes which form the subject of them. . . . Cortez was not a vulgar conqueror. He did not conquer from the mere ambition of conquest. If he destroyed the ancient capital of the Aztecs, it was to build up a more magnificent capital on its ruins. . . . If he was greedy of gold, like most of the Spanish cavaliers in the New World, it was not to hoard it, nor merely to lavish it in support of a princely establishment, but to secure funds for prosecuting his glorious discoveries.

The French attempts to settle Florida in 1564 were chronicled in Theodor de Bry's *Grand Voyages*, published in 1591. The expedition led by René de Laudonnière founded what is now St. Augustine and was later massacred by the Spanish. The narrative of this expedition was written by artist Jacques le Moyne, who escaped the massacre and managed to return to England. His extraordinary illustrations—all of the Florida Indians, which appear on 42 leaves of this work— rank with the best visual records of American Indians before the 19th century. They show all aspects of native life, including settlements, ceremonies, wars, agriculture, hunting, and preparation of food. They also show scenes of the French settlers and their involvement with the Indians.

Antonio Herrera's *General History of the Vast Continent and Islands of America* was the first edition in English of one of the primary accounts of the early Spanish conquest of the New World. It was originally published in Madrid, 1601 to 1615. Herrera was the official historian to Spain's King Philip II, and was able to examine many documents that were later destroyed, making his work an invaluable primary-research source. He wrote:

The generality of mankind were so far from imagining that there could be any such regions as the West Indies, that it was look'd upon as an extravagant notion to think of any such thing; for it was believed that the land terminated at the Canary Islands and that all beyond them to the westward was sea; and yet some of the ancients gave hints that there were such countrie. . . . The admiral . . . Christopher Columbus had many reasons to believe that

■ Plates from de Bry's *Grand Voyages*.

there were other countries because being a great cosmographer and having much experience in navigation he considered that the heavens being round and moving circularly above the earth that the water compacted together formed a globe or ball of the two elements and at the part discovered was not all the earth but that there was still much undiscovered . . . and ought to be inhabited because God had not created it to lie waste.

Christopher Columbus had negotiated a settlement with Ferdinand and Isabella of Spain as payment for his discoveries, but it did not foresee the extraordinary wealth and colonies that were to develop in coming decades. By 1508, colonists could not be controlled, and Columbus's son, Diego, began a series of lawsuits with Spain to clarify the settlement terms and make them workable. These lawsuits were inherited by Christopher Columbus's grandson, Luis, who in 1536 settled them. He received the

FOR THE
COLLECTOR
AND HISTORIAN

The era of early American exploration is very difficult to collect. It has always been considered an important historical period, and consequently has been collected by institutions for centuries. There never was very much manuscript material created during this period, and today surviving material is extremely rare. The important books that are occasionally available fetch significant prices, and artifacts, except for silver bars, are almost nonexistent.

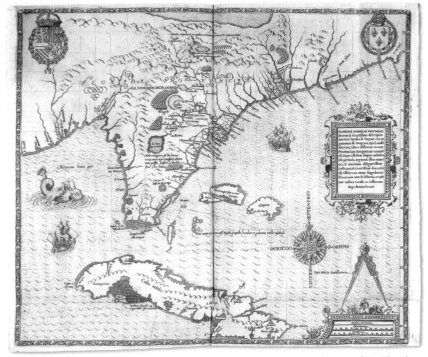

■ This map from de Bry's *Grand Voyages*, 1591, is one of the most elaborate of the Florida peninsula to appear in the 16th century using the names assigned by the French and Spanish.

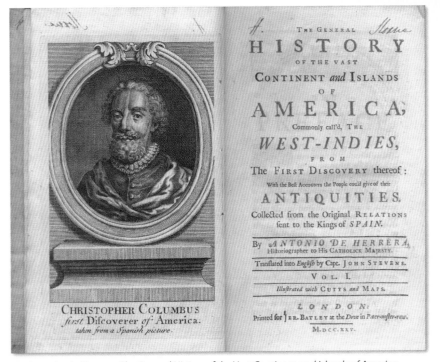

■ Antonio de Herrera, *The General History of the Vast Continent and Islands of America, Commonly Call'd the West Indies, from the First Discovery*, London, 1725–1726.

title of duke of Veragua, the fiefdom of the island of Jamaica, and an annuity of 10,000 ducats.

During the 17th century, Jamaica was gradually colonized under the control of Columbus's heirs, the dukes of Veragua. Eight Spanish families created large plantations on the island, and immigration there was discouraged unless controlled by the Columbus family. By 1650 only 3,000 people, including slaves, inhabited Jamaica.

This peaceful and profitable situation changed abruptly in June 1655, when England invaded the island. The Spanish were ejected by 1658, and the Columbus family lost its most valuable asset.

Not every European in America was seeking only gold or the Christian conversion of native souls. Louis Hennepin wrote of his reasons for traveling to America in *A New Discovery of a Vast Country in America*, published in 1698:

> Men are never weary of pursuing the objects they have in view; such as present them with millions of ravaging qualities, capable to afford 'em both satisfaction and instruction. The wonders they there meet with are so surprising and enchanting (as it were) that they are necessarily engaged to survey the same with all possible exactness in order to satisfy their natural curiosity and inform their minds. . . . They're never weary of making new discoveries. They're indefatigable in rambling through unknown countries and kingdoms . . . not mentioned in history; feasting their minds with the satisfaction of gratifying and enriching the world with something unheard of, that no thought could ever reach before. 'Tis true, such enterprises expose 'em to infinite fatigue and danger; but the hopes they've conceived of contributing thus to the public good, and advancing the glory of God, and at the same time gratifying their natural inclinations, are their chief solace and comfort, encouraging them to suffer all with constancy and pleasure.

■ Christopher Columbus's heir, the duke of Veragua, in this 1671 document presents to the queen of Spain his case for compensation in the loss of the island of Jamaica to the English. Jamaica had been given to Columbus nearly 200 years earlier, by Ferdinand and Isabella, as part of his compensation for his discoveries.

■ Jacques Gravier, June 20, 1699. In this letter, the pioneer missionary to the Ottawas and founder of the Illinois mission writes to his superior in France. Gravier was in Michilimakinac (present-day Michigan).

THE STATE OF THE FRONTIER MISSIONS IN 1699

"It is not hard to inform you of the state of our missions this year," wrote Jesuit missionary Jacques Gravier to his superior in France, in mid-1699.

The flight of those who, not wishing to obey, betook themselves too far . . . off regions has made things here so calm. . . . The absence of the whiskey traders who were the main cause of all that disorder, principally among the troops, who had nothing better to do than to engage in trade . . . has laid to rest all the riotous living for the duration of the winter and the spring. We already notice that our savages are beginning to be much more restrained, more modest in church, and more diligent at prayer than they were before. If there were no French here, or at least if those who came here would engage in commerce only according to the regulations necessary . . . to prevent things from degenerating, our missions would certainly make more progress in the spread of Christianity, and we would have truly Christian churches instead of the empty shells of a religion still in its infancy, which cannot prosper when it has before its eyes so many bad examples, and never seems anybody who is interested in its success, no matter how obligated the government may be to take an interest in it.

The reestablishment of the traders in this area must be prevented at all costs. The reinstallation of the troops, which, far from being necessary, are to the contrary very dangerous, will serve only to disrupt and harm the ordinary commerce of travelers and the advancement of our faith in a manner that will hurt our missions seriously. Ever since they came here, there has been nothing but universal corruption, with which they infected the spirits of our savages . . . resulting from their way of living. All the services they claimed to render to the King can be categorized into four principal occupations.

The first is the establishment and maintenance of a public Tavern for the consumption of spirits where they are forever trading with the savages, in spite of our opposition to it.

The second is to go, on the orders of the commandants, from one outpost to another for the sole purpose of transporting their merchandise and whiskey by means of a sort of Postal Service which they have formed together. . . . In order for it to operate properly, the commandants look the other way to avoid seeing the disorganization and illegal activities all of their solders. . . .

The third is turning therefore it into a place, the proper name of which I'm ashamed to repeat, where women have learned that their bodies can take the place of goods and that this merchandise is worth more than beaver pelts. The result is that at present it is the most usual, most constant, and most popular means of exchange, no matter what is done to discourage its proliferation. All the soldiers allow the women free access to their houses, and from morning until night, they spend the entire day after entire day at the men's firesides, engaging in interviews and acts most appropriate to their commerce. It takes place only at night, the crowds during the day being too big to allow them to work, although it often happens that the soldiers arrange with each other to leave a house vacant so they don't have to wait until night.

The fourth way the soldiers spend their time is gambling in the places where the traders meet. Sometimes things get so involved that, not content with spending all day at it, they stay there all night. And it happens all too frequently that in the heat of the games they forget to keep score, and that increases the disorderly in this. They are so headstrong that the gaming is almost always accompanied by drinking; drunkenness results in quarrels breaking out between them. The quarreling in front of the savages is doubly scandalous; first of all because they see them drunk, and secondly because they see them brawling with each other.

I am not aware of any other occupations besides these. . . . There is no reason to station troops here now, nor is there any reason to reestablish their base here after their recall, unless these kinds of services to the King are deemed necessary.

CHAPTER 2

THE FIRST EASTERN SETTLEMENTS

The Western pursuit of the American dream began to emerge in the 17th century.

By 1610 Spain was at the peak of its power in the New World. France, its main potential rival, had been establishing trading posts in the interior to develop the fur trade and had shown little interest in land. When England began sending expeditions to America in the early 1600s, its interest focused not on the gold and silver sought by the Spanish, nor on the development of trade like the French, but on acquiring land for settlement.

1550..............................St. Augustine, Florida, is settled.
1607, May 13 ....Jamestown, Virginia, is settled by 214 colonists.
1609..............................60 Jamestown settlers survive.
1620, November 9........The *Mayflower* with 103 Pilgrims lands in Massachusetts, having left
                                     England September 6; that winter, 46 would die.
1621..............................The Pilgrims have the first Thanksgiving, inviting 90 Indians; it is prepared
                                     by four women and two girls.
1624–1626.....................New York City (New Amsterdam) is settled by the Dutch.
1634..............................Maryland is settled by Lord Baltimore.
1638..............................Rhode Island is settled by Roger Williams.
1664..............................The English take New York City from the Dutch.
1681..............................William Penn settles Pennsylvania.

Jamestown in Virginia was established in 1607, and by the time of Sir Walter Raleigh's death on the scaffold in 1618, it had a population of 600. Like Massachusetts, the Virginia colony had taken root under the leadership of Captain John Smith. Virginia flourished under both a system of religious freedom (for its inhabitants) and free enterprise. Both colonies traded American resources for English products.

By the end of the 17th century, English colonists from various settlements along the Eastern seaboard had begun a steady migration westward. While the movement from New England was very orderly, resulting in systematically organized new towns, the movement from the South had the more informal flavor of a "real west," with many kinds of groups, small and large, founding new settlements.

Sir Walter Raleigh sponsored three expeditions from 1584 to 1587 to the southern coastal area he named *Virginia*, after England's "Virgin Queen," Elizabeth I. Raleigh's first expedition explored the coast from Florida to North Carolina; in 1585 he sent settlers who founded the colony on Roanoke Island, and later he sent settlers to Virginia.

■ Shown here is a receipt signed by Sir Walter Raleigh to the "Knight Captain of the Isle of Wight" for Raleigh's expenses in housing 100 soldiers on the Isle of Wight "for her Majesty's service in Ireland." After the successful invasion of Ireland, Raleigh was awarded 40,000 acres.

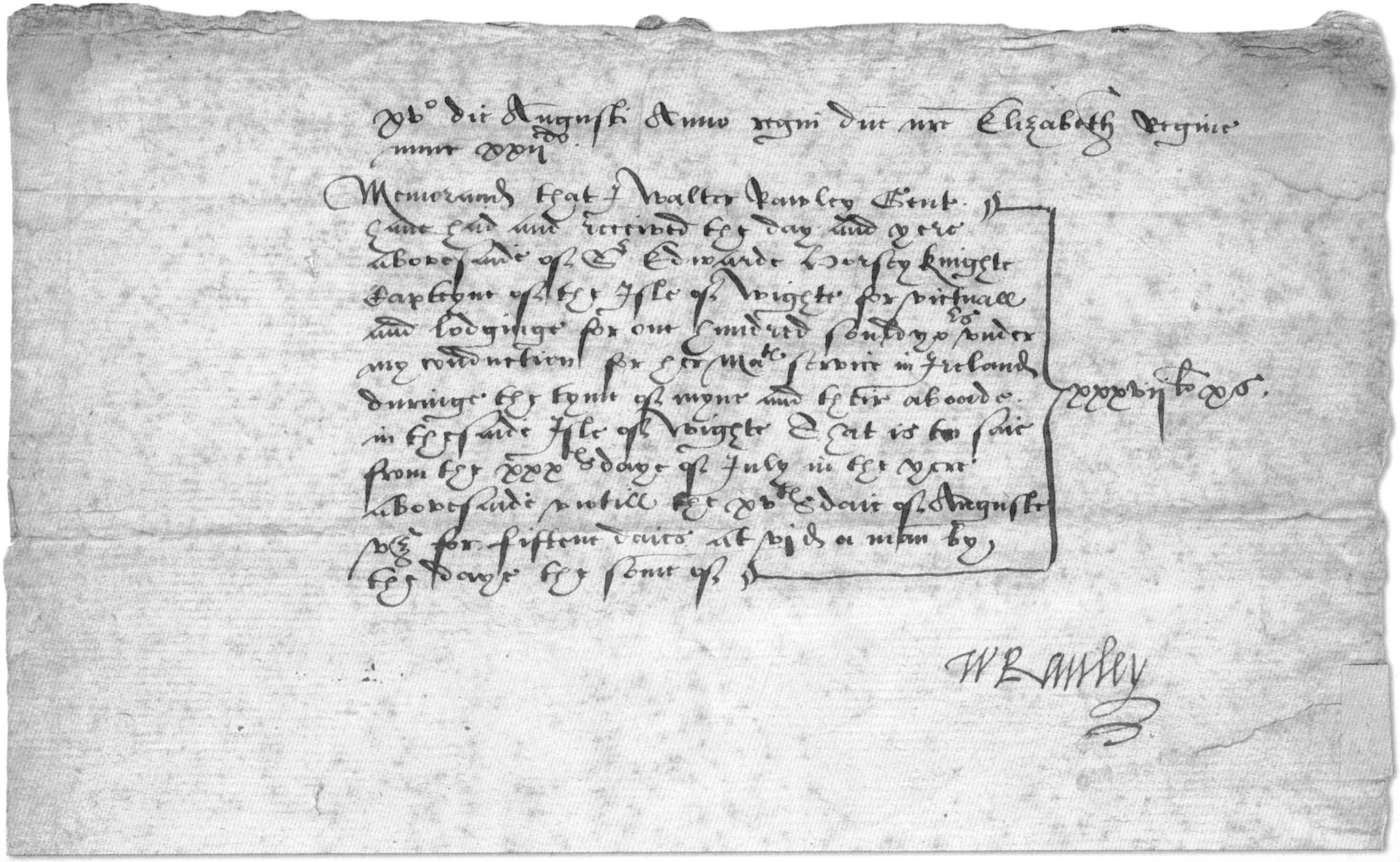

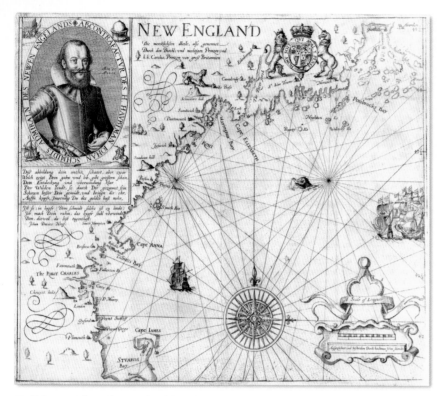

■ This map is from the 1616 book by John Smith that inspired settlers to New England. "Here every man may be master and owner of his owne labor . . . and by industrie quickly grow rich" (*A Description of New England: Or the Observations, and Discoveries, of Captain John Smith*).

John Smith's *A Description of New England* was the English pilgrims' principal guide to their American haven. Based on Smith's two visits to the New England coast in 1614 and 1615, this book did much to encourage later settlement in the region. It preceded by four years the sailing of the *Mayflower*. Smith named Plymouth, and described the place as "an excellent good harbor, good lands, and no want of anything but industrious people." The primary objective of Smith's first voyage, which was financed by a group of London merchants, was to search for whales and gold mines. The first visit was relatively brief but it afforded ample opportunities for trading with the Indians and for collecting much geographical and natural-history information. On his second voyage, in 1615, Smith met with less success. Thwarted by storms and pirates, he was eventually taken prisoner by sailors on a French warship. It was during his captivity that he wrote his *Description of New England*, which was destined to inspire future adventurers with descriptions of the opportunities awaiting them in the region.

■ Deed of land from Paupsunnuck, wife of Panneasum, to John Punchon of Springfield, Massachusetts, May 4, 1663. "The sd Paupsunnuck wife of Pannesun [sic] . . . in consideration of 150 fadam of wampum & some Coates & other thing . . . & sell . . . aforesd tract of land . . . for ever free from any Incumbrance & molestation of any Indian."

The map pictured, from 1616, was based on surveys made by Captain Smith for the Council for New England. Considered the foundation of New England cartography, it stands as the first map to bear the name *New England* (the region was known as North Virginia before the publication of Smith's book). The names of the settlements were changed by Prince Charles from their original Indian names to those used today. The map depicts the area from the present-day Penobscot Bay in Maine to Cape Cod. Smith wrote,

> And of all the foure parts of the world that I have yet seene not inhabited, could I have but meanes to transport a colonie, I would rather live here than any where: and if it did not maintaine it selfe, were wee but once indifferently well fitted, let us starve. ... [H]ere every man may be master and owner of his owne labor and land; or the greatest part in small time. If hee have nothing but his hands, he may set up this trade; and by industrie quickly grow rich; spending but halfe that time wel, which in England we abuse idleness.

FOR THE
COLLECTOR
AND HISTORIAN

Collecting artifacts, manuscripts, and books from the period of the first Eastern settlements is less difficult than acquiring material from America's early exploration, but the availability of such items is still very limited. Some early colonizers, such as William Penn, signed many land grants, but the material of others (for example, Roger Williams, the religious freedom leader who founded Rhode Island) is virtually unique in private ownership. John Smith's books on Virginia and New England are very rare and expensive. Perhaps the least expensive artifacts are the coins of the British and French colonies; they offer a window into these early times for relatively modest sums.

William Bullock, in his 1649 guide for prospective immigrants to Virginia, wrote,

> The principal motive, that drew the author to this work was ... finding many gentlemen have unsettled themselves with a desire to better their fortunes in remote places. ... Men are dispersed abroad in several small numbers at great distances from each other which is very uncomfortable ... whereas if they had been all directed to any one good place they might have been in this time a great and flourishing people: in finding also ... that this country of Virginia is abundantly stored with what is by all men aimed at ... health and wealth so there wants nothing to their happiness ... but good instructions ... I thought that man should take the stranger by the hand and lead him to it showing him not only the richest mines but also how to dig them.

■ The New England shilling, minted in 1652, was the first coin produced in the English New World. Originally the Massachusetts Bay Colony operated on a barter system. The most frequentlyy traded items included dried fish, furs, grains, musket balls, and, after 1627, wampum. The latter were strings of beads made from certain types of shells, circulated as a form of currency among the Indians.
   During this period, civil unrest in England leading to the execution of King Charles I and the defeat of Royalist forces gradually emboldened the New England colonies to become more independent, and in 1652 colonists passed an act establishing their own mint. Ten to fifteen coins from this mint are believed to have survived.

■ Massachusetts Pine Tree shilling, dated 1652, minted some time between 1667 and 1674.

■ A Lord Baltimore sixpence, minted 1658/1659. For decades after Catholics seeking religious freedom first colonized Maryland, tobacco remained its main crop and medium of exchange, with musket balls and gunpowder serving as small change. By requiring every one of Maryland's 5,500 householders and freeman to exchange 60 pounds of tobacco for 10 shillings of the new silver coins, the colony put 2,750 pounds (currency) into circulation. Eventually the coins vanished from circulation and the colony reverted to barter; in 1706 hemp, a staple crop, became legal tender.

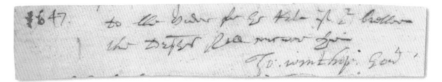

■ John Endicott led a group of colonists who landed at Salem, Massachusetts, in 1628. He served as governor at various times, including the year 1661, when he signed this document.

■ William Penn founded Pennsylvania on Quaker ideals. In this document signed October 28, 1681, he conveys 5,000 acres of land 12 miles north of Newcastle town for the sum of 100 pounds.

■ John Winthrop arrived in Salem in 1630 and, like John Endicott, served as governor of the Massachusetts Bay Colony for many years. He signed this document as governor in 1647.

■ The London Elephant token, 1666–1694, is believed to have been brought to Pennsylvania in 1682 by the Quakers. The origins of this coin are unknown; variations circulated in different colonies.

■ Peter Stuyvesant, May 15, 1664. The administrator of Dutch settlements in America, Stuyvesant forced the colony of New Sweden (present-day Delaware) to surrender and was later forced by the British to surrender New Amsterdam (later renamed *New York*). Four months before that surrender, Stuyvesant confirmed with this document a grant of land to Hendrick Sweerse on Long Island.

■ This Indian Peace medal of King George II, 1757, depicts an Indian and a Quaker sharing a peace pipe. The medal was struck and distributed by a Pennsylvania Quaker group known as the Friendly Association for Regaining and Preserving Peace with the Indians by Pacific Means.

■ Richard Nicolls was the first English governor of New York. In this 1668 document, he reaffirmed the rights of proprietorship for 500 acres of land purchased under the Dutch from Jonas Bronck, who had bought the present-day Bronx from the Indians in 1639.

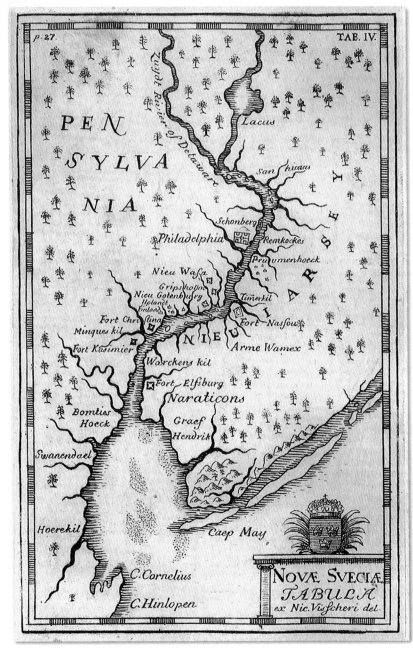

■ This map and illustration are of the Swedish settlement on the Delaware River, from John Campanius Holm's *Account,* published in Stockholm, 1702. The Swedish colony of Fort Christina was established in what is now Wilmington, Delaware, in 1638. After years of rivalry with both the English and the Dutch, the Swedes were driven from their colony by the Dutch in 1655.

■ Benjamin Worsley was English secretary for trade and plantations. In this long and important letter of December 14, 1668, he gives his reasons for fearing the resolution of King Charles II "not only to disowne but to Restraine ye Trade of ye Pirates" of Jamaica, "especially if ye said order should be . . . directed to be executed with Rigour or hastinesse" and he estimates the connivance of the Jamaican government "in ye profit so in ye Guylt of ye said Roving trade." Worsley insists the pirates should not be driven into the French camp and that a deal should be made to keep them loyal.

3 CROSSING THE APPALACHIANS AND SETTLING THE MISSISSIPPI RIVER VALLEY

By the mid-1700s America was dividing into two groups, just as those who first settled America had separated from Europe. Those who lived in the coastal settlements were oriented toward European—specifically English—thinking along class lines, and those living inland bordering the mountains were looking west to realize their dreams of self-betterment. The back-country settlers thought in terms of north-south, not just east-west, because the barriers of the mountains united them with a common interest in fur trading, hunting, fighting Indians, and farming, and they shared a dislike of land titles and boundaries.

1750.............................The Cumberland Gap is discovered.
1778.............................Daniel Boone blazes his Wilderness Road through the Cumberland Gap
        and founds Boonesboro, in what will become Kentucky.
1804.............................Boone is visited by Lewis and Clark setting out on their expedition.
1820.............................Boone dies in Missouri.
1827.............................Davy Crockett is elected to Congress.

They also shared a contempt for those on the East Coast who controlled legislation, especially regarding trade, for their pacifying attitude toward Indians and their legislative action giving vast tracts of land to favored friends.

In response to an Indian uprising, British negotiators offered the Proclamation of 1763, which prohibited settlement west of the crest of the Appalachian Mountains. This was ignored by the back-country settlers, who had no regard for agreements made by England. Land speculators from the East, including George Washington and Benjamin Franklin, ignored it as well.

The settlement of the land over the mountains began midway in the mountain chain, as Daniel Boone led settlers over old hunting trails into Kentucky. The movement through the Cumberland Gap was the greatest westward movement of the time (between 1775 and 1800, it is estimated that 300,000 people "went west" through the gap). During the American Revolution the Indians sided with the British, who could produce manufactured trade goods that the Americans could not. The Westerners fought their own battles, led in the Northwest by George Rogers Clark and in the Southwest by local leaders, and their victories saved the West for the United States in the Revolution's 1783 peace negotiations.

The most imperative task of the new American government was organizing the western lands. The older colonies, such as Virginia, had huge claims on the wilderness, while Maryland claimed nothing. The non-claimant colonies threatened the Union and prevailed. The wilderness would be divided and sold by the federal government under the terms of the Ordinances of 1785 and 1787. The West was open to the pursuit of the American Dream.

Henry Popple's "Map of the British Empire in America" was the best and most famous map of colonial North America issued up to the date of its publication, 1732. The map, which is divided into 20 sections, is on a grand scale and, if assembled, results in a rectangle more than eight feet square. Its coverage extends from the grand banks off Newfoundland to about 10 degrees west of Lake Superior, and from the Great Lakes to the north coast of South America. Several of the sections are illustrated with handsome pictorial insets, including views of New York City, Niagara Falls, Mexico City, and Quebec, and inset maps of Boston, Charlestown, Providence, Bermuda, and several other areas.

Popple produced the map under the auspices of the Lord Commissioners of Trade and Plantations to help settle disputes arising from the rival expansion of British, French, and Spanish colonies. Despite its importance and large scale, the map does contain a number of inaccuracies—reflective of the state of cartography at the time, and all the more noticeable because of its large size.

One of the best descriptions of America at this time appeared in 1797 in Gilbert Imlay's *Description of the Western Territory*, the most informative work on the West at the end of the 18th century. It was entitled "Remarks for the Information of Those Who Wish to Become Settlers" and was written by Benjamin Franklin:

> The governments in America give every assistance to strangers that can be desired from protection, good laws and perfect liberty. Strangers are welcome because there is room enough for them all and therefore the old inhabitants are not jealous of them, the laws protect them sufficiently so that they have no need of the patronage of great men; and everyone will enjoy, in security, the prophets [sic] of his own industry: but if he does not bring a fortune with him he must work and be industrious to live. . . . The government does not hire people to become settlers. Land being cheap . . . so that the property of a hundred acres of very fertile soil may be obtained at an easy rate; hearty young men . . . may easily establish themselves. . . . Multitudes of poor people from England, Ireland, Scotland, and Germany have . . . in a few years become wealthy farmers; who in their own countries where all the lands are fully occupied and the

■ Henry Popple's "A Map of the British Empire in America with the French and Spanish Supplements Adjacent Thereto . . . ," London, 1732.

FOR THE
COLLECTOR
AND HISTORIAN

Collector interest in this area is focused on documents of the leading participants, most of which are rare but occasionally obtainable. Letters of settlers are very rare, but less frequently sought after. Contemporary books are generally available, as are artifacts such as Kentucky rifles, at reasonable prices. It is an interesting area to collect, with almost as many peaks and valleys of rarity and cost as the terrain this material is concerned with.

A MAP
of the BRITISH EMPIRE in
AMERICA
with the FRENCH and SPANISH
SETTLEMENTS adjacent thereto
by Hen. Popple.

wages of labor low could never have emerged from their low position wherein they were born. . . . The increase of inhabitants by natural generation is very rapid in America. . . . Hence there is a continual demand for more artisans of all the necessary and useful kinds to supply those cultivators of the earth with houses and with furniture and with utensils . . . which can not so well be brought from Europe. Tolerable good workmen in any of these mechanic arts are sure to find employ and to be well-paid for their work; there being no restraints preventing strangers from exercising any art they understand, nor any permission necessary. If they are poor they begin first as servants or journeymen; and if they are sober, industrious, and frugal they soon become masters, establish themselves in business, raise families, and become respectable citizens. Persons of moderate fortunes . . . who having a number of children to provide for are desirous of bringing them up to industry and to secure estates for their posterity have opportunities of doing it in America which Europe does not afford.

The establishment of manufacturers has rarely succeeded in America, the country not being yet so ripe as to encourage private persons to set them up; labor being generally . . . too dear and hands difficult to be kept together, everyone desiring to become a master and the cheapness of land inclining many to leave trades for agriculture. Things that are bulky and so small [in] value as not well to bear the expense of freight may often be made cheaper in the country than they can be imported and the manufacturer of such things will be profitable whenever there is a sufficient demand. . . . The government of America does nothing to encourage such projects; the people are by this means not imposed on either by the merchant or mechanic: if the merchant demands too much profit on imported shoes they buy of the shoemaker; and if he has too high of a price they take them of the merchant; thus the two professions are checks to each other. [The] Shoemaker however has on the whole a considerable profit upon his labor in America beyond what he had in Europe as he can add to his price a sum nearly equal to all the expenses of freight and commission . . . and the case is the same with the workmen in every other mechanic art. Hence it is that artisans live better and more easily in America than in Europe.

In the old long settled countries of Europe all arts, trades, professions, farms, etc. are so full that it is difficult for a poor man who has children to place them where they may gain or learn to gain a decent livelihood. The artisans who fear creating future rivals in business refuse to take apprentices but upon conditions of money . . . which the parents are unable to comply with. . . . In America the rapid increase of inhabitants takes away that fear of rivalship and artisans willingly receive apprentices from the hope of profit by their labor during the remainder of the time stipulated after they shall be instructed, hence it is easy for poor families to get their children instructed.

The almost general mediocrity of fortune that prevails in America obliging its people to follow some business for subsistence, those vices that arise generally from idleness are in a great measure prevented. Industry and constant employment are great preservations of the morals and virtue of a nation.

Britain's superintendent of Indian affairs in America, Sir William Johnson, addressed the "brethren and friends of Oshquago" in an undated letter from this era, concerning Indian relations with the French:

I have no news now worth sending you, only what the Senecas & Oneidaes brought me a few days ago, about the French's threat[e]ning to cut of[f] all the Six Nations, which as I am sure you have heard from the Oneidaes. . . . I have often told the Six Nations that the French would some time try to do such a thing, as I know they have it in their Heart altho they speak fair with their Lips. The Oneidaes have asked me & the 2 Mohawk Castles to be ready when called to go to the meeting at Onondaga, where the Belts now are from the Chenundadies, Twightys & other Nations from the Westward. I hope [the] On[on]dagaes or Oneidaes will call y[ou]r People to [the] Meeting and some of every Nation living on Susquahana; if not, I will invite them there myself if I go. There was a great Alarm at Scohare lately, but I did not beli[e]ve a word of it, for I expected if there was any Enemy to come that Way against us, you would let me know it. So I did not mind it; I was angry with the Germans for making such an Alarm.

During the Revolutionary War, George Washington wrote a letter to Brigadier General James Potter, concerning the Indians. "I have recd . . .

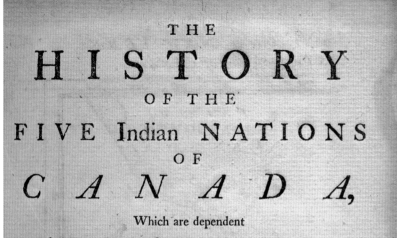

THE

HISTORY

OF THE

FIVE Indian NATIONS

OF

CANADA,

Which are dependent

On the Province of NEW-YORK in AMERICA,

AND

Are the Barrier between the ENGLISH and FRENCH
in that Part of the World.

WITH

Accounts of their Religion, Manners, Customs, Laws, and Forms of
Government ; their several Battles and Treaties with the *European* Nations ; particular Relations of their several Wars with the other *Indians* ;
and a true Account of the present State of our Trade with them.

In which are shewn

The great Advantage of their Trade and Alliance to the *British* Nation,
and the Intrigues and Attempts of the *French* to engage them from us ;
a Subject nearly concerning all our *American* Plantations, and highly
meriting the Consideration of the *British* Nation at this Juncture.

By the Honourable CADWALLADER COLDEN, *Esq;*
One of his Majesty's Counsel, and Surveyor-General of New-York.

To which are added,

Accounts of the several other Nations of *Indians* in *North-America*, their
Numbers, Strength, &c. and the Treaties which have been lately
made with them.   A Work highly entertaining to all, and particularly useful to the Persons who have any Trade or Concern in that Part of
of the World.

LONDON:

Printed for T. OSBORNE, in *Gray's-Inn*.   MDCCXLVII.

your ideas of the kind of War necessary to be carried on against the Savages for the more effectual Security of our Frontier," he wrote, "with your opinion of the most practicable Route of penetrating the Indian Country. Your ideas correspond in a good measure with my own. . . . I have turned my thoughts and taken some measures towards carrying on an expedition against the Indians of the Six Nations . . . the more suddenly a Blow of this kind can be struck especially against the Indians, the more will the weight of it be felt."

Washington's expedition broke the power of the Six Nations and freed the frontier from the horrors of Indian warfare. Secretary of State Thomas Jefferson, writing to General Daniel Smith after the war, in 1791, noted that "The opposition made by Governor Blount [of North Carolina] & yourself to all attempts by citizens of the U.S. to settle within the Indian lines without authority from the General government is approved and should be continued." He looked forward to communications becoming easier once the government set up better lines of postal delivery:

■ These pages are from Cadwallader Colden's *The History of the Five Indian Nations of Canada, Which Are Dependent on the Province of New-York in America, and Are the Barrier Between the English and French in That Part of the World,* published in 1747. For decades, this was the only reliable colonial history of the Iroquois. The book influenced British and American policy throughout the mid- to late 1700s.

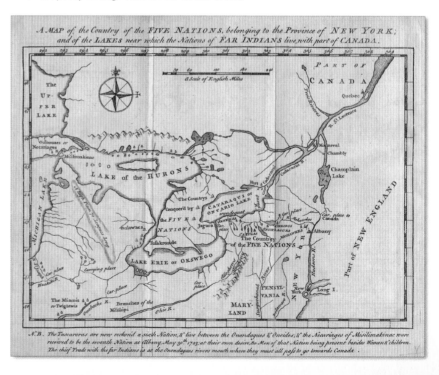

"There being a prospect that Congress, who have now the post office bill before them, will establish a post from Richmond to Stanton, & continue it thence towards the S.W. government a good distance, if not nearly to it, our future correspondence will be more easy, quick & certain."

Frontiersman Daniel Boone first heard about Kentucky from hunters around 1766; in 1769, he and a group of hunters went through the Cumberland Gap and were captured by the Shawnee. After escaping, he spent several years exploring Kentucky. By 1773, land speculators became interested in the region for settlement, and conflict with the Indians, who saw Kentucky as their hunting area, was constant. In 1775 Boone cut the Wilderness Road through Cumberland Gap and founded Boonesboro. Settlers followed him in such huge numbers that they soon overwhelmed the Indians.

In John Filson's *The Discovery, Settlement, and Present State of Kentucky*, 1793, Daniel Boone wrote, "Thus we hold Kentucky, lately an howling wilderness, the habitation of savages and wild beasts, become a fruitful field; this region, so favorably distinguished by nature, now becomes the habitation of civilization. . . . [W]here wretched wigwams stood, the miserable adobes of savages, we behold the foundations of cities laid, that, in all probability, will rival the glory of the greatest upon earth."

George Rogers Clark organized and led frontiersmen in defense against Indian raids in 1776 and 1777. He gained the approval of Virginia's governor, Patrick Henry, for the expedition to conquer the Illinois country, and saved the Kentucky region for the colonies.

Writing in *Travels to the West of the Allegheny Mountains*, 1802, F.A. Michaux noted that

> More than half of those who inhabit the borders of the Ohio, are again the first inhabitants, or as they are called in the United States, the first settlers, a kind of men who cannot settle upon the soil that they have cleared, and who under pretence of finding a better land, a more wholesome country, a greater abundance of game, push forward, incline perpetually towards the most distant points of the American population, and go and settle in the neighborhood of the savage nations, whom they brave even in their own country. . . .
>
> Such were the first inhabitants of Kentucky and Tennessee, of whom there are now remaining but very few. . . . They have emigrated to more remote parts of the country, and formed new settlements. It will be the same with most of those who inhabit the borders of the Ohio.

■ Letter from George Washington to Brigadier General James Potter, March 2, 1779, on "the kind of war necessary to be carried on" against the Indians.

Sir   Philadelphia Dec. 24. 1791.

I have to acknolege the receipt of your favors of Sep. 1. and Octob. 4. together with the report of the Executive proceedings in the South Western government & from March 1. to July 26.

In answer to that part of yours of Sep. 1. on the subject of a seal for the use of that government, I think it extremely proper & necessary, & that one should be provided at public expence.

The opposition made by Governor Blount & yourself to all attempts by citizens of the U.S. to settle within the Indian lines without authority from the general government approved, and should be continued.

There being a prospect that Congress, who have now the post office bill before them, will establish a post from Richmond to Stanton, & continue it thence towards the S.W. government a good distance, if not nearly to it, our future correspondence will be more easy, quick & certain. I am with great esteem Sir

your most obedt.
& most humble servt

Daniel Smith esquire.   Th. Jefferson

■ From Philadelphia Thomas Jefferson wrote this December 24, 1791, letter to General Daniel Smith. Both men discouraged U.S. citizens from settling in Indian territory without government approval.

Dear Sir   Philadelphia July 12. 1792.

The President set out yesterday for Virginia, and I shall follow him tomorrow, and shall not return here till the last of September, consequently shall not again write to you before that date. nothing interesting has occurred since your departure, except some attempts on the part of the state of Vermont to extend their jurisdiction a little closer to the British forts than has hitherto been done. we have received a complaint from mr Hammond on the subject and shall endeavor to keep matters quiet till we see whether there is any hope of their doing us justice voluntarily. — I think we shall have no campaign against the Indians this year. there is some ground of expectations that they will accept of peace, as we ask nothing in return for it. the public papers will be sent you from my office regularly during my absence. I leave this with mr Taylor, not knowing how or when it will be sent. I am with great & sincere esteem Dear Sir

Your most obedt.
& most humble servt

Mr. Pinckney   Th. Jefferson

■ On July 12, 1792, Jefferson wrote to Charles Pinckney, "I think we shall have no campaign against the Indians this year. There is some ground of expectations that they will accept of peace . . . as we ask nothing in return for it."

■ This powder horn, inscribed MY LIBERTY ILE HAVE OR DEATH, 1773, is also carved with a rough sketch of hills, three houses nestled in a valley, and a small compass with an arrow pointing north. Beginning during the French and Indian War and continuing throughout the Revolutionary War, regular soldiers, militiamen, farmers, and others used such horns to hold the black powder that fired their muskets and rifles. Because the horns were a highly visible part of their accouterments, the men would often have them decorated by professionals or would carve them themselves. There were all kinds of designs: some horns show a map of a particular region; others refer to a particular campaign or battle, depict specific locations, or show when and where the owner served in the war. Examples are known commemorating a particular regiment or company, and others refer to a particular ship or naval battle.

■ A Kentucky rifle made by Jonathan Dunmyer, .30 caliber bore, with powder horn, shot pouch, and knives, circa 1850.

■ This early-1800s flintlock pistol is attributed to Peter and Daniel Moll, Allentown, Pennsylvania.

■ The earliest Indian Peace medals of the United States were individually engraved by silversmiths and bear the date of George Washington's inauguration, 1789.

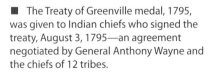

■ An Eastern woodlands frontier jacket, lined with silk and decorated with beadwork, circa 1825–1850.

■ This Athapascan poncho-style shirt was most likely owned by a trapper in the mid-1800s.

■ The second American Indian Peace medal, 1792: George Washington has replaced the female figure.

■ The Treaty of Greenville medal, 1795, was given to Indian chiefs who signed the treaty, August 3, 1795—an agreement negotiated by General Anthony Wayne and the chiefs of 12 tribes.

■ By this January 29, 1780, Land-Office warrant, George Rogers Clark would receive "five hundred & Sixty Acres of Land . . . for recruiting his Battalion & in lieu of the bounty of 750 Dollars & in Consideration of the Sum of two hundred & twenty four pounds."

■ In this 1788 indenture, Daniel Boone transferred 125 acres of land in Kentucky.

■ Letter signed by George Rogers Clark in Louisville, Kentucky, October 15, 1792. "Baptists de Guoin, Chief of the Kaskaskias Tribe of Indians, has ever been a friend to the Whites together with his Tribe."

■ In this April 3, 1821, letter, Andrew Jackson (later elected president of the United States) writes, "July will compel me . . . to set out for . . . Pensacola, to be ready to receive the Floridas, and to organize the governments of thereof." This southern coastal region was taken by the United States from the Spanish; Jackson served as its military governor.

■ President Andrew Jackson comments on the Erie Canal in this June 17, 1827, letter: "I have witnessed with delight the progress of the New York Canals."

THE CANAL THAT OPENED THE WAY WEST

When a canal across New York State was first proposed, Dewitt Clinton (then mayor of New York City) supported the idea. President Thomas Jefferson thought it was a "little short of madness" and the mayor's opponents called the proposal "Clinton's Folly." But when Clinton became governor of New York State in 1817, $7 million in funds for a canal from the Hudson River to the Great Lakes were quickly approved. On July 4, 1817, unskilled workers broke ground in Rome and started west. The Erie Canal (between Albany and Buffalo) opened on October 26, 1825, and was hailed as the greatest engineering marvel in the world. The canal—363 miles long, 40 feet wide, 4 feet deep, with 18 aqueducts

■ Davy Crockett wrote this January 3, 1829, letter from the House of Representatives, to the Honorable James Clark of Kentucky. In it, he defends what some called a rough-and-tumble demeanor.

■ Fortescue Cuming, *Sketches of a Tour to the Western Country . . .*, Pittsburgh, 1810.

and 83 locks—shortened by half the travel time from the East Coast to the gateway to the West (the Great Lakes) and reduced shipping costs by 90 percent.

More than an engineering feat, the Erie Canal proved to be the key that unlocked an enormous series of social and economic changes. Its effect was immediate and dramatic—it opened the only trade route west of the Appalachians, prompted the first great westward migration of American settlers, turned Rochester into the nation's first boomtown, and made New York City the busiest port in the United States. The explosion

of trade was spurred by freight rates from Buffalo to New York of $10 per ton by canal, compared with $100 per ton by road. In 1829, some 3,640 bushels of wheat were transported down the canal from Buffalo. By 1837 this figure increased to 500,000 bushels; four years later it reached one million. In nine years, canal tolls more than recouped the entire cost of construction. Prior to the Erie Canal's building, New York City was the nation's fifth-largest seaport. Within 15 years of its opening, New York was the busiest port in America, moving tonnages greater than those shipped by Boston, Baltimore, and New Orleans combined.

be an account of my first visit to the President of the Nation. . . . I presume Sir that you have a distinct recollection of what passed at the dinner . . . and you will do me the favor to say distinctly, whether the inclosed publication is not false. I would not make this appeal, if it ware not, that, like other men, I have enemies who would take much pleasure in magnifying the plain Rusticity of my manners in to the most unparalleled grossness and indelicacy. I have never enjoyed the advantages which many have abused, but I am proud to hope that your answer will show, that I have never so far prostituted the humble advantages I do enjoy, as to act the part attributed to me.

■ *The Hunter's Shanty in the Adirondaks*, a lithograph by Currier & Ives, 1861, romanticized life in the mountains.

■ An original 13-inch barrel of Kentucky Rifle Gunpowder, circa 1840.

DAVY CROCKETT DEFENDS HIS BACKWOODS MANNERS

Shortly after the opening of Congress on December 3, 1827, the freshman congressman from Tennessee, David "Davy" Crockett, was invited to dinner at the White House. Crockett had already attracted attention in the capital for his backwoods appearance and rough-and-tumble manners, and rumors that he had behaved boorishly in front of President John Quincy Adams were soon circulating among his Whig detractors. When the story found its way into print, Crockett was moved to refute it publicly in a letter to Representative James Clark of Kentucky.

Forbearance Ceases to be a virtue, when it is Construed into an acquiescence in falsehoods or a tame submission to unprovoked insult. I have seen published . . . a Slander . . . purporting to

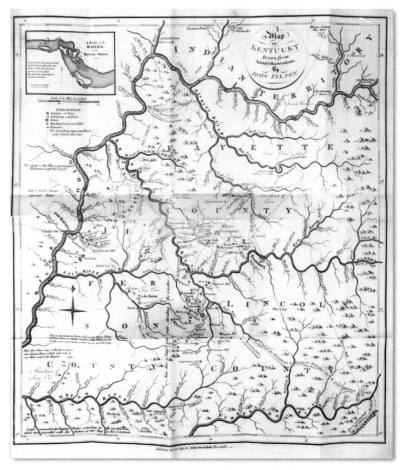

■ The first map of Kentucky is from John Filson's 1793 book *The Discovery, Settlement, and Present State of Kentucky. And an Introduction to the Topography and Natural History of That Rich and Important Country; Also Colonel Daniel Boon's [sic] Narrative of the Wars of Kentucky.*

■ Davy Crockett's almanac, published in 1838, contains the story of Mike Fink, the Ohio boatman—"half horse and half alligator," according to Crockett—and a number of yarns concerning fights with bears, snakes, and wildcats.

■ "Snowy Heron or White Egret," plate 49 (page CCXLII), from *Birds of America, Drawn from Nature*, by J.J. Audubon. The engraved surface of the original measures 22 by 18-3/4 inches (on a page overall measuring 36-1/4 by 24-3/4 inches). This illustration is the only one in *Birds of America* in which Audubon portrayed himself. The artist is at lower right.

■ This circa-1830 manuscript by John James Audubon is entitled "Hospitality [in the Woods]." Probably written while Audubon was in Edinburgh, Scotland, in late 1829 or early 1830, the manuscript was originally published in that city in 1831 as Episode XV of the first volume of *Ornithological Biography*, as the text accompaniment to *Birds of America*. In this episode, Audubon vividly describes an incident of frontier travel in the Kentucky woods where he and a fellow traveler were royally entertained by settlers after having lost their way in a storm. It provides Audubon with the perfect anecdote to illustrate the pure and frank hospitality of the American frontier.

SETTLING THE MISSISSIPPI RIVER VALLEY

Realizing the dreams of Americans to settle the Mississippi River Valley was a lengthy process. The new United States had to solve a number of major problems before it could deal with how to distribute the land and settle the area.

In the early 18th century, Spain owned the west bank of the Mississippi River, and French trading posts occupied much of the land to the east. The French and Indian War, 1755 to 1763, resulted in a treaty that forced out the French. The Treaty of Paris, 1783, which ended the American Revolution, recognized the right of the new United States to these lands but left Britain with seven frontier posts. These outposts enabled the British to both continue the fur trade in what would be American territory, and maintain their relationships with the Indians there. Those relationships acted as a buffer between the U.S. territory and the waterway systems vital to England's fur trade in the West and around the Great Lakes.

■ The French explorer Robert de La Salle led an expedition in 1684 to the Gulf of Mexico coast (in present-day Texas) to found a French colony. The next two years he spent awaiting reinforcements that never came, while internal tensions in the expedition party grew. In the end, La Salle and his men determined to return to Canada via the Mississippi River, but one of the company assassinated La Salle near the Trinity River and the company split up. Some of the survivors reached Canada by way of the Mississippi and Arkansas rivers. Among them was Henri Joutel, who wrote the premier account of the expedition, *Journal Historique de Dernier Voyage Que Feu M. De Lasale Fit Dans le Golfe de Mexique, Pour Trouver L'Embouchure, & Le Cours de la Riviere de Missicipi, Nommee a Present la Riviere de Saint Louis, Qui Traverse le Louisiane . . .*, 1713.

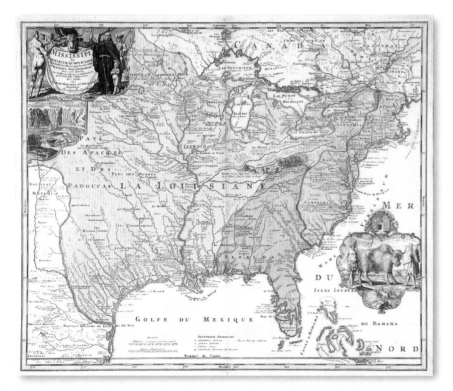

■ Map of the Mississippi Valley (Homann, Nuremburg, 1759–1784), with insets showing Niagara Falls and an Indian family with a buffalo and an opossum.

The Ordinances of 1785 to 1787 established the methods for developing the area and provided that only the government could negotiate treaties with the Indians to obtain land. While various states were claiming huge tracts (for example, Virginia claimed most of the Northwest), settlers were moving into the Mississippi River Valley without regard to land titles or whether the land still belonged to the Indians.

By 1790, settlers were moving north across the Ohio River, and Congress was being pressured by settlers and speculators to acquire lands from the Indians. The extensive forests that covered the present-day states of

Ohio, Indiana, and Illinois were rich in furs, and the Indians had no desire to give up the lands that supported their livelihood.

American frontiersmen firmly believed that the British posts providing arms, ammunition, and other supplies to the Indians incited the attacks on American settlements.

The Indians could be formidable enemies. In the fall of 1791, when General Arthur St. Clair, governor of the Northwest Territory, tried to build forts on the Maumee River to counter British influence, a surprise Indian attack near today's Fort Wayne inflicted more than 900 casualties on his 2,000 men. St. Clair, laid up in his wagon with gout, was hauled to safety, but few other officers survived. News of the defeat struck fear along the frontier, intensifying the clamor for removal of the British.

The Treaty of Greenville, after General Anthony Wayne's victories over several tribes, opened most of the territory to settlement by forcing the Indians to give up much of their land. Other treaties forced other tribes to give up their lands in the Mississippi River Valley, which was about to be overwhelmed with speculators and unscrupulous promoters. The biggest problem confronting the United States—navigation of the Mississippi River—still remained. Negotiations with Spain resulted in the Pinckney Treaty, which gave Americans free navigation of the Mississippi and the right to ship goods through New Orleans for three years free of customs duties.

Suddenly, with three treaties—statesman John Jay's (the Treaty of London of 1794), Greenville, and Pinckney's—the Mississippi River Valley was open . . . until the War of 1812 closed the frontier once more.

During the intervening 17 years, Americans who were crowded into the area east of the mountains exploded into the West. It was the first opportunity they had to go west and pursue their dreams; fertile farming land was selling for $2 to $3 an acre compared to $14 to $50 an acre in New England. Other emigrants wanted to escape the religious establishment, taxes, or the rigid social order. In the Southern states, farm soil was exhausted and yields had declined. This, in addition to the same incentives and pressures motivating Northerners, propelled Southerners to movement. The American Dream was marching westward.

George Washington had sent John Jay to London to negotiate a treaty with Great Britain that would settle issues concerning the western parts of the United States. These issues had been left unresolved in the treaty ending the American Revolution. Jay had been one of the three American commissioners in negotiating that treaty. His first draft of a new treaty was filled with proposals most advantageous to the United States.

■ This extraordinarily important September 1782 letter by John Jay, at the time negotiating the treaty that ended the American Revolution, addresses the French foreign minister's assistant—who had been appointed to mediate the dispute, but in fact was conspiring with England. Jay writes, "I have received . . . your remarks on the Western limits of the United States and a description of the line you Propose as a conciliatory one between Spain and them."

In his manuscript notes (pictured), Jay responded to counterproposals presented by the British foreign secretary, Lord Grenville, on August 30, 1794. Jay headed the manuscript "notes to all of objections to settlements project." It detailed the points the United States and Great Britain had not resolved in a meeting in September 1794.

The first seven (of eighteen) objections Jay noted are

1. In what Capacity are they so to remain? As British Subjects or American Citizens? If the first, a Time to make their Elections shd. be assigned.
2. If His Majesty's Subjects are to pass into the American Territories for the Purpose of Indian Trade, ought not American Citizens to be permitted to pass into His Majesty's Territories for the like Purpose.
3. If the Am[erica]n Indians are to have the Priviledge of trading with Canada, ought not the Canada Indians to be priviledged to trade with the U.S.?
4. If goods for Indian Trade shall be introduced Duty Free by British Traders, how is the introduction of other Goods with them to be prevented? And for this Priviledge, operating a Loss to the Am[erica]n Revenue, what reciprocal Benefit is to be allowed?
6. Why confine the mutual Navigation of the Mississippi to where the same bounds the Territory of the U.S.?
7. Why shd. Perpetual commercial Priviledges be granted to G.B. on the Mississippi etc., when she declines granting perpetual Commercial Priviledges to the U.S. anywhere?

Not everyone found the Indians the only problem. Andrew Chute, a physician, wrote to his sister and brother-in-law from Independence and Westport, Missouri, 1835: "I am living snugly in a log hut in the West. . . . Business of all kinds is very profitable and none more so than the practice of medicine, but physicians are exposed more than all others to the various causes of disease, and the sickness and mortality among them are very great."

Concerning the state of religion among the Indians and other Westerners, he wrote, "The great mass are sunk in the grossest ignorance and indifference to religion. There is certainly a field for Christian effort. . . . It is lamentable to see a population sufficiently large to constitute an entire state . . . almost entirely destitute of moral instruction. . . . Though Sabbath breaking, intemperance, profanity, falsehood, and impurity prevail . . . I never heard one syllable uttered by a preacher against them."

■ The Treaty of Amity, Commerce and Navigation, better known as Jay's Treaty, was signed on November 19, 1794. In this document, John Jay notes his concerns in the negotiations.

FREE NAVIGATION OF THE MISSISSIPPI RIVER

"I wish disagreeable consequences may not result from the contentions respecting the navigation of the River Mississippi," George Washington wrote to the French chargé d'affaires in mid-1785.

> The emigrations to the waters thereof, are astonishingly great; and chiefly of that description of People who are not very subordinate to Law & good Government. Whether the prohibition from the Court of Spain is just or unjust, politic or otherwise; it will be difficult to restrain a people of this class from the enjoyment of natural advantages. [Spain should] enter into such stipulations with Congress as may avert the impending evil, & be mutually advantageous to both Nations.
>
> After the explicit declarations of the Emperor, respecting the Navigation of the Scheldt, and his other demands upon Holland, he will stand I think, upon unfavorable ground; for if he recedes, his foresight & judgment may be arraigned, and if he proceeds, his suit may be involved. But probably I am hazarding sentiments upon a superficial view of things, when it will appear, ultimately, that he has had important objects in view, and has accomplished them.

Washington's letter, expressing his views in favor of the free navigation of the Mississippi River, reflects explicitly on the negotiations that were currently taking place between the Spanish minister, Don Diego de Gardoqui, and John Jay. His support was based on his belief that if "trade would go down the Mississippi as soon as Spain had the wisdom to welcome it, this was an indirect argument for the development of the Potomac.... [Goods] ... could be delivered to the Ohio far more cheaply and more quickly via the Potomac than by the long, long voyage back up the Mississippi against the current" (Douglas S. Freeman, *George Washington*). The issue of free navigation was important to the inhabitants of the interior Mississippi Valley at a time when the river was their main highway of commerce and its mouth was owned by a foreign power. The establishment of the right was an important step in the world wide liberation of commerce. It was first granted by France, which then owned Louisiana, in favor of Great Britain and was a by-product of the territorial settlement at the end of the French and Indian War. ... At the same time France ceded Louisiana to Spain.... During the American Revolution both British subjects and American citizens claimed the right of free navigation and Spain permitted both of them to navigate it for a time—the British until 1779, when Spain went to war with Britain, and the Americans until 1784, when Spain closed the river to all foreigners, mainly in the hope of checking the growth of American settlements in the West. (*Dictionary of American History*)

■ In this June 21, 1785, letter to the French chargé d'affaires, George Washington identifies the free navigation of the Mississippi River as the critical issue in opening the American West.

DEFENDING THE LOUISIANA FRONTIER

The governor of Upper Louisiana, Benjamin Howard, reflected the Western perspective when he wrote to Robert Wickliff from St. Louis on May 26, 1812, discussing at great length his actions

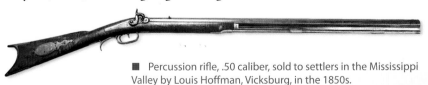

■ Percussion rifle, .50 caliber, sold to settlers in the Mississippi Valley by Louis Hoffman, Vicksburg, in the 1850s.

In another letter to Robert Wickliff, September 5, 1813, Howard wrote, "organizing about 1000 men for an Expedition against the Indians in the neighborhood of Peoria, they have come down and settled at their former village. . . . If I had those men I could have taken high ground with our numerous enemies in this quarter; with my present force, to annoy them partially is all I can expect."

The constant problem of white settlers moving onto Indian lands was a concern of fair-minded Easterners.

> General Arthur St. Clair, the governor of the Northwest Territory, was frequently faced with the issue. He wrote from Cincinnati on July 16, 1796, to General James Wilkinson concerning Zachariah Coxe, who had started an illegal settlement on the Ohio River. It is important to the public interests the settlement made by Coxe, below the mouth of the Cumberland, should be broken up, and that he himself should be made prisoner. . . . Upon the presumption that the Lands, upon which the Settlement is formed, are a part of those allotted to the Chickasaws by the Treaty of Hopewel in 1786 . . . [i]t is declared to be lawful for the military force of the United States to apprehend every person who shall be found in the Indian Country over and beyond the boundary-line between the United States and the Indian Tribes.

■ Julian Dubuque discovered lead deposits on land controlled by the Fox Indians in 1785 and received sole permission to work the mines on the Iowa side of the Mississippi River. He built a smelting furnace and opened a trading post, developing it into a thriving trade with the Indians. He was the first permanent white settler in Iowa. This promissory note was signed by him in 1809, the year before he died and was accorded the burial honors of a chief of the Fox Indians.

for the defences of the frontier. . . . When they hear of the late [miseries] in Indiana, and the deplorable state of the Country, the people running off . . . the Govr. sending his wife away and fortifying his own house. What would have been our situation if no preparations had been made. We have not the strong and intrepid populations of Kentucky to call upon in the moment of difficulty and confusion. Our strength is not great but our plan of defence is settled and now understood by the people. Each man on the frontier is fixed and has made up his mind to make a stand, and altho we may be attacked and injured yet the enemy will feel too, but perhaps I feel more alive on this subject than you.

■ Remington "over and under" pistol, commonly used by riverboat gamblers.

■ A flintlock pistol made by Henry Deringer.

THE IMPRESSIONS OF TRAVELERS VISITING THE UNITED STATES

Laurence Oliphant, in *Minnesota and the Far West*, wrote the following in 1855:

> The impressions of a traveller visiting the United States of America . . . for the first time are so totally unlike those which he has experienced in the course of his rambles in the Old World, that he at once perceives that, in order to the due appreciation of the country he is about to explore, an entire revolution must be effected in those habits of thought and observation in which he has hitherto indulged. . . . Instead of moralising over magnificence in a process of decay, he must here watch resources in a process of development—he must substitute the pleasures of anticipation for those of retrospection—must be more familiar with pecuniary speculations than with historical associations—delight himself rather in statistics than in poetry—visit docks instead of ruins—converse of dollars, and not of antique coins.

The Immigrants Guide to the Western States of America, by John Regan, published in Edinburgh, Scotland, in 1852, begins,

America is the land of freedom, not withstanding her Negro slavery! Freed from the antiquated and absurd traditions of European states which weigh like an incubus upon the energies of their people and in the enjoyment of an unencumbered energy she stands forth the most favored land under the broad heavens. . . . The great immigration field in the Mississippi Valley consisting of the states of Illinois, Iowa, Minnesota, Wisconsin, Michigan and Indiana, embraces a territory 360,000 square miles or three times the extent of Great Britain and Ireland, of surpassing fertility, watered by a system of rivers unequaled in the world. To this fine country would I direct the attention of immigrants. . . . There is all the difference in the world between the American seaboard and the interior in the manners of the people. On the coast the manners of older countries in some measure prevail and a just estimate of the true character of the people can not be formed from that source. . . . In the United States an industrious man has a tenfold better opportunity of improving his condition than here. How few working men in this country are laying up anything for old age and infirmity? Do they not find that all their weekly earnings are barely sufficient to meet their weekly wants? What must they expect when sickness and old age come upon them? There was once upon a time when

■ These scenes of the Mississippi River are by Henry Lewis, from the mid-1800s.

one might have said 'the hand of the diligent maketh rich' and relied upon it under all circumstances. We have come to a poor pass indeed when in our native land such an axiomatic proverb as that must be taken with many exceptions. . . . He who will not arise . . . and make the proverb good deserves the fate that awaits him.

The author then outlined the basic rules for immigrants to America:

To purchase land there is as easy as to rent it here. . . . The country is everywhere well-watered. . . . The country is fertile to a remarkable extent. . . . The people are essentially democratic, like their institutions: they are an educated people without which a democracy could not subsist. . . . Work! Work!! Work!!! must be the order of the day with all who immigrate to better their fortunes. To honest and prudent industry everything will be conceded. To indolence and imprudent movements nothing but disappointment. The roughness of first appearances must not be minded. The vigorous and resolute hand put forth in all discouraging appearances will melt as the mists of the morning before the rising sun. . . . The New World supplies territory while the Old World supplies people. . . . To all who feel themselves pinched and straitened in this Old World from no fault of their own I would say WESTWARD, HO!

Henry Lewis traveled along the Mississippi River from Minnesota to New Orleans in 1847 and 1848, making numerous sketches and watercolors of the scenery on and along the river. His goal evidently was to paint a 500-yard-long panorama of the river. The fate of that mass of work is unknown but in 1851 Lewis retired to his native Germany, where he produced *Das Illustrirte Mississippithal*, published in Dusseldorf, 1854 to 1858. This work was intended to give German immigrants a better idea of America. Lewis's depictions of the valley of the Mississippi at mid-century are outstanding.

■ *The Jolly Flat Boat Men*, a large engraving made by the American Art Union in 1847, from the painting by G.C. Bingham.

THE LEWIS AND CLARK EXPEDITION

After Louisiana was ceded by France to Spain during the French and Indian War, the Spanish allowed Americans free navigation of the Mississippi River. This right was vital to the settlers of the Mississippi Valley, Kentucky, Ohio, and Tennessee, for whom the river provided a waterway to the rest of the world.

1803..Napoleons sells Louisiana to the United States.

May 14, 1804 ....The Lewis and Clark expedition begins.

November 20, 1805................The expedition reaches the Pacific Ocean.

March 22, 1806.....................The expedition leaves the Pacific.

September 23, 1806...............The group returns to St. Louis after two years, four months, and ten days.

When Napoleon Bonaparte demanded that Spain, which he had virtually annexed, give Louisiana back to France, the Spanish readily agreed—there was no choice, and Louisiana was not a profitable colony. Before the transfer was made public—just before Thomas Jefferson became president—Spain closed the Mississippi River to Americans. Americans in the West realized the threat to their commerce, and Jefferson realized Napoleon's potential threat to America.

If France owned the land west of the Mississippi, and France and England went to war (as seemed inevitable), England would likely move into Louisiana and close the Mississippi River—much more effectively than Spain could do.

Jefferson was surprised by Napoleon's offer to sell Louisiana, and a deal was struck (for $15 million) that doubled the size of the United States. But the topography was unknown and rumors of a water route across the vast West persisted.

Presents for Indian Tribes Taken on the Lewis and Clark Expedition

12 dozen pocket mirrors	288 knives
4,600 sewing needles	8 brass kettles
144 small scissors	Vermilion face paint
10 pounds of sewing thread	20 pounds of assorted beads, mostly blue
Silk ribbons	
Ivory combs	5 pounds of small white glass beads
Handkerchiefs	
Yards of bright-colored cloth	288 brass thimbles
130 rolls of tobacco	Armbands
Tomahawks that doubled as pipes	Ear trinkets

■ The most important part of the Lewis and Clark report was their map, which was sold separately from the two-volume account of the expedition. It is extraordinarily rare and is not usually found in the first edition.

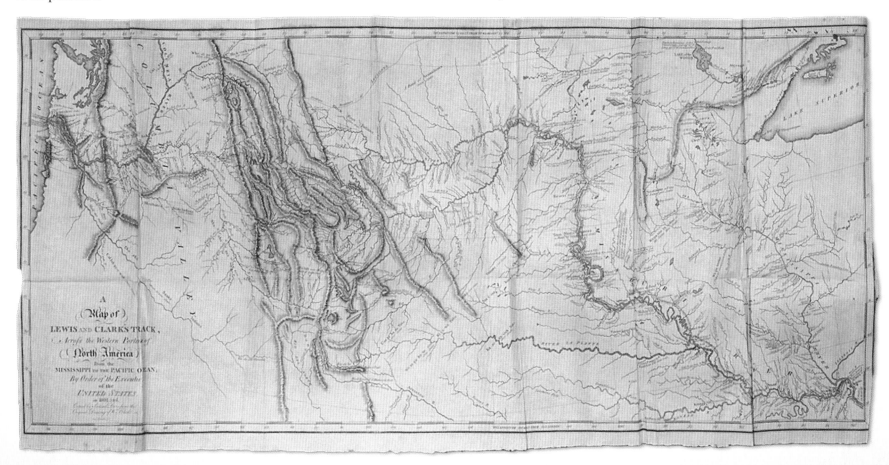

The primary objective of the Lewis and Clark expedition was to find that rumored water route across the continent. In this they could not succeed—because it did not exist. The expedition also had many important scientific objectives. Their mapping of the territory to the Pacific and their natural-history research was of tremendous importance to the new nation. The dreams of westward expansion now reached to the Pacific.

One famous medal related to Lewis and Clark (from a set of three, examples of which were taken on the expedition) depicts a family scene in a typical American room, circa 1796. In the background, a woman is weaving on a large vertical loom. In the foreground another woman, dressed in a flowing skirt, uses a foot-treadle–powered spinning wheel. At the left, a young child beside the spinner's chair watches an infant in a cradle. At the right is an open fireplace with andirons and, above it, a kettle suspended on a chain, and several utensils. John Trumbull, who designed the medal, said, "It is meant to convey an idea of domestic tranquility and employment." Collectively, the trio have come to be known as the Seasons medals, although they don't actually depict different seasons. An example of the Season medal known as "The Home" is pictured herein. Although the specific pedigree of this particular medal is not known, it is quite likely that it was taken on the Lewis and Clark expedition and was

■ This Season medal, given to the Indians by the Lewis and Clark expedition, bears a scene representing the American family. This design is known as "The Home"; the others in the three-medal set are "The Shepherd" and "The Farmer."

presented to an Indian. Their journal records that 55 silver specimens (of various designs) were taken along on the trip. Pieces made for other purposes were not fitted with suspension loops.

The History of the Expedition Under the Command of Captains Lewis and Clark, to the Sources of the Missouri, Thence Across the Rocky Mountains and Down the River Columbia to the Pacific Ocean, Performed during the Years 1804-5–6, was first published in Philadelphia, 1814. It was the official account of the most important exploration of the North American continent.

R.M. Osborne, a U.S. agent in the newly acquired Louisiana Territory, wrote to the chief of the Osages on the River Arkansas on August 10, 1805, that he was forwarding to the governor of Louisiana, James Wilkinson, the chief's request for official recognition of his tribe:

> As it seems to be your wish to have both a commission and flag from the American government as a testimony of their friendship towards the people of your nation, I shall by the first convenient opportunity transmit to the governor of Louisiana & commander in chief of the army a copy of your commission with the substance of your message to me. Until his pleasure is known I would recommend to you to live in perfect friendship with the white people who may occasionally come among you, and endeavor to cultivate the friendship and esteem of your neighbours. It is a duty encumbent on you to keep the young men and women of your tribe in habits of industry & sobriety and prevent as much as possible the introduction of ardent spirits and such other kinds of merchandise as tend to corrupt their morals, their minds, and dispositions. Should the white people of America learn that your conduct is such as merit it, they will no doubt feel every disposition to treat you as friends wherever they meet with you.

FOR THE
COLLECTOR
AND HISTORIAN

Everything concerning the Lewis and Clark expedition is rare. Anything signed by Meriwether Lewis, who died at a very young age, is very rare. Documents and letters of William Clark, who served in many official capacities after the expedition, are frequently available though not inexpensive. All of the Peace medals carried by the expedition are very rare; fewer than 10 examples of the large Peace medal are known to exist. There are no known artifacts that were taken on the expedition. The official account of the expedition is rare, but frequently available are other accounts, including one published before the official one in 1814.

The U.S. Model 1803 Harpers Ferry flintlock rifle is the type carried by the Lewis and Clark expedition.

Joshua Wingate

HISTORY

OF

THE EXPEDITION

UNDER THE COMMAND OF

CAPTAINS LEWIS AND CLARK,

TO

THE SOURCES OF THE MISSOURI,

THENCE

ACROSS THE ROCKY MOUNTAINS

AND DOWN THE

RIVER COLUMBIA TO THE PACIFIC OCEAN.

PERFORMED DURING THE YEARS 1804—5—6.

By order of the

GOVERNMENT OF THE UNITED STATES.

PREPARED FOR THE PRESS

BY PAUL ALLEN, ESQUIRE.

IN TWO VOLUMES.

VOL. I.

PHILADELPHIA:

PUBLISHED BY BRADFORD AND INSKEEP; AND ABM. H. INSKEEP, NEWYORK.

J. Maxwell, Printer.

1814.

■ Title page from *History of the Expedition Under the Command of Captains Lewis and Clark.*

■ The large-size Jefferson Indian Peace medal in silver—Lewis and Clark carried three of this size (four inches in diameter) for the chiefs of the Mandans, Arikaras, and Omahas. President Jefferson himself also presented prominent chiefs brought to Washington with the largest medal. Fewer than 10 specimens are known. Lewis and Clark also carried 13 medium-size silver medals and 16 smaller ones.

■ This June 7, 1803, letter posted from Paris—by Robert Livingston and James Monroe to Secretary of State James Madison—notes some worry that France might not carry through with its agreement to sell Louisiana.

Gaining the friendship and respect of the Indian tribes they would encounter was one of Lewis and Clark's major goals. Indian leaders in the Mississippi Valley and especially along the Missouri had long been accustomed to gifts of silver medals from the British, French, and Spanish, and Lewis and Clark had to prepare accordingly.

AMERICA'S FEAR: WILL NAPOLEON BACK OUT OF LOUISIANA SALE?

In late April 1803, France agreed to sell its Louisiana territory to the United States. Five and a half weeks after the Treaty of Cession and its two accompanying conventions had been signed, Robert R. Livingston (American minister to France) and James Monroe (special envoy)

discussed, in a 12-page letter, the final stages of the Louisiana Purchase. They expressed to Secretary of State James Madison their anxieties that France might back out of the deal, as it appeared the Republic was experiencing seller's remorse.

On November 9, 1806, Meriwether Lewis wrote from Louisville, Kentucky, to Secretary of War Henry Dearborn. He requested a partial payment of $400 toward compensation of William Clark for their recent western expedition: "My bill of exchange No. 115 of this date in favor of Capt. William Clark for the sum of four hundred dollars is in part monies due him for his services while on the late expedition to the Pacific Ocean," wrote Meriwether Lewis to Secretary of War Henry Dearborn in late 1806, "and which when paid will be charged to me on the faith of my final settlement with the United States relative to the said Expedition."

■ Lewis's letter of November 9, 1806, to Henry Dearborn.   ■ William Clark wrote this letter on November 15, 1810, as the U.S. agent for Indian Affairs, in St. Louis.

Six weeks earlier, Lewis and Clark had returned to St. Louis after their western exploration. Lewis arrived in Washington on December 28. There, he made recommendations to Congress to reward the participants. Stephen E. Ambrose in *Undaunted Courage* wrote that Lewis had already, in an initial report to President Jefferson, paid tribute to Clark, stating that "he is equally with myself entitled to your consideration and that of our common country." . . . That put it directly before the president," according to Ambrose. "Lewis wanted him as captain and co-commander. This was what he had promised, what Clark had earned. To Lewis, any other action was unthinkable." Lewis and Clark each received a total of $7,262 in compensation.

"When you are at Washington," William Clark wrote as superintendent of Indian Affairs in 1810,

Your attention to certain points . . . would conduce much to the safety and quiet of this detached part of the Country. . . . A Military Establishment & Factory at pra[i]rie de Chien. . . . The Boundary line run in conformity with the Sae & Fox Treaty. The Osage annuities given them at the Factory on the Missouri, at the time of running the line agreeably to the Osage Treaty which is indispensable, arrangements made to build Blockhouses & a Horse mule, and a Black smith furnished at the Fort. . . . Medals of four Sizes made solid, with the impression of the present president, the proportion to one large medal 4 second 6 third and 12 fourth size. Flags in proportion to the medals. Blank commissions for Indian chiefs [suited] to the medals.

CHAPTER 5
THE FUR TRADE

The fur trade and, to a lesser degree, fishing were France's principal interests in the New World. The Indians' knowledge that France didn't want their lands (Quebec was founded on unoccupied ground) gave the French a distinct advantage over the English in pursuing the fur trade business.

■ Tools of the fur trade: Plains rifle by H.E. Dimick, St. Louis, .44 caliber, circa 1850s; various traps and knives; together with beaver skins and a beaver skin hat.

FOR THE COLLECTOR AND HISTORIAN

Some of the artifacts of America's early fur trade, specifically trade axes and guns (except for Hawkens), are frequently available to collectors. Very few documents or letters are ever offered on the market. Generally, while almost everything related to the fur trade is rare, collector interest is not so overwhelming as to make offerings as expensive as one might imagine.

France's competition with the English and Dutch increased as the Indians' desire for European trade goods continued to grow. The European countries played on intertribal rivalries, at first in the East, and then farther west as the supply of pelts was depleted. The Iroquois, backed by the English, attacked French traders to keep them out of the fur-rich Mississippi Valley, but in 1701 the French and Iroquois made peace, and the English began open competition and warfare with the French, eventually driving them out of North America.

The Hudson's Bay Company became the dominant force, later rivaled by the North West Company. But after the Louisiana Purchase and the Lewis and Clark expedition, the Americans became an important factor in the fur trade. One of the first American expeditions was led by Manuel Lisa, and another by William H. Ashley. Both expeditions went up the Mississippi and Missouri rivers, establishing trading posts and beginning the period of the mountain men—the independent fur trappers and explorers who roamed the West in pursuit of their dreams of riches.

John Jacob Astor's American Fur Company, which had started dealing in furs on the New York frontier, was designing a global monopoly. Astor intended to take over the Western fur trade by setting up trading posts across the West and establishing his major trading post, Astoria, at the mouth of the Columbia River. From there, his ships would take furs directly to the Orient and bring back trade goods.

After establishing Astoria, Astor's ship went north to trade. All of the crew were killed and the ship was blown up by natives. When Astor and his partners learned of the outbreak of the War of 1812 and the threat from British ships he sold out to the Canadian North West Company. With that the American Fur Company was essentially out of the Western fur trade.

Eventually the Hudson's Bay Company took over the North West Company. In the United States territory, the Rocky Mountain Fur Company came to dominate the fur trade. Their success was fueled by the innovative practice of the annual rendezvous. Instead of establishing posts throughout the West, the company brought trade goods to annual meetings in various mountain locations, allowing the trappers to stay in the mountains and trap without having to travel east with their furs. The company prospered until the mid-1800s, when the silk hat became the fashion rage in Europe and the beaver hat's popularity declined.

The fur trade provided tough and self-reliant young men the opportunity to pursue the American dream of riches, and the legends of the mountain men have been an important part of the lore of the Western pursuit of the American dream ever since.

■ An exceptionally early document "Drawn at Michilimackinac," August 1, 1661, by Robert Giguiere. "Messrs. Giguiere will load the surplus of pelts that they will be able to carry in the canoe that . . . Perrot must furnish them for their trip, without having to leave when the pelts belonging to . . . Perrot have been loaded."

■ Henri de Tonty was a pioneer fur trader and explorer. He signed this contract with two voyageurs (French fur transporters), August 18, 1686, together with an inventory of trading goods. The contract gives Tonty (the holder of one of only 25 royal permits) half the proceeds of their fur trading and allows the two voyageurs to take general trade items of their own on the trip. The inventory of trade goods illustrates what they believed would be most appealing to the Indians at this early time. Tonty had just returned from a voyage down the Mississippi in search of La Salle's lost expedition when he wrote this document.

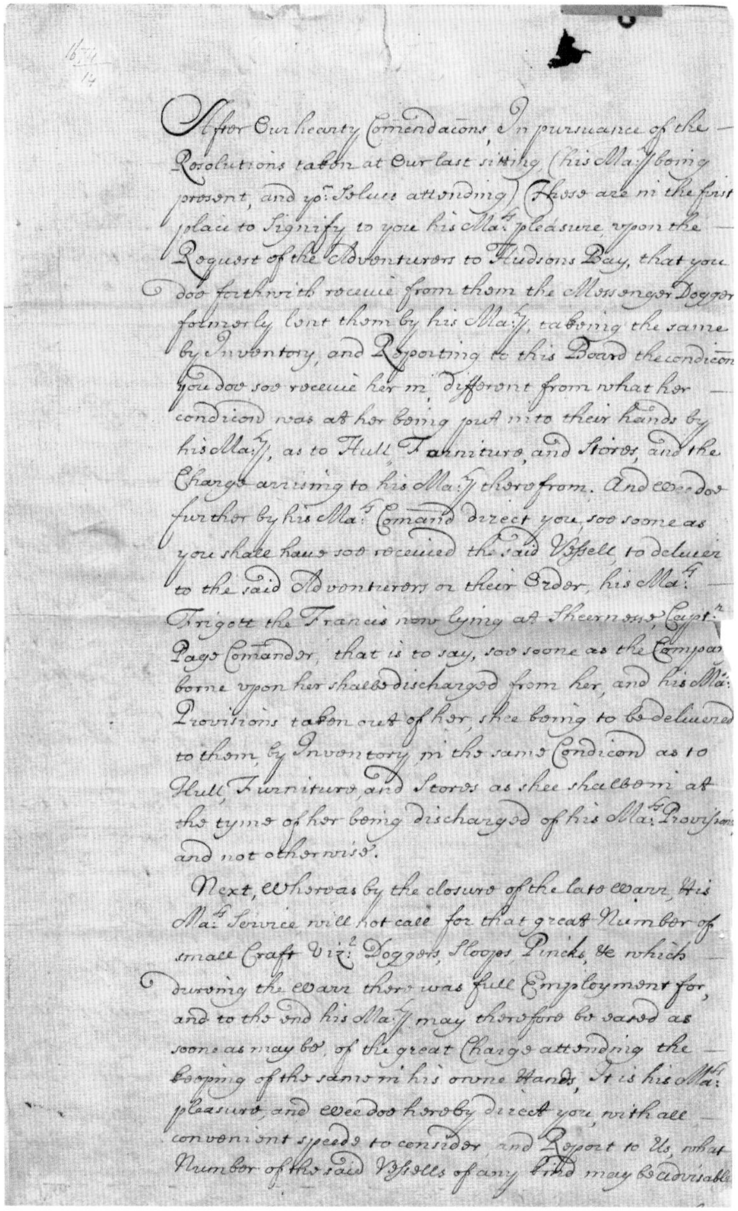

■ This Hudson's Bay Company medal, made after 1801, was used as a gift to friendly Indians.

■ A portrait of King George III graces this Hudson's Bay Company silver friendship medal from the late 1700s.

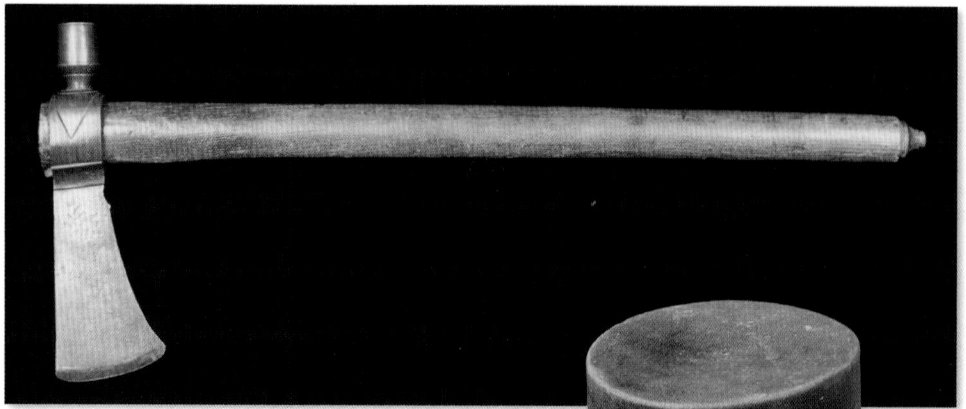

[handwritten letter, left column]

■ Hudson's Bay Company—letter signed by Prince Rupert, Sir George Carteret (one of the proprietors of New Jersey), and other members of the Admiralty Board, March 9, 1673/74. "To the Principal Officers and Com: of his Ma: Navy," concerning the early affairs of the Hudson's Bay Company, which was organized by Prince Rupert and other influential Englishmen and chartered in 1670 as The Governor and Company of Adventurers of England Trading into Hudson's Bay, for the purpose of seeking a northwest passage and engaging in fur trade in the untapped vast area northwest of Lake Superior.

■ This classic Hudson's Bay Company pipe tomahawk, circa 1770–1790, marked "Parkes" with a British broad arrow on the reverse, was used as a treaty gift.

■ The label on the silk lining inside this classic beaver tall hat (circa 1800–1815), depicting two beavers on a riverbank, reads, "Stillman, Manufacturer and Dealer in Hats, Caps and Furs . . . Hartford, Conn."

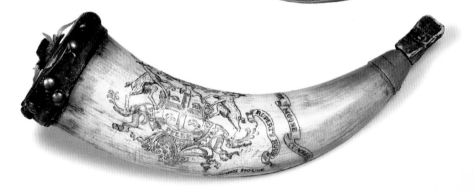

■ The crest of the Hudson's Bay Company is engraved on this 19th-century gunpowder horn.

■ Hudson's Bay Company scrip for one pound sterling, issued at York Factory on Hudson Bay, 1821.

of the manufacturers; and have been, and still may be, obliged to witness the exportation of these furs to Europe, to enrich and encourage foreign, to the injury and ruin of domestic, manufactures. This your memorialists consider a hardship and a serious evil to their country, and to remedy it, humbly request the serious attention of Congress.

[We] suggest to the wisdom of congress, the propriety of regulating by law, the mode of selling the furs . . . [to] the manufacturers and a fair price to the government. The mode which your memorialists beg leave to suggest is a sale by public auction, at such times and places as may enable the manufacturers and others generally to attend. . . . The government will receive a full price, and the American manufacturer, whether of large or small capital, be enabled to obtain a sufficient supply.

The island of Michilimackinac (present-day Mackinac), between lakes Huron and Michigan, was at the center of the fur trade from its beginning to its decline in the 19th century. It contained the vital waterways to the West, as well as to the Chicago area and to the Mississippi River. Trade goods were assembled in Montreal in the winter and then sent by boat to Michilimackinac, where the island post was the distribution and trading center for the entire fur trade in the northern part of the continent.

In a very interesting 1806 *Memorial of Sundry Manufacturers of Hats in . . . Philadelphia*, 46 hatmakers in Philadelphia petitioned Congress to make more furs available to American hatmakers, rather than sending them to Europe.

> That your memorialists are engaged in a branch of manufactures of considerable importance; that owing to the regulations with the Indian tribes on our frontiers, they are obliged to depend for a very large proportion of furs, the raw materials of their manufacturers, on the government of the United States; that the mode at present adopted by the agent for Indian affairs in vending these furs is, in the opinion of your memorialists, improper and disadvantageous to the manufacturer, and to the interests of the government.
>
> By the plan now in operation, the agent for Indian affairs exercises a complete control over the sale of these furs, and may dispose of them at what places, for what prices, and in what quantity he may deem most proper. Thus are your memorialists dependent on the will of an individual, for the raw materials

At the time the North West Trading Company was proposed, John Jacob Astor first consolidated his holdings in the American Fur Company and made plans to circumvent the St. Louis control of the fur trade in the far west by planning a central depot at the mouth of the Columbia River. This depot, Astoria, was established in 1811.

■ A draft of the articles of association of the North West Trading Company, Boston, 1808. The articles state the plans for a proposed enterprise whose principal objective was to establish a permanent settlement at the mouth of the Columbia River as a site to deposit trade goods and a safe haven for ships.

(handwritten document, upper left)

(handwritten document, upper right)

■ René Auguste Chouteau was a cofounder of the city of St. Louis, and an important fur trader. This document is one he signed July 2, 1811, as administrator of the estate of Iowa pioneer Julien Dubuque.

■ A fur-trade musket with an exceptionally long barrel (47-1/2 inches), made by Barnett, 1800, for the North West Company.

■ This frontier percussion pistol was handmade from available parts, using a "J. Henry and Son" treaty-rifle lock, the barrel marked with a small "U.S." at left breech, plainly and simply full-stocked to the muzzle.

■ Manuel Lisa, an early fur trader and explorer, pioneered trading forts on the Mississippi River. In this document of August 25, 1817, Lisa sold a parcel of land north of the town of St. Louis.

■ The Jack and Samuel Hawken percussion conversion pistol, .48 caliber, circa 1825, was the earliest known pistol produced by the Hawkens' St. Louis workshop.

■ This invoice of McTavish Frobisher & Co., Agents, NW Co., was signed in Montreal, May 5, 1806. A list of sundries forwarded from Montreal by the North West Company to River St. Maurice included blankets, cloth, Russian sheeting, cotton, Irish linen, colored thread, stitching needles, scalpers, awls, fire steels, gun flints, fishing lines, round beads, cod lines, files, scissors, blank books, paper, ink powder, quills, lead pencils, sealing wax, tea, ox-hide shoes, portage collars, men's Montreal hats, wool hats, beaver ruffs, corn, peas, gunpowder, molasses, pork, butter, spirits, wine, brandy, sugar, carrot tobacco (tight bundles of tobacco leaves rolled up in linen and bound with cord for shipping), salt, soap, mattresses, a tent with poles, biscuits, flour, pork, and kegs.

■ In this contract for voyageurs (Montreal, January 17, 1820), Allard and LaFleur agree to "make the journey in winter for three years in the dependencies of the Northwest of Upper Canada." Archibald McLeod, who played a leading role in the struggle between the North West Company and the Hudson's Bay Company for control of the Western fur trade, signed on behalf of the company.

THE BUILDING OF ONE OF AMERICA'S GREAT FORTUNES

A letter from fur trader and financier John Jacob Astor to his agent, Robert Stuart, who negotiated with the Indians, reveals the business savvy that made Astor into America's first millionaire. "Of our deer skins of 1822/1823," wrote Astor, "nearly all are sold but all the furs and most of the bear skins of that year as well as all the deer of this year remain unsold. . . . The people are everywhere and every day getting poorer and as many articles of manufacture which are now very low can be used in place of deer skins and furs they receive the preference. . . . It is absolutely necessary that our imports and our expenses be lessened. . . ." He continues with a discussion of fur prices.

Go on steadily & as sparingly as possible. Perhaps next season our hatters will use Raccoon and that some of them may come your way to buy them at 40 cents. I would rather sell than purchase. Otter are always good & worth from 3 1/4 to 3 3/4 or even 4$ to us. Beare 3$. Costs have got to be very low & we should only pay 1 1/2 for good fisher, 1$, Lynx 1 to 1 1/2$. Deer should [be] 33 cents Red 30 & gray 24. Beaver & muskrat as the Price may be in New York.

[Handwritten letter — John Jacob Astor, October 7, 1823]

■ Robert Stuart, agent for the American Fur Company, issued this coupon "Good to W. McGulpin for baking fifty loaves bread." (Michilimackinac, April 30, 1825.)

■ John Jacob Astor sent this October 7, 1823, letter from Germany to Robert Stuart at Michilimackinac.

■ John Jacob Astor's American Fur Company silver medal, bearing his profile, was given by the company's Upper Missouri Outfit (note the "U.M.O." on the reverse) to the tribes it traded with—the Mandan, Hidatsa, Assinoboine, and Yankton Sioux. Fort Union, the Upper Missouri Outfit's base, was a square-shaped stockade just north of the confluence of the Yellowstone and Missouri rivers. There are six known examples of this medal, all struck between late 1832 and 1843.

Fort Union was in competition with the Hudson's Bay Company. In 1831, the agent in charge of Fort Union proposed to Pierre Chouteau Jr., who managed the company in the West, that they obtain Indian Peace medals from Washington. The secretary of war replied that the company could issue its own "ornaments," but they would not be considered official medals of the United States. Astor had medals struck in late 1832. In 1843, the government prohibited the company from minting and distributing any more medals after the Hudson's Bay Company complained that Astor's company had usurped the authority of the federal government through their production and distribution. The number minted is unknown.

In 1810, Robert Stuart became a partner in John Jacob Astor's Pacific Fur Company. During an 1812 expedition to the Columbia River, he was chosen as a courier to carry dispatches overland to Astor. After a perilous journey, attended by extreme privation and suffering, over a route which in considerable part had never before been seen by white men (he discovered South Pass, which became the gateway through the mountains), Stuart arrived in St. Louis on April 30, 1813.

From 1820 to 1834, he was the head of the American Fur Company for the Upper Lakes Region.

■ A copy of the Van Buren Indian Peace medal, this 1843 presentation medal was made in St. Louis at the direction of Pierre Chouteau Jr. & Company (Upper Missouri Outfit) after the distribution of the Astor medal was prohibited by the government. Chouteau's blatant copy of the federal design was noticeably larger and cast in pewter rather than silver. The secretary of war ordered Chouteau to cease distribution of the medals almost as soon as he started presenting them to Indian tribes. Four to six examples are known.

■ 21-inch "Arkansas Toothpick" Bowie knife made by J.S. Silver around the 1860s.

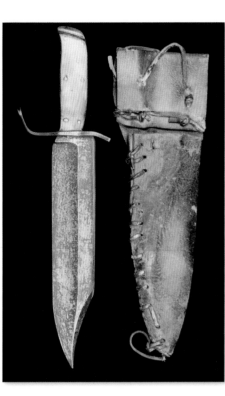

■ The North West Company's 1820 Beaver token was the only circulating currency in the Pacific Northwest. It is believed to represent one beaver skin. All known examples were unearthed in the Columbia and Umpqua river valleys in Oregon.

■ This massive Bowie-type knife and handmade scabbard measure 16 inches overall.

■ A deer-foot handle gives extra character to this frontier knife.

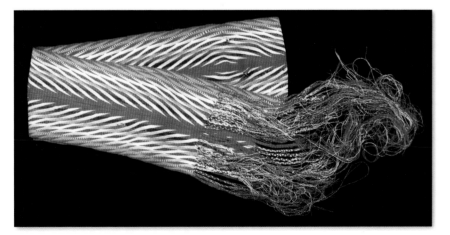

■ L'Assomption sashes are named after the village in Quebec where many were made. These were traded extensively throughout North America by fur traders, and many voyageurs wore them as part of their regular attire. The sashes were not only decorative but also functional—the key to an individual's trunk, in which his every possession was usually stored, was often attached to one end.

THE LEGENDARY MOUNTAIN MAN

Jedediah Smith was a legendary American explorer, fur trapper, and mountain man, the first white man to reach California overland from the east, pioneering the route across Nevada and over the High Sierras. He was one of the most important men in the fur trade, quickly rising to form a partnership to buy out General William H. Ashley's trading company. Having survived many hair-raising (and potentially hair-losing) encounters with bears and Indians, he was killed by Comanches in 1831 while searching for water when leading a caravan down the Santa Fe Trail. He was 31 years old. "I have been under the necessity of going forward with a partnership amounting to a part of My Capital," Smith wrote a few months before his death,

but Shall Still, unavoidable accidents excepted, have eight, or perhaps ten thousand Dollars, in March, or April next, which Could not be vested in any way to please me so well, as to have it aid both my Friend and me. . . . I received from Mr. Kyle a price Current of Nov. 10th, together with such information as that Gentleman was able to collect . . . but Since I wrote, We have engaged a Gentleman (Gen. Wm. H. Ashley) to take our Furs forward to Philadelphia and N. York and dispose of Same. . . . Mr. Keyte has now removed from St. Louis, near to a Small Town, called Chariton, in this State.

After the perusal of these two Letters, which I have had the pertinacity to write, it is hardly necessary for me to tell you that I am much more in my element, when conversing with the uncivilized Man, or Setting my Beaver Traps, than in writing Epistles.

■ Letter signed by mountain man Jedediah Smith, St. Louis, November 24, 1830.

William Sublette was involved in the early fur trade, joining General William Ashley's pioneering expedition up the Missouri River; he was one of a small group of trappers led by Jedediah Smith that made many discoveries of new routes in the Rocky Mountain. Sublette became the major organizer of the fur-trading rendezvous in the Rockies and the chief supplier of trade goods. In the lengthy handwritten letter pictured (to his former mentor and now business associate), he writes from "Walnut Creek near the Arkansaw," September 24, 1831:

We have had some hard blocks since we left St. Louis. On our way out to Santa Fe we lost Mr. Minter, killed on the Pawnee fork we suppose by the Pawnees. . . . Mr. J.S. Smith was killed on the Cimeron . . . by the Comanches. We met with no other losses by Indians and arrived in Santa Fe July 4th. The trace to Santa Fe has been well watched by different nations of the Indians this season, annoying the traders of there and back to this place. We have not lost any man as yet on our return and but few animals. . . . We are now within 260 miles of Independence. . . .

Young Mr. Austin Smith is in company. Mr. Peter Smith and Mr. Parkman is in the Spanish country. I don't think they have made any money. . . . We equipped Mr. Thomas Fitzpatrick out from Taos . . . with about 40 men and supplies. . . . [W]e heard from Milton Sublette by the Santa Fe trappers.

William Tilton formed the Columbia Fur Company with former employees of the Hudson's Bay and North West companies who had been displaced when those two companies merged. John Jacob Astor bought

"Smith was killed on the Cimeron," wrote William Sublette in a September 1831 letter. *"The trace to Santa Fe has been well watched by different nations of the Indians this season."*

■ This is probably the most perfectly preserved example of a Plains rifle by J & S Hawken. It was originally purchased around 1840 (directly from the St. Louis gunsmiths) by Dr. James L. Jones, who, according to his descendants, brought the rifle back to Pennsylvania as an important frontier artifact. He preserved it as a pristine example of the most famous and popular rifle of the mountain men. The rifle is 47-3/4 inches long and .49 caliber.

them out in 1827 and their territory became the Upper Missouri Outfit of the American Fur Company. He wrote to his father from Galena, Illinois, March 24, 1830, explaining how, after five years in the fur trade, he was in debt:

It may seem strange to you that after residence of Eleven years in this western country . . . risking my life & health for gain that I should still be so poor, but such is the fact and to account for it I will give you a sketch of . . . the last Eleven Years. The first 3-1/2 years I spent in St. Louis as a clerk principally in an auction house. . . . I received a salary for my services of $400 and board, this just about paid my expenses. . . . I associated myself with five other young men like myself, obtained a credit for about $20,000 worth of Indian goods and went into the Indian country.

In this business I spent five years returning every spring to St. Louis with my peltries for supplies. We traded on the Upper Missouri as high as the Yellow Stone—on the Upper Mississippi above the falls of St. Anthony and up the St. Peters to its source. . . . The last year we returned to St. Louis, furs and peltries to the amount of $90,000, yet . . . we wound up our business at the end of five years with a loss of $2,000 per share. This was owing to the great opposition in prices we had to contend with in the Am. Fur Co. together with a loss in one Spring . . . by the rise of the Missouri River of about $10,000. I settled my $2,000 by a note.

Robert Stuart, head of the American fur Company in the upper Great Lakes region, became a partner in John Jacob Astor's Pacific fur Company in 1810. During an 1812 expedition to the Columbia River he was chosen as a courier to carry dispatches overland to Astor. After a perilous journey, attended by extreme privation and suffering, over a route which in considerable part had never before been seen by white men (he discovered South Pass, which became the gateway through the mountain), he arrived in St. Louis in 1813.

■ Robert Stuart's missive to Ramsay Crooks, dated November 10, 1822, provides a lengthy report on activities in Stuart's area.

In a lengthy handwritten report to Ramsay Crooks, the head of the New York division of the company, Stuart writes from Mackinac, November 10, 1822:

> The season is so far advanced, that the navigation of the North River must be closed. . . . McKinzie has arrived at the Prairie with $40,000 worth of goods—Lockwood with $18,000 worth. . . . He . . . [r]equested to bring him next spring for a Montreal, 1 pr: fine linen made into shirts: and to get 3 prs: pantaloons off cloth. 1 body coat & 1 suitout, all of fashionable colors. . . . You will have to watch McKinzie, this winter yet, for I have direct and positive information. . . . That's an attempt is to be made to trammel the trade. . . . [H]is maxim . . . is to prevent the Indians hunting altogether. . . . [D]o not neglect to let me know as soon as practicable all you may learn of the new opposition as it may be of consequence to know what their movements are likely to be. . . . [W]e are to have a monthly express this winter, so you can write often. . . . [U]nless we crush their ambitious views . . . at once . . . they will soon show themselves in every section of the country. Could you reconcile the interests at St. Louis, and make a general arrangement, it would give them death blow to all their hopes; he has too much sagacity not to further the project forward and would at once give us the control of the whole country.

THE ROCKY MOUNTAINS FUR RENDEZVOUS: THE TRADE AND SOCIAL FAIR OF THE WILDERNESS

The rendezvous is perhaps the most properly romanticized event in the American West. Originally conceived by William Ashley as an efficient means for the fur trappers in the mountains to sell their pelts and buy supplies, the first rendezvous was held in 1825. For the next 15 years it was the great gathering of mountain men, company trappers, supply caravans from St. Louis and large numbers of Indians from various tribes. After the hardships and isolation of the winters in the mountains, the trappers flocked to the rendezvous (mostly held in Wyoming), where trading, drinking, gambling, games of all types, and, perhaps most important, squaws were the activities. It was a carnival where letters from home, newspapers, and gossip brought trappers in touch with St. Louis

■ In a document written at the 1830 rendezvous (held just east of the Wind River Mountains in Wyoming, July 28), Thomas Fitzpatrick, one of the pioneer fur traders and trail makers in the Rocky Mountains, wrote a four-line promissory note as agent for Smith, Jackson & Sublette: "As a settlement of all acct, up to this date with [Martin?] Irroquois there appears a balance due by us to him of fourteen hundred & fifty two dollars forty cents which we promise to pay him on demand." On the verso is an autographed document signed by William Sublette acknowledging payment in full "on the watters of Columbia Aug 28th 1832" signed by the Iroquois trapper Martin Sword, to whom Fitzpatrick wrote the promissory note. The transaction was witnessed by Robert Campbell, an early trapper, trader, and entrepreneur who supplied goods to the 1832 rendezvous and the following year challenged the supremacy of Astor's American Fur Company on the Upper Missouri by building a rival trading post. Sublette and Campbell built Fort Laramie in 1834.

and the East. The rendezvous made great commercial sense for all involved but their most important aspect was the contact between whites and Indians of many different tribes.

William H. Ashley founded and organized the brigade-rendezvous system that established the fur trade in the Rocky Mountains and fostered

■ Alfred Jacob Miller went west in 1837 as the artist on the expedition organized by William Drummond Stewart. Miller was the first artist to travel the Oregon Trail and the only one to experience in person the Rocky Mountains during the height of the fur trade, the rendezvous, and the mountain men. He produced hundreds of sketches as well as paintings, and his watercolors are arguably the most important in relating a sense of the traders, the Indians, the rendezvous, the Rocky Mountains, and the Oregon Trail. This watercolor of the *Flat Heads & Nez Percé* was painted circa 1858–1860.

■ William H. Ashley's order for supplies.

the mountain men. A letter signed from St. Louis, November 24, 1831, paints a picture of the supplies hauled to a rendezvous. Ashley ordered the following from a New Orleans merchant: 1,200 pounds of coffee; 2,500 pounds of first-quality brown sugar; 300 pounds of rice; 4 boxes of prepared chocolate; 14 pounds each of raisins and Hyson tea; and 1 hogshead of highest-proof rum—all to arrive in St. Louis on February 15.

■ This contract, signed at the 1833 rendezvous in Wyoming, started the Rocky Mountain Fur Company.

A contract forming a new Rocky Mountain Fur Company was written and signed at the 1833 rendezvous, which started at the mouth of Horse Creek in the Green River Valley in Wyoming on July 15. The document was signed by the legendary mountain man Thomas Fitzpatrick, as well as Edmund T. Christy, and it bears the name of Jim Bridger, who was illiterate and could not sign. It was witnessed by Robert Campbell and Louis Vasquez (an early pioneer in the fur trade, and Jim Bridger's partner in the famous Overland way station Fort Bridger).

Nathaniel Wyeth wrote from the 1834 rendezvous after being double-crossed on providing trade goods. He described his plan to build a trading fort on the Oregon Trail.

Wyeth had gone to Oregon in 1832, pioneering the Oregon Trail and stopping at the Rocky Mountain fur rendezvous. The ship he had sent to the Oregon coast with trade goods did not arrive and he returned east in 1833, again stopping at the rendezvous. He made a contract with William Sublette to provide the trade goods for the 1834 rendezvous, but when he arrived in the Rocky Mountains, the Rocky Mountain Fur Company did not honor their contract and had bought trade goods already. Wyeth wrote to his brothers in Baltimore, from the rendezvous in what is today Wyoming,

> Ham's Fork of the Colorado of the West Latt 41-45 Long 112-35,
>
> All well, but I am afraid not doing as well as might be expected, but will do all I can, and then 'trust to providence' for the rest. My affairs here are in too unsettled a state to express an opinion of the event. I shall write to you again by the vessel, in the mean time I am going about 150 miles west of this to build a fort, and that done shall proceed to the mouth of the Columbia to build another there for fishing, then the De[vi]l knows where, after beaver. . . . Believe me, that old kindness is not diminished; on the contrary, I look back to the fondness that has so long sweetened our intercourse, as the brightest spot on memory's green, and the brighter for the darkness and desolation which encompasses me. . . . Is money scarce? If I knew so I would indite[?] the blackest kind of a Letter and dip my pen in gall and wormwood and indulge my own fancy while tallying with yours. Affairs in this region are going bad. Murder is rife, and distrust among themselves makes the whites an easy prey to the Indians. There has been little Beaver caught and of that little I get less

Nathaniel Wyeth wrote this letter from Ham's Fork after being double-crossed at the 1834 rendezvous.

> than I ought. As yet there is no positive indication of the event of this business. I shall do all I can and if those at home do not get discouraged it will yet turn out well but of this I am afraid.
>
> I leave the above [rendezvous] 1 July and then go about 150 miles to Lewis River to make a fort for trade thence to the Columbia to build another, then try . . . trading with a party. I shall write you . . . and I hope to have good news to send but if not shall send nothing. . . .
>
> Here are plenty of Buffaloe and other good things to eat and so far no Indians to trouble us but continued watching is tiresome and at last men get willing to lie down and take their chances.

Wyeth took his trade goods from the rendezvous north, as he said he planned to do in this letter, and built a fort on the Snake River called Fort Hall to compete with the Rocky Mountain Fur Company, which had reneged on their contract at the rendezvous.

CHAPTER 6

THE INDIANS

The history of the American Indians is far too complex to even attempt a brief summary of the historical context. It might be easier to summarize the history of the Europeans. That the Indians' treatment by the largely white European settlers is, along with slavery, the darkest part of American history is disputed by no one. The modern view of the Indians, however, is frequently just as extreme, and wrong, as the early settlers' view that all the Indians were savages and that "the only good Indian is a dead Indian."

1804.............................Lewis and Clark visit the Mandan Indians, a tribe of 1,250 members
1837.............................Smallpox decimates the Mandans; between 125 and 550 survive

Many tribes were peaceful and very spiritual. Their systems of beliefs addressed the fears of the unknown that concern all religions. They also addressed their own relationship with nature and combined both into complex rituals and beliefs. They were preyed upon by Christian missionaries obsessed with "saving" the so-called heathens and destroying their native beliefs.

Many other tribes were barbaric in their constant wars with other Indian tribes, with some enslaving or torturing their captives. Many of the lands that the white settlers drove the Indians from had been violently taken by them from other Indians who were then annihilated or driven further west.

The Western pursuit of the American dream was the Indians' worst nightmare.

Trade between colonists and Indians was very important for both parties on the frontier. The Indians had pelts, and the colonists had manufactured articles and metal products, such as axes and guns. Silver ornaments became important trade items in the 18th century and eventually dominated trade. The average Indian wore much more silver jewelry (see the illustrations on pages 70 and 71) than white men or women did. Most of the early silver jewelry was made by European silversmiths in Montreal, London, and Philadelphia and other American cities.

■ This spontoon blade pipe tomahawk dates from circa 1830–1840. The tack-decorated haft is charred in the middle from being left too close to a fire. Pipe tomahawks were more symbolic than functional and were often carried during ceremonies or treaty talks as symbols of power and status.

■ Classic pipe tomahawk with tack-decorated haft.

The Indians began to make their own jewelry around 1800, using the silver from coins, primarily Spanish ones, and tableware.

Many of those visiting the Indians did so to convert them to their own religion. A letter signed by 25 Christian brothers in Philadelphia, September 18, 1812, is addressed "to the Chiefs and others of the Seneca Nation of Indians residing at Cattaraugus." It is typical of the attitude of James Lloyd Breck, a Christian missionary to the Indians and settlers on the Wisconsin and Minnesota frontier, who wrote vivid firsthand accounts of Native American life and the trials and rewards of missionary endeavor in 1850.

■ *The Travelers Meeting with Mandan Indians, Near Fort Clark* shows Prince Maximilian of Germany and artist Karl Bodmer.

FOR THE COLLECTOR AND HISTORIAN

Indian artifacts are probably the most available and reasonably priced collectibles of western American history, and have been collected since whites began to visit tribes in the early 19th century. There is a very broad market in all price ranges, and meaningful collections can be formed that represent the complex cultures of the many very different tribes.

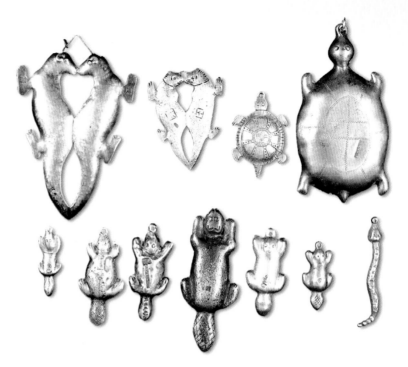

An order for silver trade jewelry, an agreement between John Jacob Astor of the American Fur Company and William Thomson, silversmith, who would make gorgets ($2.16 each), armbands ($2.75), wristbands ($2.16), brooches (62 1/2 cents), earwheels (86 cents), earbobs (10 cents), crosses (5 cents), and large brooches ($3.50), December 23, 1816.

Animal effigies were worn essentially as good luck talismans. Beavers represented wealth and good trading, and turtles represented longevity. The kissing otters were very popular. These are by various makers, including the Hudson's Bay Company, generally dating to 1750–1800.

An unusual neckpiece made by Simon Curtis in Montreal, circa 1797–1801, features engraved tomahawks on the gorget. Gorgets were worn by colonists as badges of military authority and rank. The shape quickly became popular with the natives as symbolic of the power of the moon.

■ Crosses with arms of equal length represented north, south, east and west; when a fire was set for a council meeting, four logs were placed in the form of a cross by some tribes. The popularity of various forms of crosses in trade jewelry had more to do with the Indians' own beliefs than the Europeans' association of crosses with Christianity.

■ Crowns represented social status within tribes. The one on the left was crafted by Ignace Delzenne, Quebec, 1765–1776, the one on the right by Simon Curtius, Montreal, 1797–1801.

■ A receipt for the $500 annuity for lands in Western New York. Signed by Red Jacket, chief of the Senecas, in Buffalo, New York, June 15, 1824; also signed by ten other chiefs and warriors. It reads: "We the undersigned Chiefs and Warriors of the Seneca Nation do acknowledge to have received by Jasper Parrish Sub-Agent of the United States to the Six nations of Indians Five hundred dollars in full for the Annuity due us." The Senecas had given up their lands in Western New York in exchange for this annuity. Along with names like Uncas, King Phillip, and later Geronimo and Sitting Bull, Red Jacket remains one of the most recognizable figures in the history of American Indians. Known as a great orator, he pursued a policy of friendship with whites, but opposed the cession of Indian lands to the United States and efforts to train Indians in the white man's civilization. Red Jacket became his name because of the richly embroidered scarlet jacket that was presented to him by a British officer shortly after the American Revolution as a reward for his services.

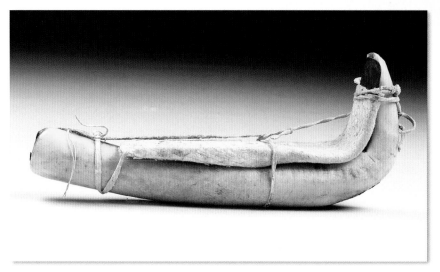

■ This Plains buffalo hide scraper, circa 1880, 12 1/2 inches long, has unusual brass tack and screw ornamentation. The metal scraper was possibly made from an old file that has been sharpened, then wrapped in buffalo hide. Work on buffalo hides was almost exclusively done by women.

■ Plains pictorial buffalo hide, Northern Cheyenne or Sioux, of unusually large scale (100 by 80 inches), drawn in a classic and refined Cheyenne style, and faintly signed in one area, "Kills-Eagle." It was probably collected at Standing Rock Agency circa the 1870s.

The pictographs on the hide shown here illustrate a series of episodes from the life of Kills-Eagle (Wan-Bli-Kte). These include confrontations with Crow and scenes of horse capturing, a group of red-painted horses circling the central field, and participation in a particular but unknown exploit. Two of the equestrians are wearing elaborate headdresses, the horses have galloping hooves and elongated necks, and one of the enemies in the confrontation is clad in a cloth kapote.

Kills-Eagle was with the "hostiles" at Rosebud during the Custer campaign. While he did not participate in the Battle of Little Big Horn, his personal account of the events was reported in the *New York Herald*, October 6, 1876.

In his 1992 book, *The Native American Heritage: A Survey of North American Indians*, Evan M. Maurer wrote, "By the third quarter of the nineteenth century, Plains warrior-artists had become increasingly interested in using more detail in the representation of figures, horses, clothing, and military equipment. They also were developing a style in which they depicted men and animals in full action described by a greater variety of poses and movements."

In *Letters and Sketches: With a Narrative of a Year's Residence Among the Indian Tribes of the Rocky Mountains*, 1843, Pierre-Jean De Smet wrote: "The call of the Rockies was not immediately answered. The Catholic Church and fledgling Jesuit mission and novitiate at the frontier's edge had few men and fewer resources for such a far-flung mission."

Jacqueline Peterson wrote of De Smet in *Sacred Encounters: Father De Smet and the Indians of the Rocky Mountain West*:

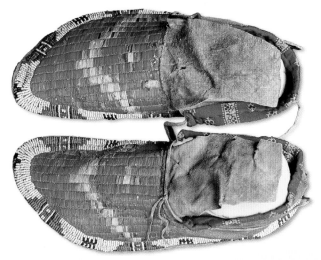

■ Sioux moccasins decorated with dyed porcupine quills, as well as with beads, late 19th century.

In 1839 . . . at St. Joseph's mission . . . at Council Bluffs, they found a man whom the Plains Indians later called "good-hearted," a thirty-eight-year-old Flemish Jesuit named Pierre-Jean De Smet. For De Smet, the appeal came as a voice crying from the wilderness. He visited the Salish at the Rocky Mountain Rendezvous of 1840. . . . The following year . . . De Smet and his European confreres . . . set out for the Bitterroot Valley of western Montana. . . . St. Mary's mission to the Flathead . . . became for De Smet the imagined heart of an "empire of Christian Indians," a wilderness kingdom in the uncontaminated reaches of the Rocky Mountains.

For a privileged moment in 1841–1842, the mission seemed to prosper. The Salish at St. Mary's settled into a rigorous daily routine of prayer and song, catechism, and agricultural labor. . . . Missions to the neighboring Coeur d' Alene, Pend Oreille, Colville, Kootenai, and Blackfeet tribes were opened in rapid succession.

Nonetheless . . . the Salish resisted Catholic authoritarianism, the concepts of sin

■ A superb Northern Plains beaded and fringed hide woman's dress, probably Blackfoot. Of elegant proportion, constructed of Indian tanned hide, sinew sewn with glass pony beads in white, blue, and black; faceted basket beads in blue and black; Russian trade beads, translucent and blue; white porcelain beads; olivella shells; red, green, and black wool; glass seed beads; red-dyed porcupine quillwork and metal thimbles, with open sleeves and uneven hemline; circle discs and three rows of scalloped beadwork on shoulders; fringe on shoulders and overall.

According to Jacqueline Peterson's *Sacred Encounters,* "This dress was one of several patterns sent by De Smet to Belgian relatives and patrons following the meeting in 1859 between General Harney and Plateau Chiefs at Fort Vancouver. The cut of the yoke, the ponybead circles at shoulders, and the uneven him line all suggest Blackfeet manufacture. De Smet may have acquired the dress on his return trip to St. Louis at Fort Benton, on the upper Missouri River."

and hell, and the imposition of European social, political, and economic values that directly challenged native norms. The Salish wanted Christian power and protection for their own ends, but they weren't interested in farming or making peace with their Blackfeet enemies. . . . [T]he prayers of the Flathead "consisted in asking to live a long time, to kill plenty of animals and enemies, and to steal the greatest number of the [enemies'] horses possible."

Within scarcely a decade of its founding, St. Mary's mission and the Jesuit missions to the Colville and Blackfeet were closed, their native residents apostatizing due to disease and missionary demands for change far in excess of spiritual conversion. . . .

After 1847, and for the remainder of his life, De Smet was an advocate for peace. . . . De Smet lent his charismatic presence as a trusted military and government emissary in treaty negotiations with reluctant or hostile Indian nations, among whom he was well known. . . .

His most controversial role involved a mission to the camp of Sitting Bull during the Fort Laramie treaty negotiations of 1868. Although he failed to persuade Sitting Bull of the government's good intentions, he brought in a sufficient number of Sitting Bull's people to secure the treaty and diffuse the threat of immediate war. The Fort Laramie treaty was a hollow victory, however. Government promises were broken within less than a decade, and war, however futile, became the only honorable alternative for the Sioux.

■ This Winnebago scalloped-edge bow dates from circa 1880.

■ These Southeastern beaded hide and cloth moccasins, possibly Cherokee, are constructed of Indian tanned hide, black cloth, and yellow silk; decorated with white, pink, orange, three shades of blue, and two shades of translucent red and green beads; and embellished on the uppers and cuffs with stylized elements. 10 3/4 inches long, these were collected by Father Pierre-Jean De Smet.

■ Sioux child's moccasins, late 19th century.

■ Kiowa Comanche long-fringe moccasins, circa 1860.

■ This ensemble of war shirt, leggings, and headpiece, circa 1820–1830, belonged to an important Mandan warrior whose exploits and battlefield achievements are chronicled in the remarkable series of painted pictographs. The wash of black paint over the right shoulder and yellow over the left shoulder indicates that the owner, while alone, killed and scalped an enemy. The column of early 19th-century pipes represents the number of war parties he led, while the 13 painted horse quirts show the number of horses stolen and given away. Captured horses are also indicated by the series of parallel lines on the shirt sleeves and leggings. The feat of touching your enemy in battle and living to talk about it was commonly referred to as counting coup. The Mandan people were almost entirely wiped out by smallpox in 1837, making material from this group among the rarest of all Native American art.

■ On this Arapaho woman's dress from the Central Plains, circa 1840–1850, the hide is decorated with extensive beadwork and trade cloth. Very few Arapaho women's dresses are known.

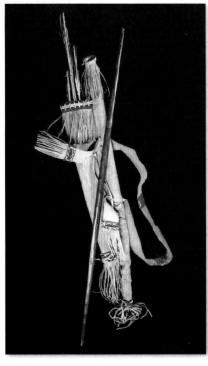

■ Bowcase and quiver, bow, and arrows, Southern Plains, circa 1865.

■ This Crow shirt dates from circa 1870.

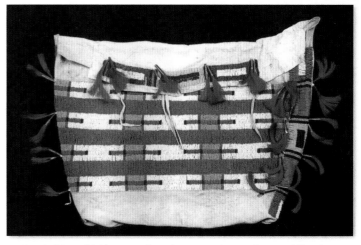

■ Beaded "possible" bags, such as this, were often tied to a saddle when traveling and at other times hung inside a tepee.

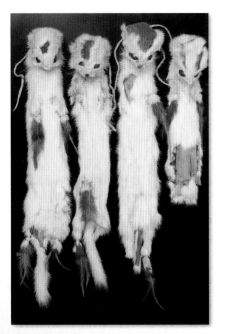

■ Blackfoot ermine medicine that belonged to the family of Weasel Tail, a prominent Blackfoot chief, 19th century. The ermines were prized for their pure white color; these are adorned with pieces of cloth, dyed feathers, leather thongs, and brass beads. They were part of a medicine man's bundle and used in ceremonies. The four ermines represent the four directions; the sacred colors were black, white, red, and yellow.

■ An Eastern Apache man's coat, circa 1880, is made of painted hide with calico and stroud cloth. It boasts extraordinary twisted and dyed fringe with mescal beans, beadwork trim, and brass and silver buttons.

■ Flintlock Springfield M1807 Carbine (also known as the Indian Carbine). Only two other original examples are known.

■ Sioux Council pipe with quill-wrapped ash stem and ribbon decoration. The catlinite bowl with lead inlay in the form of a hunter aiming his gun at a stag, geese in flight, the head of another stag, and the head of a bird. The original collection paper on the stem reads: "Sioux Indian pipe used in councils of war brought from America by Alfred Boyd 1868." 46 inches long.

Pipe smoking, though sometimes casual, was usually spiritual or ceremonial. It was the most widely practiced Indian ritual, and pipes were smoked before important affairs were discussed.

Catlinite is a red stone found only in Minnesota at a site the Indians consider sacred.

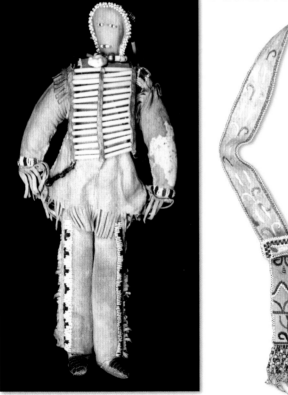

■ Shown here is a classic Plains male doll.

■ This turtle effigy bustle fetish, Northern Plains, is probably Lakota Sioux in origin and circa 1870s. The turtle is finely carved out of catlinite; this stone was considered sacred. It was believed to represent the blood of the earth and was used solely for ceremonial purposes, most notably pipe bowls. The turtle is attached to a rosette of cut feathers and quills, which were attached to a dance bustle.

For many Indian tribes, the turtle symbolized Mother Earth and was associated with the time of Creation. Different tribes had slightly different beliefs, but most held a number of them in common. Some referred to the earth as Turtle Island; the thirteen sections on the turtle's back represented the thirteen moons of the year. Others viewed the world as resting on the back of the Big Turtle and believed that when he got tired and changed position, earthquakes occurred. Because the turtle could breathe air but also lived under the sea, it was thought to be an instrument of the Creator. The turtle was celebrated during dances for its gift of fertility as well.

■ A Sioux shot pouch from the upper Missouri River area, made of hide, porcupine quills, glass beads, and commercial cloth. In faint ink on the back of the lower panel is the inscription "presented to—St. Louis, August 12, 1841 from R J Watson to G Parson 1841 at Ticcadonncaville."

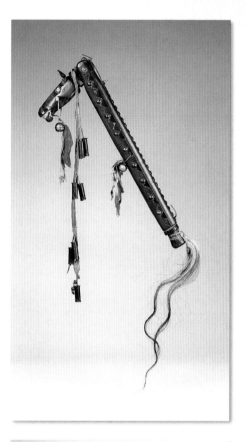

■ Lakota Sioux bird effigy spoon made from cow horn, late 19th century. Spoons and bowls were the Indians' principal eating utensils.

■ Shot pouch and powder horn, probably from the upper Missouri, circa 1850. The horn is likely earlier and came from a cow, not a buffalo. The bandolier is indicative of tribes in the Northern Plains mid-century, notably the Metis; their work is frequently mistaken for that of the Sioux. The Metis inhabited both sides of the Missouri and worked in the fur trade. The pouch designs also indicate a Missouri River tribe. They share similar materials and were evidently made at the same time using designs influenced by different Missouri River tribes. The pouch, bandolier, and horn are all most likely Missouri River Metis or Fur Trade, showing the influence of many tribes of the area.

■ A Cheyenne beaded hide baby carrier. The sinew-sewn hide carrier is mounted on a wood framework with two projecting forked back slats, each decorated with openwork and metal tacks and stained with deep red pigment. The carrier's white lazy-stitched background is decorated with a geometrical motif. Pairs of triangles intersecting at their top points, rectangles, pairs of smaller triangles arranged in a forklike design, and a narrow band encircling the carrier are rendered in dark blue, bright blue, yellow, green, and translucent red beadwork. 39 inches long.

Laced into the cradleboard, the child could be carried on the mother's back, hooked onto a saddle, or leaned against a tree or tepee. Elaborate cradles were customarily made by the new father's sister.

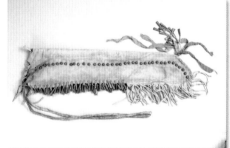

■ Shown here is a southern Plains Commanche horse raider's medicine man's bundle composed of a wood "horse stick" with cylindrical shaft and decorated with incised design and brass tacks, in a fringed hide case decorated with brass shoe buttons, ribbons, and tin rattlers, circa 1860–1870.

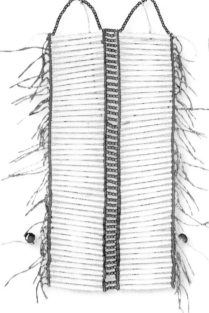

■ An early courting flute, or flagelot, is wrapped with bullsnake skin and dates from circa 1860. The bullsnake was the enemy of the rattlesnake, and the Indians believed it had great powers. Flutes were also used for enjoyment as well as courting rituals.

■ Jicarilla Apache drum, wood with hide heads, both painted, one with moon and star motifs. Northern New Mexico, circa 1900.

■ Sioux breastplate made of bone pipes with a center panel of brass trade beads, hawk bell on one side, and an 1875 military button on the other, circa 1880.

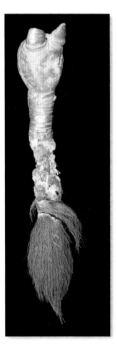

■ Northern Plains beaded and fringed hide tobacco bag, probably Blackfoot, circa 1875.

■ Sioux tobacco bag, circa 1875. Tobacco was sacred to the Indians, who mostly smoked it for ceremonial and religious purposes.

■ Northern Plains buffalo hoof rattle, circa mid-19th century, which has been repaired numerous times with various cotton strings and patches of tepee canvas attached to a buffalo tail. This rattle likely played a prominent role in religious ceremonial life.

■ This early Northern Plains doll, circa 1860–1870, is made from buffalo hide; the head is adorned with buffalo hair, and the face is painted. Collected by Father Martin, as written in ink on the right leg.

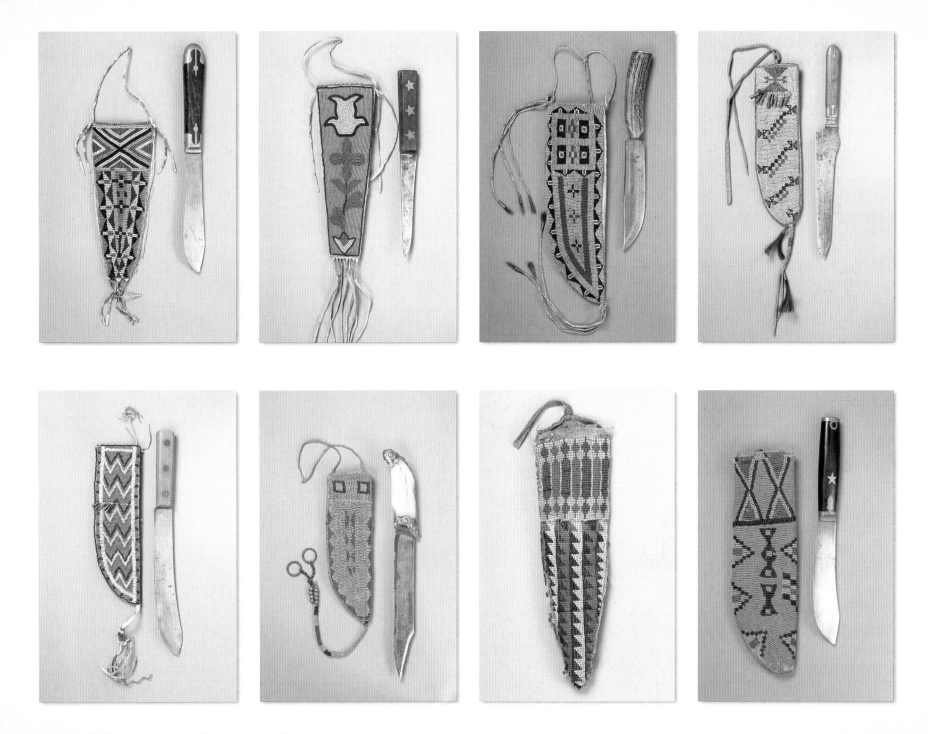

■ Beaded knife sheaths were usually presented as gifts.

The use of peace medals, which were almost always silver, began in the early 18th century, first by England, followed by France and Spain. The medals were seen by the Indians as physical evidence of the alliance and friendship that was declared in the indecipherable treaties they were signing. They were awarded not only at treaty signings but also for allegiance to Britain in war and by the Hudson's Bay Company to establish firm commitments in the fur trade.

The United States, beginning with George Washington's administration (see chapter 3), continued the practice, but with a very limited number of medals. Jefferson saw the necessity of medals for the Lewis and Clark expedition (see chapter 4) and began the practice of having Indian Peace Medals with the obverse showing the president's portrait and name, and the reverse engraved with clasped hands, a tomahawk crossing a peace pipe, and the legend "Peace and Friendship." The medals were minted in three sizes through the presidency of Zachary Taylor and, from then until Grant, in two sizes, and finally in one size through the administration of Benjamin Harrison. The large Thomas Jefferson medal, the first produced, was by far the largest (105 mm); the size was reduced by Madison to 76 mm.

The medals were distributed not only at treaty signings but also at visits to the White House by important Indians, as well as on tours of the Indian country by important government officials, by expeditions (notably Lewis and Clark's), and later by Indian agents according to a set of regulations drawn up in 1829:

> They will be given to influential persons only. The largest medals will be given to the principal village chiefs, those of the second size will be given to the principal war chiefs and those of the third size to the less distinguished chiefs and warriors. They will be presented with proper formalities and an appropriate speech. . . . Whenever a foreign medal is worn it will be replaced by an American medal.

The medals carried the full weight of the Indians' national allegiance during the commercial and military wars with England. They were also prized by their recipients as symbols of friendship and are seen being prominently worn particularly in the portraits by Thomas L. M'Kenney and James Hall (see pages 70 and 71). Many Indians were buried wearing their medals, while others passed them down through the generations.

Paintings shown on pages 68 and 69 are from Prince Alexander Maximilian of Germany's book *Reise in das Innere Nord-America in den Jahren*

■ George III Medal, the classic design given to Indians, circa 1776–1814. The impressive size (3-inch diameter) of these silver medals was very influential in attracting Indians throughout what is now Canada and North America to the British side and began the tradition of the Indians expecting expensive gifts.

■ A later George III silver Indian Peace Medal, dated 1814, given to Indians for their support in the War of 1812.

■ The first English Indian Peace Medal to be widely distributed, the King George I medal in copper.

■ Louis XVI Indian Peace Medal, 1774, presented to Hakosayee.

■ Franklin Pierce Indian Peace Medal with the reverse design changed from the clasped hands and the "Peace and Friendship" inscription to one showing the white man and the Indian in front of an American flag, with a plow and axe between them and pastoral scenes on either side.

■ James Monroe. "Peace and Friendship."

1832 bis 1834, published circa 1839–1841, which is generally considered the greatest and most important color-plate book on the American West.

Prince Maximilian was already an experienced naturalist and explorer when he began his preparations for his trip to North America, including retaining the skilled artist Karl Bodmer to prepare illustrations of the journey. He arrived in the spring of 1833, and traveled as far upstream as the American Fur Company post of Fort McKenzie in present-day Montana. He spent the winter at Fort Clark, near the Mandan Indian villages. During this prolonged stay, he and Bodmer had ample opportunity to observe the Indian tribes of the Upper Missouri in their full glory. Bodmer carefully recorded scenes of Indian life in watercolors. In the spring of 1834, they returned to Europe and devoted the next five years to preparing the text and plates for this publication.

As a painter, Bodmer was scrupulously realistic, and his portraits of the unspoiled West could never be duplicated. Four years after his trip, half of the Blackfoot and virtually all the Mandan Indians were dead from smallpox.

In the preface to his *Travels in the Interior of North America, 1832–1834*, Prince Maximilian noted,

A large portion of [North America] which only a few years ago was covered with an almost uninterrupted primeval forest and a scanty population of rude barbarians has been converted by the influx of immigrants from the Old World into a rich and flourishing state, for the most part civilized and almost as well-known and cultivated as Europe itself. Large and flourishing towns with fine public institutions of every kind have risen rapidly and every year add to their number. Animated commerce, unfettered unlimited industry have caused this astonishing advance of civilization. . . . The tide of immigration is impelled onwards wave upon wave and it is only the sterility of the Northwest that can check the advancing torrent.

■ Abraham Lincoln medal, the reverse showing the advantage of civilized customs over those of the Indian.

■ Karl Bodmer, *Bison Dance of the Mandan Indians.*

Another important source of period paintings of Native American life is George Catlin's *North American Indian Portfolio: Hunting Scenes and Amusements of the Rocky Mountains and Prairies of America*, published in 1844. This large-folio volume contains 25 hand-colored lithographs.

George Catlin was the first artist to observe the native tribes of the Plains Indians and to illustrate their habits and customs from firsthand observation. His belief in the noble savage, unspoiled by contact with the outside world, sustained him as he crossed and recrossed the country—from the Mississippi to the Rockies—gathering raw material for his Indian gallery.

In 1844, Catlin published the *Portfolio* as a means of publicizing the cause of preserving the vanishing Indian culture. His tableaux of Indian life demonstrate "the struggle for survival that was thought to shape the force and independence of savage character" (Ron Tyler, *Prints of the American West*, page 31).

Catlin appealed to his audience with the thrill of the hunt and tribal games and the mystery of Indian ritual. But Catlin's crusade to preserve the "wildness" of the Indians was in vain; within only a few years of his visit in 1832, the Mandan tribe had been wiped out by disease, and the noble savages were no longer untouched by the authority of European civilization.

■ Bodmer, *Moennitari Warrior in the Costume of the Dog Dance.*

■ Bodmer, *Mandan Indians.*

■ George Catlin, *Wi-Jun-Jon.*

■ *Ball-Play Dance* is from George Catlin's *North American Indian Portfolio.*

■ M'Kenney and Hall, *Ki-On-Twog-Ky or Corn Plant, a Seneca Chief.*

■ M'Kenney and Hall, *Wa-Pel-La, Chief of the Musquakees.*

Wi-Jun-Jon, or the Pigeon's Head Egg (depicted on page 69), was a young Assiniboine much admired by his tribesmen. Catlin met him when Wi-Jun-Jon was on his way to Washington. He painted a portrait of the Indian in his native costume. In Washington, Catlin wrote, "He travelled a giddy maze and beheld amid the buzzing din of civil life their tricks of art, their handy works and their finery. He visited their principal cities. He saw their forts, their ships, their great guns, steamboats, balloons, etc.,

and in the spring returned to St. Louis where I joined him . . . on their way back to their own country."

Catlin's model for the unspoiled Indian who had lured him to the West was now completely taken over by his experiences on the East Coast. He wore a blue army uniform and the high-crowned beaver hat, and he carried an umbrella, a large fan, and a small keg of whiskey. Wi-Jun-Jon's tales of what he had seen in the East were impossible for his tribesmen to

■ M'Kenney and Hall, *A Winnebago.*

■ M'Kenney and Hall, *Keokuk, Chief of the Sacs and Foxes.*

believe. After listening to him for three years, they came to believe that he was an evil wizard, and assassinated him.

One of the most important 19th-century works on the American Indian and one of the most important color-plate books produced in America in the age of lithography is Thomas L. M'Kenney and James Hall's *History of the Indian Tribes of North America, with Biographical Sketches and Anecdotes of the Principal Chiefs*, published in three large-folio volumes in Philadelphia between 1836 and 1844. M'Kenney, the Com-

missioner of Indian Affairs, collaborated with prolific Cincinnati journalist James Hall to produce this work, a series of biographies of leading Indian chiefs, written by Hall, and illustrated by 120 hand-colored lithographic portrait plates based on original oils by Charles Bird King and others. It was the most elaborate color-plate book produced in the United States up to that time.

CHAPTER 7 SANTA FE

Founded in 1610, Santa Fe was the first permanent settlement west of the Mississippi River. Unlike Mexico, which had developed because of gold and silver, Santa Fe grew out of the efforts of the Spanish missionaries to convert the natives. Despite generally good relations between the two groups, the Indians sometimes led uprisings against the missionaries and temporarily took control of Santa Fe from them.

By the time of the Lewis and Clark expedition, Americans had started using the Santa Fe Trail. The Mexicans feared these aggressive Americans who were following their "manifest destiny" across the continent and established a ban on foreigners' trading in New Mexico. In 1810, a group of American traders was jailed for eleven years. Other groups were arrested and their goods taken. Even explorer Zebulon Pike, who had blundered into Santa Fe territory, was arrested and not returned to the United States for some time.

In 1821, a revolt resulted in Mexico's breaking away from Spain, and Santa Fe was open to trade with the Americans. The trail itself was difficult—it was almost entirely desert, and the threat of Indian attack along its entire length was very real. Jedediah Smith, the great explorer and mountain man, was killed by Commanches on the trail in 1831. Nevertheless, the Americans came, and the first groups to arrive made enormous profits, as did the Mexicans. In 1824, traders brought a wagon train from Missouri carrying merchandise that cost them $35,000 to Santa Fe and sold it there for $190,000. Soon Mexican traders got into the business and began sending pack trains full of their trade goods north. In the early to mid-1830s the director of customs at Santa Fe charged $500 per wagon. Everyone was following their dreams of wealth—the Spanish, Mexicans, and Americans alike.

By 1840, New Mexico feared it would be taken over by the Americans in Texas who claimed Santa Fe and Taos as part of Texas. In response to rumors that the New Mexicans would revolt, the Texans raised an army of 300 to support the New Mexicans in their revolution. The Texans' information was incorrect. In fact, the New Mexicans were more fearful of the Texans and preferred to remain a part of Mexico. The members of the ill-conceived Texas expedition continued on toward Santa Fe but, neither being properly supplied nor knowing the route, became lost. The Texans were eventually found by the New Mexicans, who arrested them and marched them 2,000 miles to Mexico City and prison. Six years later in 1846, General Stephen Watts Kearny led 1,700 troops to take Santa Fe. The small force of occupation he established before moving on to California was able to quell uprisings in Taos and Santa Fe. The American takeover of New Mexico was the first part of driving the Mexican government south of the present-day border.

FOR THE
COLLECTOR
AND HISTORIAN

The books about Santa Fe, the trail, and trade are generally not expensive. Letters are rarely encountered but relatively inexpensive. Anything signed by **Kit Carson** is rare and costly.

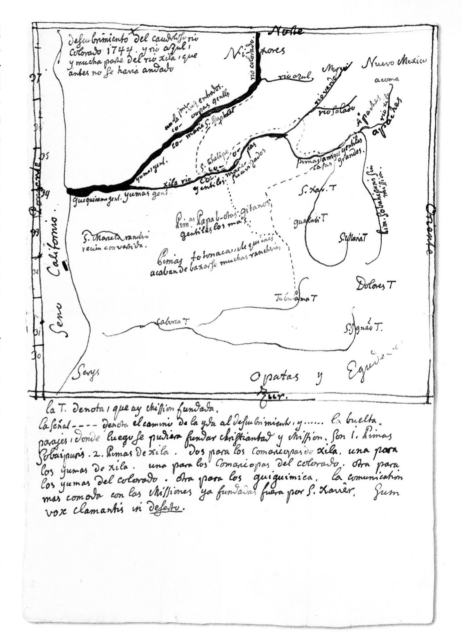

■ This map of explorations of the Colorado River in New Mexico is accompanied by a lengthy letter from the Jesuit missionary Gaspar Estiger, dated June 6, 1745, to his superior general in Mexico City. In it he reports on the Indians in the area, missions, the route, and the prospects of spreading the missions further. The map measures 8 1/2 by 7 1/2 inches.

■ Yoke used on the Santa Fe Trail. This type of yoke remained in use in the Santa Fe area until the late 19th century.

■ Josiah Gregg's *Commerce of the Prairies: Or the Journal of a Santa Fe Trader During Eight Expeditions Across the Great Western Prairies, and a Residence of Nearly Nine Years in Northern Mexico,* 1844, is the best contemporary account of the Santa Fe Trade. Gregg vividly described the scene on the trail: "'All's set!' is finally heard from some teamster—'All's set' is directly responded from every quarter. 'Stretch out!' immediately vociferates the captain. The 'heps' of drivers—the cracking of whips—the trampling of feet—the occasional creak of wheels—the rumbling of wagons—form a new scene of exquisite confusion. . . . 'Fall in!' is heard from headquarters, and the wagons are forthwith strung out upon the long inclined plain."

■ *Zuni, New Mexico,* by H.B. Mollhausen, lithograph, 1858. Mollhausen accompanied the 1853 Pacific Railroad Survey across northern New Mexico and Arizona, and published his plates and account of the journey in 1858.

Benjamin Bonneville, the Western explorer whom Washington Irving wrote about in the *Adventures of Captain Bonneville*, wrote a lengthy letter to the quartermaster general of the army in November of 1848. He discussed in detail his opinions about the Santa Fe Trail, particularly the problem with Indians and the need for setting up posts at critical points. His letter (shown at right) reads in part:

> If a post were established on the Canadian River, where the Texas line crosses it; you see at once, the advantage such a post would possess. The Indians and the Texans would each advance their settlements under its protection, & it would become the rallying point for all traders, wishing to participate in the trade of the prairies. It would be supplied with quite as much ease as, Fort Washita has ever been and I think that an Agent for Indians, established here, might readily acquire the happy influence over the Wild Man of the Plains. . . .
>
> Until New Mexico became ours, I was strongly of opinion, that some day we would be compelled to establish a post . . . somewhere not far from Bent's fort, to overawe our Indian population and to give an eye to our trade with Mexico: but, now that Santa Fe is ours—we have in this point, everything to be desired. I observe . . . so many plans for a rail road to the Pacific Ocean. . . . [N]o one seriously, will believe, a rail road can be safe, until the route be enveloped by the settlements, at least sufficiently, to secure the track from injury by the Indians. Until this period arrives, we may content ourselves with looking at Santa Fe, as the only true door, to our new territories.

Kit Carson became a national hero as John C. Fremont's guide; the reports Fremont wrote publicized his expeditions, himself, and Kit Carson's abilities in the wilderness. In a lengthy letter to Carson written from Fort Davis, Texas, in 1860, De Witt Peters, a physician on the frontier, wrote,

> I am back again in the army & am the Surgeon of this Post which is 200 miles south of El Paso & about 90 miles from the Rio Grande. I was doing well in New York but not being satisfied with City life I made up my mind to wander out on the frontiers again.
>
> Fort Davis where I am at present stationed is on the California Overland Mail route. . . . [H]ow bold the Comanches are here. . . .

Benjamin Bonneville's November 1848 letter to the quartermaster general of the army.

The soldiers turned their lead mules around & tied them to the wagon wheel which they also locked & then received the bucks. The Indians charged & the soldiers received them with several volleys from their minnie muskets. Two horses (Indian) were killed & two head Indians were mortally wounded when the red men ran but returned & attacked an ox train behind (loaded with Government supplies). They killed a Mexican Teamster; broke a wagon to pieces & carried off several animals together with such articles selected from the wagon as they fancied. For three

■ *Grand Canyon of Arizona From Hermit Rim Road,* by Thomas Moran, 1912. Lithographed in 1913 for the Atcheson, Topeka and Santa Fe Railroad.

We have had a tedious and tiresome journey thus far. . . . We started from Fort Leavenworth on the 17th of May—our own party consisted of about 30 men on horse back. We had an Escort of 50 Dragoons, with 35 six mule waggons carrying baggage and provisions for 150 days, for each man. . . . Santa Fe is nothing under the Heavens but a collection of mud houses [and] as you

weeks every train passing a place called "Johnson's M . . ." has had to fight & several have lost all their animals. These Indians have white men & Mexicans with them and are armed to the teeth, even down to Navey sized revolvers. The Mexican spoken of above was killed with this kind of ball as I saw the case & know it to be a fact. For some reason they do not trouble the mail or the mail stations though often, seen by the mail party. We need cavalry in this section very much & no doubt will have some soon as the Mexican affairs on the Rio Grande are being summarily quieted. There was a boy arrived in San Antonio said to have been rescued recently from the Indians of the Plains by you. He came down by the mail in Company with several officers. His Father is a German who lives near Fort Mason & I learned that this pernicious old Father felt very [sad] at having to pay some thing for the boys expenses. The boy liked or at least said he liked living with the Comanches & wished he was back again. The Indians here generally prefer mule meat to that of cattle which they rarely run off, only sometimes killing enough to supply their temporary wants.

In a letter written from Santa Fe, dated July 17, 1849, Edward T. Tremaine describes the Santa Fe Trail, Santa Fe, and his expectation that he will be leaving shortly for California guided by Kit Carson:

■ In this document signed by Kit Carson, dated March 31, 1859, he acts as Indian agent in certifying that he has purchased wheat, corn, tobacco, and other supplies at the "lowest market price."

approach it looks very much like a large brick yard before the bricks are burnt. The houses are all of one story & built of what the natives call Adobes, a sun burnt brick—they are nothing more than sods, cut from the ground about 15 x 8 inches thick, dried in the sun until they are hard enough to handel, & then put up with mud—the roofs are all flat, there is no regularity to the streets & the natives are a most miserable looking set of beings. We shall remain here probably a week longer and then proceed direct to San Francisco on Pack Mules with Kit Carson as our guide—where we expect to arrive in about 40 days. We anticipate a hurried and tiresome journey & we all wish most heartily that it was accomplished, but we are possessed with considerable patience & perseverance & I doubt not that we shall finaly get there.

■ Carte-de-visite photograph of Kit Carson.

■ Carson became a national hero as John C. Fremont's guide; the reports Fremont wrote publicized his expeditions, himself, and also Carson's abilities in the wilderness. Carson's friend DeWitt Peters wrote a flattering biography of him in 1874.

KIT CARSON'S
LIFE AND ADVENTURES,

FROM FACTS NARRATED BY HIMSELF,

EMBRACING EVENTS IN THE LIFE-TIME OF AMERICA'S

GREATEST HUNTER, TRAPPER, SCOUT AND GUIDE,

INCLUDING

VIVID ACCOUNTS OF THE EVERY DAY LIFE, INNER CHARACTER, AND PECULIAR CUSTOMS OF ALL

INDIAN TRIBES OF THE FAR WEST.

ALSO, AN ACCURATE

DESCRIPTION OF THE COUNTRY,

ITS CONDITION, PROSPECTS, AND RESOURCES; ITS CLIMATE AND SCENERY; ITS MOUNTAINS, RIVERS, VALLEYS, DESERTS AND PLAINS, AND NATURAL WONDERS. TOGETHER WITH A FULL AND COMPLETE HISTORY OF THE

MODOC INDIANS AND THE MODOC WAR.

BY

DEWITT C. PETERS,

BREVET LT.-COLONEL AND SURGEON U. S. A.

HARTFORD, CONN.:
DUSTIN, GILMAN & CO.
QUEEN CITY PUBLISHING CO., CINCINNATI; M. A. PARKER & CO., CHICAGO, ILL.; FRANCIS DEWING & CO., SAN FRANCISCO, CAL.
1874.

CHAPTER 8

EXPLORATION AND SCIENTIFIC EXPEDITIONS

Organized expeditions played a crucial role in America's westward expansion and the pursuit of the dreams of hundreds of thousands of Americans. The quintessential expedition was that of Lewis and Clark, which was organized by Jefferson and paid for by the government. The character of its two leaders and, to varying degrees, every member of the expedition made it successful and, more fundamentally, enabled the party to survive. There were multiple reasons for the expedition, but unlike other expeditions, it depended on two people: Meriwether Lewis, who focused on Jefferson's scientific goals, and William Clark, who mapped the topography and organized and led a small group of men—and one crucial woman, Sacagawea—on a nearly impossible trip.

Earlier organized expeditions—for example, Cook's and Vancouver's—were relatively large-scale naval endeavors. Alexander Mackenzie's expedition was more akin to that of Lewis and Clark. Both had the real goal of finding a water route across North America, and neither could find such a route . . . because there isn't one. Mackenzie was the first to cross the continent, but the route is today almost unknown because of its tortured course across very unappealing and difficult terrain.

After the Lewis and Clark expedition, Zebulon Pike and Stehen H. Long led expeditions to the Southwest. Pike was particularly inept as an explorer and managed to be arrested by Santa Fe authorities and led to Mexico. Both explorers described the Southwest as a wasteland and set back enthusiasm for Western exploration and expansion for decades. Both created the vision of the "Great American Desert." Long's report, written by Edwin James, called this region "almost wholly unfit for cultivation."

Although John C. Fremont was inept at carrying out the goals of his expeditions, this self-styled "pathfinder" was of great importance because of the maps produced by his expedition's skilled German cartographer, Charles Preuss. Fremont's national reputation as an explorer was largely the result of his talent for self-promotion. His romantic reports greatly increased popular interest in the West.

William H. Emory led an important expedition to the Southwest just after the Mexican War and spent six years surveying the new 1,800-mile southern border. His report is a major work on the West and was the first reliable information on the border area. By the time of the Civil War, the West was essentially explored and mapped.

The great geographical and geological surveys of the West from the post–Civil War period of 1867 to 1879 include Clarence King's *Report of the Geographical Exploration of the 40th Parallel.* The book contains more than 4,000 pages of text and hundreds of plates, illustrations, and maps. It was a landmark publication in American science. Ferdinand Hayden con-

FOR THE
COLLECTOR
AND HISTORIAN

All of the expedition reports of this period can be collected, but they range widely in price. Letters are not seen on the market.

Captain James Cook

■ Captain James Cook was the British mariner and explorer who charted the Pacific Coast of North America and did extensive exploration throughout the Pacific.

Drawn by J.Webber.   The Landscape Eng.by.Middiman

An OFFERING before CAPT. COOK, in the SANDWICH ISLANDS.

ducted an 1870 survey that explored and documented today's Nebraska, Wyoming, Utah, and Colorado but is perhaps best known for taking along the photographer William Henry Jackson. Jackson produced photographs that gave Americans a sense of the reality of the beauty and scale of the terrain.

The Grand Canyon area remained one of the last geographical mysteries until the 1869 expedition of John Wesley Powell. In the summer of that year, Powell's expedition discovered the canyon's last unknown mountain range, the Henry, and last unknown river, the Escalante. He

■ *An Offering Before Capt. Cook in the Sandwich [Hawaiian] Islands.* From *James Cook: A Voyage to the Pacific Ocean, Undertaken by the Command of His Majesty, for Making Discoveries in the Northern Hemisphere . . .* , 1784, three volumes.

■ The first explorer to record crossing the continent was Alexander Mackenzie.

also studied the Indians he encountered and reported all his findings in his *Canyons of the Colorado*.

These expeditions provided the maps and information for the great Western pursuit of the American Dream.

The greatest explorer of the 18th century was Captain James Cook. The account of his third voyage was based on his journals and those of James King, who succeeded Captain Cook as commander after the renowned explorer's murder in Hawaii. The third voyage was undertaken to continue the British survey of the Pacific, but most particularly to search for a northwest passage from the western side. Sailing in 1776, they discovered the Hawaiian Islands. The expedition then thoroughly

■ This signed letter by Alexander Mackenzie, from Fort La Truite, September 3, 1790, was written on the expedition that led him to the Arctic Ocean via the McKenzie River, two years before the voyage of discovery during which he became the first explorer to record crossing the continent. Mackenzie wrote to Alexander Fraser, "I Expected to have found Some Chipewians . . . to get Canoes to go to winter to Lac de Carribou. I found Several Campments. . . . One of my men Lost his woman here going out. . . . It is supposed that she is among with the Indians. . . . [O]rder him a three pound Blanke[t] . . . which he Lent him 5 years Since at the Beaver River."

explored and charted the northwest coast from the Bering Straits along the coast of Alaska and Canada, as far south as present-day Northern California. On returning to Hawaii in 1778, the expedition was at first received warmly by the natives. After the British sailors were forced to return to the island to repair a mast shortly after departure, trouble developed, which led to a tragic series of events in which the great navigator was killed.

■ "Costumes of the Inhabitants of San Francisco" from Jean-Francois La Perouse's *Voyage de la Perouse Autour de Monde* . . . , Paris, 1796–1797, about the greatest of 18th-century French voyages to the Pacific. The French navigator made an extensive survey of the northwest coast of America and published detailed maps and descriptions.

Alexander Mackenzie's 1801 book *Voyages From Montreal* is a classic of North American exploration. It describes the extraordinary travels of the author in 1789, when he discovered the Mackenzie River, and in 1793,

■ *View of San Francisco During Fishing Season* appeared in Jean-Francois La Perouse's *Voyage de la Perouse Autour du Monde . . .*, published in Paris, 1796–1797.

when he crossed the continent to the Pacific Coast of British Columbia and returned. Besides a narrative of his travels, Mackenzie also provided an excellent history of the fur trade in Canada, as well as vocabularies of several Indian languages. Mackenzie was sent on the expedition to find a water route to the Pacific by the North West Company, which was anxious to supply its fur trading posts from the Pacific rather than from Montreal. Mackenzie's route, however, was too difficult to be commercially useful.

V O Y A G E S

FROM

M O N T R E A L,

ON THE RIVER ST. LAURENCE,

THROUGH THE

CONTINENT OF NORTH AMERICA,

TO THE

FROZEN AND PACIFIC OCEANS;

In the Years 1789 and 1793,

WITH A PRELIMINARY ACCOUNT

OF THE RISE, PROGRESS, AND PRESENT STATE OF

THE FUR TRADE

OF THAT COUNTRY.

ILLUSTRATED WITH MAPS.

BY ALEXANDER MACKENZIE, ESQ.

L O N D O N:

PRINTED FOR T. CADELL, JUN. AND W. DAVIES, STRAND, COBBETT AND MORGAN, PALL-MALL; AND W. CREECH, AT EDINBURGH.

BY R. NOBLE, OLD-BAILEY.

M.DCCCI.

■ The title page of Mackenzie's book *Voyages From Montreal, on the River St. Laurence, Through the Continent of North America, to the Frozen and Pacific Oceans; In the Years 1789 and 1793, With a Preliminary Account of the Rise, Progress, and Present State of the Fur Trade of That Country*, London, 1801.

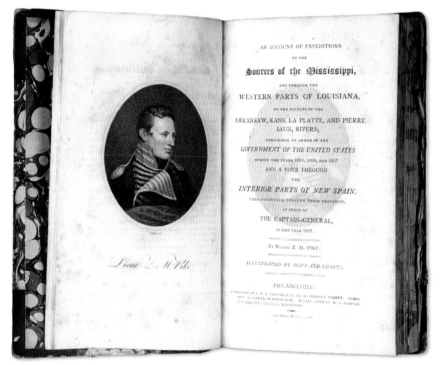

■ Zebulon M. Pike's *An Account of Expeditions to the Sources of the Mississippi, and Through the Western Parts of Louisiana . . .*, 1810, was the report of the first U.S. government expedition to the Southwest, and one of the most important of all American travel narratives. It includes an account of Pike's expedition to explore the headwaters of the Arkansas and Red rivers, his earlier journey to explore the sources of the Mississippi River, and his visit to the Spanish settlements in New Mexico. The maps that resulted from this expedition were the first to exhibit a geographic knowledge of the Southwest based on firsthand exploration and are considered milestones in the mapping of the American West.

CHAPTER 9

TEXAS

Prompted by the panic of 1819, Moses Austin began the colonization of Texas with 300 families on a grant of 200,000 acres obtained from the Mexican government. When he died in 1821, his son Stephen went to Texas to carry out the project. By 1832, as a result of his unremitting labor, perseverance, foresight, and tactful management, Austin's several colonies had about 8,000 settlers. Other impresarios with similar grants brought the territory's Anglo-American population to about 20,000.

Stephen Austin believed in and supported the relationship his colony had with Mexico. A prosperous colony was of great importance to him, and good relations with Mexico were at the heart of his plans. He steadfastly urged his colonists to appreciate their relationship with Mexico, to obey its laws, and to become loyal Mexican citizens.

The Texas colonists, however, saw themselves as the Texas vanguard of the pursuit of the American dream, and, as Americans, wanted a say in how the colony was governed. The success of the colonies led to more American settlers—more than Austin could handle—and the newcomers were much less tolerant of Mexican rule. By 1832, the Texans had organized a committee that met in San Felipe and presented Mexico with proposals for independent Mexican statehood for Texas.

Austin showed his skill as a diplomat when he tried to induce the Mexican government to make Texas a separate state in the confederation, so that the American settlers might have the liberty and self-government they considered indispensable. When this attempt failed, he recommended in 1833 the organization of a state without waiting for the consent of the Mexican congress, and was thrown in prison.

In 1832, as Mexican political leader Antonio López de Santa Anna continued to rise in power, Sam Houston arrived in Texas. A natural military and political leader, he quickly joined the independence movement and played an increasingly important role in the struggle as the Texans' unhappiness with Mexico grew.

FOR THE
COLLECTOR
AND HISTORIAN

The history of Texas has always been of great interest to both private and institutional collectors. Documents signed by Stephen Austin and Sam Houston can be found without difficulty, but William Barret Travis, who commanded the forces at the Alamo, is very rare. Antonio López de Santa Anna is frequently available. Anything concerning the Alamo is very rare and in great demand. The many books published during the early years of Texas's history are relatively inexpensive.

■ Stephen Austin was in St. Louis on February 12, 1832, when he wrote this letter, which reads, "I have recd your letter and the maps by Mr. [Rhodes] Fisher who arrived safe with his family. . . . The affair of Genl Santana [Santa Anna] has made no disturbance in Texas, and every thing here is peace and quietness and I think I will so remain. We are very much imposed in this remote corner of the nation to be misled or deceived by false rumours and reports. Such was the case during the whole of last month or the latter part of December. Great pains had been taken to impress upon the minds of many here, and on mine, amongst the rest, that the govt. intended to break us up—It was incorrect and I therefore wish you to <u>burn</u> the two last letters I wrote you, one in December & one in January—I leave in a few days for the seat of govt."

Houston urged the Texans to be calm. By mid-1835, Santa Anna had become dictator of Mexico. When the Texans learned of his plan to send a Mexican army on a punitive mission to Texas, they organized resistance and the Texas Revolution began. The Texans defeated the first forces Santa Anna sent. As Houston suspected he would, Santa Anna then sent better troops. In March 1836, he personally led 3,000 troops against the 183 Texans defending the Alamo, massacring all of them. Six weeks later, 800 Texans, under Houston's tactical leadership, caught Santa Anna's army of 1,250 and killed or captured all of them.

Texas was proclaimed a republic in June 1836, and Houston was elected president, defeating Stephen Austin. About 30,000 people had settled in Texas by this time.

In 1841, John Slocum wrote to a friend in Pennsylvania from Huron County, Ohio, "[I] travelled through the settled part of Texas. Allmost all kinds of property is plenty in Texas and is worth about the same as here. Government gives evry man that gets thare this year 320 Acres of land by cultivating 10 Acres of the same."

STEPHEN AUSTIN'S ORIGINAL TEXAS COLONY

The first book in English devoted entirely to Texas was written by Stephen Austin's cousin, Mary Austin Holley. Titled *Texas: Observations, Historical, Geographical and Descriptive, Written During a Visit to Austin's Colony, With a View to a Permanent Settlement in That Country, in the Autumn of 1831*, it was published in 1833. According to Holley,

> Texas until within the last few years has been literally a terra-in-cognita. . . . [T]his is the more remarkable, lying as it does, contiguous to two enlightened nations, the United States . . . and Mexico . . . being very easy of access both by land and sea. . . . A report has reached the public here that the country lying west of the Sabine River is a tract of surpassing beauty exceeding even our best western lands in productiveness with a climate perfectly salubrious and of a temperature at all seasons of the year most delightful. The admirers of this new country speaking from actual knowledge . . . call it a splendid country, an enchanting spot. . . . All who return from this fairy land are perfect enthusiast in their admiration of it. . . . It is uncertain how long this extensive and

■ An ornate land grant from the Galveston Bay & Texas Land Company, dated October 16, 1830, giving 4,428 acres in the area shown on the map, which depicts Austin's colony.

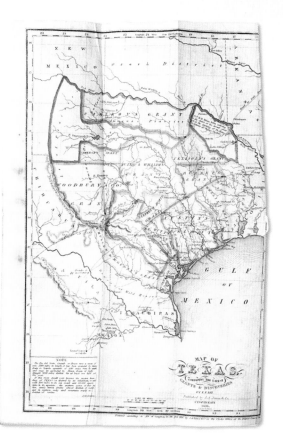

■ The map from Mary Austin Holley's *Texas: Observations, Historical, Geographical and Descriptive, Written During a Visit to Austin's Colony, With a View to a Permanent Settlement in That Country, in the Autumn of 1831.*

■ David B. Edward's map of Texas was published in his book *The History of Texas; or the Emigrant's Farmer's, and Politician's Guide to the Character, Climate, Soil and Productions of That Country . . . ,* 1836. Generally considered one of the best works written at the time of the Texas Revolution, the book describes Texas and political events up to 1835 through the eyes of a man who was not enamored of the Texans' revolt against the Mexican government.

valuable country would have remained unknown and unsettled had not the bold enterprise and perseverance of the Austins torn away the veil that hid it from the view of the world and redeemed it from the wilderness by the settlement of a flourishing colony of North Americans. . . . With the settlement of this colony a new era has dawned upon Texas. The natural resources of this beautiful province have begun to be unfolded and its charms displayed to the eyes of the admiring adventurers. A new island as it were has been discovered . . . at our very doors apparently fresh from the hands of its maker and adapted beyond most lands both to delight the senses and enrich the pockets of those who are disposed to accept of its bounties. . . . Emigration is often undertaken with expectations so vague and preposterous that disappointment if not ruin is the inevitable consequence. Not more unreasonable were the immigrants of the early history of America who expected to find streets paved with gold. . . . Those

individuals of the present day who escaping from confinement in poverty in the northern cities of America or from the slavery and wretchedness of the crowded and oppressed communities of Europe complained of their disappointments in Texas. . . . Such persons would do well to ask themselves in what part of the world they can get land for nothing, where obtained so many enjoyment with so little labor? What region combines every good? . . . A soil that yields the fruits of nearly every latitude almost spontaneously with a climate of perpetual summer must like that of other countries have a seed-time and a harvest. Though the land be literally flowing with milk and honey yet the cows must be milked and the honey must be gathered. Houses must be built and enclosures made. The deer must be hunted and the fish must be caught. From the primeval curse that in the sweat of his brow man shall eat bread though its severity be mollified there is no exemption even here. The immigrants should bear in mind

■ William Barret Travis commanded the Texas garrison at the Alamo. Shown here is an April 20, 1834, petition of Martha Hill regarding the settlement of her late husband's estate, signed by Travis.

that in a new community labor is the most valuable commodity. He sees about him all the means for supplying not only the necessaries but also the comforts and luxuries of life. It is his part to apply them to his use. He is abundantly furnished with the raw materials but his hands must mold them into the forms of art.

The inhabitants in general are composed of a class who have been unfortunate in life; as it could hardly be supposed that the fortunate except in a few instances would voluntarily make choice of a country where in they were to encounter such a number of difficulties as the first settlers had to contend with; who in a great measure were banished from the pleasures of life and almost from its necessities, so much so that many of them had to rely upon the precariousness of the chase alone for their first year's support; often times solacing themselves, men women and children on the flesh of a wild horse . . . without the satisfaction of seasoning it with salt! Although the whole country plentifully abound with that useful article, particularly near the lower waters of the Colorado.

■ Nicholas Pickford's detailed description written in Texoma, Texas, March 14, 1836, of the Battle of the Alamo, eight days earlier. "The Mexicans came in between 4 & 5000 strong & after an action of 3 Days our little band that remained alive say 7 out of 177, then begged for quarter but the Rascals gave them no other quarter than their swords & murdered every soul on the spot."

FIRST TEXIAN LOAN SCRIP.

No. 218

640 ACRES OF LAND.

CERTIFICATE OF TITLE TO SIX HUNDRED AND FORTY ACRES OF LAND.

Know all Men, That, in consideration of a Loan to the Government of Texas, negotiated by the Commissioners of said Government in New Orleans, on the eleventh day of January, 1836, *Thomas D. Carneal of Cincinnati Ohio*, is entitled to have and to hold, SIX HUNDRED AND FORTY ACRES OF LAND, of the Public Domain of Texas, according to the terms and conditions of a Contract of Compromise, made and executed on the first day of April 1836, between the Government ad interim of Texas, and the Stockholders in the aforesaid Loan; and of the Act of Congress for fulfilling and carrying into effect the said Contract of Compromise, approved the twenty-fourth day of May, 1838. This Certificate shall be authority for any duly appointed surveyor, to survey, at the expense of the holder hereof, any land, belonging to the Government of Texas, that may be selected by the said holder, at any time after the first Thursday in August next. And should the same be located on any land to which the government of Texas has not the prior right, it may be removed, and laid on other land. When the holder of this Certificate shall file the same, together with the boundaries, or field notes, of the land intended to be covered by it, in the General Land Office, a title or Patent, for the same, shall issue to the said *Thos D. Carneal*, his heirs or assigns, in the usual form.

In Testimony Whereof, I, SAM. HOUSTON, President of the Republic of Texas, have hereunto set my hand, at the CITY OF HOUSTON, this *Twentieth* day of *June* in the year of our Lord eighteen hundred and thirty-eight, and of the Independence of Texas the third.

BY THE PRESIDENT

Henry Smith
Secretary of the Treasury.

Sam Houston

SAM HOUSTON AND OTHERS

Although Sam Houston had evinced an interest in Texas ever since he was a young man—as early as 1822 he had joined a group of investors in applying for a grant of land in Texas, and in 1829, he had been invited by John Wharton to settle there—he apparently did not make his first trip to Texas until December 1832. In the spring of 1829, Houston had resigned the governorship of Tennessee following an acrimonious—and very public—estrangement from his wife. Alone and embittered, he set himself up among his Cherokee friends in the Arkansas Territory as a trader, an occupation he pursued for about four years. In the spring of 1833, he settled in Nacogdoches, where his popularity and character soon elevated him to a position of leadership in the growing agitation against Mexican rule.

Before permanently settling in Texas, he wrote an intimate and lengthy letter to a friend in New York, giving much information on his activities in the months following his retreat to the frontier. Dated from Wigwam Neasho, January 28, 1831, it is the most important Houston letter I have seen.

> I know that since we had parted, the little remaining stock of reputation remaining with me when we parted, since had been assailed by the solemn 'Report of a Committee'. . . . It was reasonable for me to suppose, that . . . my friends . . . might suppose me, only intitled to pity or contempt. Your letter was well calculated to dispel all aprehensions of the kind. . . . You do not know . . . how often, my heart has recurred to my friends of New York, in which you never fail to be embraced! You are a noble set of souls there, but I cannot be with you and therefore must solace myself with recollections of the past and hopes of a happy future to you all! I am done with goods, but not with good things I trust. In next month I hope to sell out, close my concern and migrate to some other Theater—say Natchez, and resume my profession, and do whatever else I may as, an honest & honorable man. My original design was to remain in the world as far as possible removed from scenes and circumstance which I believed it my duty to forego, and forget—but the world will not let me rest in quiet or enjoy tranquility—I am assailed when absent and my reputation must suffer too severely, unless

■ Sam Houston, president of the Republic of Texas, "in consideration of a loan to the government of Texas," gives Thomas Carneal 640 acres of land, June 20, 1838.

I return again, and by proper conduct rally around me proper aids, & after establishing a moral influence such as I can do, repel by my character the assaults, which may be directed, against my reputation. This will disappoint my enemies and gratify my friends! Furthermore mercantile business is not adopted to [my] cast or disposition! Nor if it were possible for me to enjoy all the luxuries of life, could I endure indolence, as a pass time—I must be active, or I would sink, into the horrible gulph of dissipation and debauchery!

Thus you see a sense of duty to myself and a decent respect for the feelings of my friends shall induce my course, and the things done by me, shall be directed to what I most devoutly believe, will be my countrys Glory, and her good! You speak of our Dear old Chief, and the success of his administration. From my soul, I rejoice in his Glory, and would to God, he had other, and I could add, better aids, to devise and execute his measures—who but a man just as Great as Genl. Jackson could sustain himself before the American people, with such a weight upon his shoulders as John H. Eaton. He alone is enough to break the Backbone of Atlas; or destroy any other mans moral, and political influence save the old Chiefs! But it is an evil that must cure its-self and patience must be the remedy, for the disease for any struggle to get rid of the evil, might only produce greater! As to Mr. V[an] B[uren] of your State I know, but little, but deem your remarks . . . very just, so far as I can judge! So soon as I can get settled, you will be apprised of it.

Within three months of Governor Sam Houston's marriage to Eliza Allen on January 22, 1829, the couple was estranged; on April 16, Mrs. Houston returned to her father's house in Gallatin, Tennessee, and Houston, refusing to discuss the separation, endured five days of public innuendoes before he resigned his governorship and vowed to return to life with the Cherokees. Neither Houston nor his wife ever disclosed the reason for the broken marriage, but historians have since concurred that Houston's hasty condemnation of his young wife's affection for a previous suitor—and the couple's failure to reconcile their differences before they became public—precipitated the crisis. In any event, Houston renounced

■ Title page of George W. Kendall's *Narrative of the Texas Santa Fe Expedition . . . Through Texas, and Across the Great Southwestern Prairies, the Comanche and Cayuga Hunting-Grounds, With an Account of the Sufferings From Want of Food, Losses From Hostile Indians, and Final Capture of the Texans, and Their March, as Prisoners, to the City of Mexico,* 1844.

NARRATIVE

OF THE

TEXAN SANTA FÉ EXPEDITION,

COMPRISING A DESCRIPTION OF

A TOUR THROUGH TEXAS,

AND

ACROSS THE GREAT SOUTHWESTERN PRAIRIES, THE CAMANCHE AND CAYGÜA HUNTING-GROUNDS, WITH AN ACCOUNT OF THE SUFFERINGS FROM WANT OF FOOD, LOSSES FROM HOSTILE INDIANS, AND FINAL

CAPTURE OF THE TEXANS,

AND

THEIR MARCH, AS PRISONERS, TO THE CITY OF MEXICO.

WITH ILLUSTRATIONS AND A MAP.

BY GEO. WILKINS KENDALL.

IN TWO VOLUMES.
VOL. I.

SEVENTH EDITION.

NEW YORK:
HARPER & BROTHERS, PUBLISHERS,
FRANKLIN SQUARE.
1856.

his promising career and, embittered by the controversy, which his political opponents did much to encourage, set out to live among his Cherokee friends, newly relocated by government treaty to the Arkansas Territory. He settled at Wigwam Neosho, a trading post he built near Cantonment Gibson, just north of present-day Muskogee, Oklahoma, and set up business as a contractor supplying Indian rations. Eager to protect his friends from unscrupulous agents, he traveled to Washington in early 1830 to complain to secretary of war John Eaton about fraudulent practices in the distribution of supplies This, as Houston's comment in his letter reflects, provoked a controversy with the secretary. At the same time, the scandal over the breakup of his marriage continued to rage. In April 1830, a group organized by longtime political foes of Houston's issued a report declaring that Houston's "unfounded jealousies and his repeated suspicion of her coldness of want of attachment" were the cause of the separation. The report, which was released to the newspapers, further insinuated that Houston had rebuffed attempts at a reconciliation.

Not everyone thought Texas the ideal place to settle. M. Kennett wrote of his intentions to his mother from Corpus Christi, Texas, on July 16, 1849:

> I shall be on my way for California where I hope after the elapse of a short time to be able to repair my disappointed fortune and make up for lost time in Texas. . . . The party which I leave with consist of about fifty men well armed and equiped, used to travel through a wild country, tryed soldiers who have fought all through the Revolution in Texas. The distance from here about fifteen or eighteen hundred miles to be undertaken on horseback, and with our experience in a campaign life it will be a mere execution of pleasure.

James Hamilton was enthusiastically involved in the struggle for Texas independence. Having advanced substantial funds of his own to the cause, he was honored by the leaders of Texas with a series of appointments. In 1838, the president of Texas, Mirabeau B. Lamar, made Hamilton commissioner of loans, and in 1839, Hamilton went to Europe as diplomatic agent to France, Great Britain, Belgium, and the Netherlands, where he secured recognition of Texas, as well as favorable commercial treaties. Soon, however, he became a casualty of the austerity that followed Sam Houston's return to the presidency: Texas, in effect, defaulted on $210,000 in gold owed personally to Hamilton. In 1855, he settled permanently in Texas, where he had an enormous land grant, hoping to recoup his debt through land promotion, as well as by political means. That year he wrote a letter full of the same exuberance for the future of Texas that still exists more than a century and a half later:

> [There is] an enterprise in North Eastern Texas which I regard as the most promising operation which is open to the Enterprise of those who have the sagacity & boldness to embrace it. I send you most confidentially a Pamphlet which is yet a sealed Book which I shall not issue until I have made my association with a capitalist or capitalists & made negotiation & selection of Lands. Then I shall transmit it to my friends . . . to invite them to the lovliest & most fertile region on Earth. . . .
> I send it for your sole & exclusive perusal. I have not the smallest hesitation in avowing, that I can during the ensuing Winter purchase Lands in the Country in question for $1 or $2 pr acre which in five years will certainly & inevitably bring $5 & $10 and after all the capital is replaced with a profit of 50 pCent if one half of the Lands are retained for five years

■ A letter from John B. Jones, commander of the Texas Rangers, from Austin, August 19, 1878, to Captain Pat Dolan, commanding officer of Ranger Company F. Written exactly a month after his ranger detachment had tracked down and killed the notorious train robber Sam Bass, Major Jones's letter displays his careful attention to military organization and discipline:

"I wish you to be particularly careful in reorganizing. . . . [D]rop all who have proven themselves inefficient or in any manner shown that they are not well fitted for the service in which we are engaged. We are allowed so few men that we cannot afford to keep any drone among the number. Send me report of the number of men whom you will reinlist of the present company and if you have not required number I will send you some good men whom I am recruiting from the interior counties, most of whom have been engaged in sherrifs' officers. I expect to come to the frontier in September and can bring the recruits out with me."

more, the half so retained will sell for $20 pr acre. After you have read my Pamphlet you will oblige me exceedingly if you will go to London & see Mr Peabody. He will show you my Letter detailing the terms & conditions of the association I have proposed the scope an object of which is to raise $100,000 to purchase 100,000 acres in the Region distinctly designated & laid down in the Pamphlet. Rich as Mr. Peabody is the diversion of so large a sum as $100,000 from his Banking business might be inconv[en]ient but it is quite possible he might organise under his influence & lead a Company of ten persons at $10,000 each who would be willing to go into the Enterprise. I know not how it might suit you to take a share but if it did I think I might with safety gu[a]rantee you Fifty thousand in five years for your ten at the lowest possible calculation.

As the Pacific Rail Road may never be completed to its extreme western terminus yet that it will be build from the Red River indeed from Memphis to the Banks of the Leon in less than five years cannot be doubted which will appreciate the Lands in NoEastern from 500 to 1000 pCent. This Road is already commenced. I have urged prompt action on the part of Mr Peabody as the Season for profitable operation will close in the Spring. As Mr Peabody is but imperfectly acquainted with me you can best inform him who [is] the . . . man calculated to conduct the proposed Enterprise & to give to it a successful development. Pray oblige an old friend by going to London & seeing Mr Peabody. I have requested him to show you my Letter that you may understand the whole subject. . . .

In case you do not become a share holder in the proposed association or you do not hand the printed circular to some one who is a member or Mr. Peabody deems the association of impracticable formation then return me the Pamphlet as it might accidently without your knowledge fall into the Possession of some person who might avail himself of information which I have acquired at so much cost & labor.

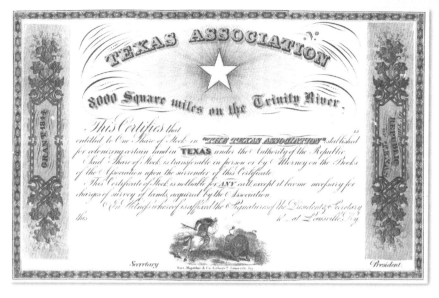

■ A Texas Association "8,000 Square Miles on the Trinity River" stock certificate from Louisville, Kentucky, 1858. It reads in part, "This certifies that _____ is entitled to One Share of Stock in 'The Texas Association' established for colonizing certain land in Texas."

■ A revolver made by Cimmaron, Houston, circa 1892; the holster is decorated with a Mexican coin.

CHAPTER 10

CALIFORNIA

California had always been somewhat neglected by Spain. Only when Russian fur hunters began to expand to the south from Alaska did the Spanish begin to establish a chain of missions up the coast. The first mission was San Diego in 1769, and eventually 21 were founded, as far north as San Francisco. Within 15 years of Mexican independence, the mission system was in decline, in part because of the expulsion of all Spanish-born missionaries.

By 1846, California was being settled by Americans pursuing their dreams of rich farmland and good weather. Its government was far removed from Mexico, which supplied neither financial support nor an army. The talk of independence was everywhere.

John C. Fremont was in California on an exploring expedition and, knowing of the growing tension with Mexico over negotiations concerning the Texas border, joined the Bear Flag Revolt, aiding an independence group that raised a "grizzly bear" flag in Sonoma on July 4, 1846. Fremont's hopes for sole glory were brief; an American squadron under Commodore John Drake Sloat occupied Monterey, and Fremont had to join forces with him and his successor, Robert F. Stockton, in the conquest of Northern California.

Stockton sent Fremont's men, including Kit Carson, by boat to take Southern California, and by August, San Diego and Los Angeles were occupied. Meanwhile, the troops that had just taken Santa Fe under Stephen Watts Kearny were still making their way to California; west of Santa Fe in September 1846, they met Kit Carson, who was heading east. Carson told them of the conquest of California. At the Colorado River, they received the news that Californios—the descendents of early settlers from Spain and Mexico—had revolted and recaptured Los Angeles, Santa Barbara, and San Diego. Kearny had to fight his way into California and, reinforced by Stockton's men and American settlers, defeated the Californios at the San Gabriel River on January 8 and 9, 1847. The Americans reoccupied Los Angeles without opposition. The tensions that arose among the occupation forces were largely the result of the traditional army-navy rivalry that continues even today. Stockton refused to recognize Kearny as President Polk's authorized commander and appointed Fremont governor. In February, orders from Washington confirmed Kearny's authority, and Fremont traveled back East, where he was court-martialed for insubordination.

FOR THE COLLECTOR AND HISTORIAN

Letters and documents from many of the major figures in pre–gold rush California are fairly available on the market, though rarely with content concerning the period. Many books are also available, and even though they are widely collected, prices are still relatively modest.

THE ESTABLISHMENT OF THE CALIFORNIAN MISSIONS

Francisco Palóu's *Relacion Historica* was the most important contemporary account of the Spanish colonization of California and the beginning of the mission system that dominated life there until the coming of the Americans. In 1769, the Spanish began to occupy upper California, mainly to forestall any possible incursions by the Russians or English. Father Junipero Serra was the chief figure in the founding of the 21 California missions that were a key part of the Spanish government there, and the story of his 15 years there encapsulates a large part of the Spanish effort. The author accompanied Serra to California, and so had first-hand knowledge of many of the events he described.

Francisco Palóu, in an autograph manuscript diary, 71 pages in length, entitled *Diary of the Expedition by Land Which Was [Done] to Reconnoiter and Discover the Environs of the Port of San Francisco in the Year 1774*, gives a day-by-day account of his own expedition from Monterey to San Francisco and back during a well-equipped and well-manned exploration to and around the San Francisco Bay area. It includes extensive and detailed observations on the Native American Indians and their customs as well as on the terrain, distances, weather, and suitability of various places for the establishment and settlement of missions.

Palóu writes,

> Diary . . . on the voyage . . . carried out in the month of November 1774 to the environs of the port of San Francisco on the coast of the Pacific Ocean of Northern California, with the purpose of occupying them with new missions entrusted to my Hispanic College of Franciscan missionaries . . . of Mexico City.
>
> We encountered . . . a large settlement of more than 30 houses, well made of grass, and when we approached many Indios came out of them armed with bows and arrows. . . . We called to the Indios, they came nearer, and many of them gave me arrows, which they consider the greatest gesture of peace, and I responded with a string of glass beads.
>
> The men were completely naked, like all the other heathens, and some of them had a hood of leather or grass to protect their back from the cold down to the waist, leaving the rest of the body uncovered, and the principal, which they had to cover. Some of them are very bearded and most of good size and corpulent. The women are covered with the leather of animals and grass instead of petticoats. . . .

V. R. DEL V. P. F. JUNIPERO SERRA

hyo de la S.ta Prov.a de N.P.S. Fran.co de la Isla de Mallorca D.y Ex.cr de Theol.a Comis.io del S.to Of.o Mis.o del Ap.l Col.o de S.n Fern.do de Mex.co Fund.r y Presid.te de las Mis.s de la Calif.a Septentr.l Murio con gr.e fama de sant.ed en la Mis.on de S. Carlos del Pu.to del N. Mont.e Rey à 28 de Ag.to del 84 de edad de 70 a. 9 m. 4 d.s hab.do gastado la mi.d de una vida en el exerc.o de Mision.es Apost.co

RELACION HISTORICA,

DE LA VIDA Y APOSTÓLICAS TAREAS

DEL V. P. FRAY JUNIPERO SERRA,

De la Regular Observancia de N. S. P. S. Francisco de la Provincia de Mallorca; Doctor, y ex-Catedrático de Prima de Sagrada Teología en la Universidad Lulliana de dicha Isla; Comisario del Santo Oficio en toda la Nueva España, é Islas adyacentes; Predicador Apostólico del Colegio de Misioneros Apostólicos de Propaganda Fide de San Fernando de México; Presidente y Fundador de las Misiones, y nuevos Establecimientos de la Nueva y Septentrional California y Monterey.

CAPITULO I.

Nacimiento, Patria y Padres del V. P. Junípero: Toma el santo hábito, y exercicios que tuvo en la Provincia antes de pretender salir para la América.

EL infatigable Operario de la Viña del Señor el V. P. Fr. Junipero Serra dió principio á su laboriosa vida el día 24 de Noviembre del año de 1713 naciendo á la una de la mañana en la Villa de Petra de la Isla de Mallorca: Fueron sus Padres Antonio Serra, y Margarita Ferrer, humildes Labradores, honrados, devotos, y de exemplares costumbres. Como si tuvieran anticipada noticia de lo mucho que el hijo que les acavaba de nacer se habia de afanar á su tiempo para bautizar Gentiles, se afana-

na-

I made the sign of the cross to them all, who were very attentive to the ceremony, which they did not comprehend, or know what its purpose was. I spoke to them in the language of Monterey some words about God and heaven, and although they were very attentive, I was not satisfied that they understood. . . .

I . . . give them a string of beads and a little tobacco. . . . They went off to smoke . . . with them the same custom and ceremony as in all the others. The chief was the first to smoke

■ Francisco Palóu's *Relacion Historica de la Vida y Apostolicas Tareas del Venerable Padre Fray Junipero Serra, y de las Misiones que Fundo en la California Septentrional, y Nuevos Establecimientos de Monterey . . .*, Mexico, 1787.

and immediately he passed the pipe on to all the others, and each took a mouthful of smoke while speaking a few words.

[I] saw the mouth that is like a narrow channel where the great estuary of San Francisco enters the Bay of the Promontories.

When ships enter via the strait they could anchor behind the island while protecting themselves from the winds, as they would be free from high seas as soon as they entered the strait.

Standing atop the cliff of the ridge . . . that forms the narrows or channel of the mouth of the estuary of San Francisco, we had a view of the Bay of the Promontories and . . . Punta de Reyes and [that] of the Guardian Angel. . . . This appears to be the Port of San Francisco.

Inasmuch as this high steep hill is the point of land that forms a wall of this southern range on the strait or channel of the mouth of the estuary of San Francisco . . . on which until the present no Spaniard or Christian had set foot, it seemed to us . . . to be [fitting to] fix on the summit the standard of the Holy Cross.

Palou's expedition is described by DeNevi and Moholy in their biography of Father Serra. Junipero Serra:

By November of 1774 . . . [Governor] Rivera was ready to undertake the reconnaissance of the San Francisco Bay area preparatory to founding the sixth mission [San Francisco de Asis]. On November 30, sixteen soldiers and Palou, along with supplies for forty days, headed north. On December 4, Palou planted a cross on the highest peak overlooking the wide entrance to San Francisco Bay. When the party returned to Monterey on December 13, Palou presented his diary to the padre president, who immediately forwarded it to the viceroy.

In *California: An Interpretive History*, Walter Bean describes the site where the sixth mission was finally founded on March 29, 1776.

For the site of the new presidio, Anza chose a point near the northernmost tip of the San Francisco peninsula. Rivera had noted, and it was one of his objections, that the whole northern part of the peninsula consisted largely of sand dunes. About three miles to the southeast of the presidio site, however, Anza found a little oasis on a creek, and here . . . he marked the site of the mission. . . . Various obstacles, including some set up by Governor Rivera, delayed the actual founding of the new establishments for several months. . . . The presidio was formally established . . . on September 17, and Father Palou formally opened the mission on October 9.

In his classic memoir *Two Years Before the Mast*, from 1849, Richard Henry Dana described California and its inhabitants in great detail, saying California was

a country embracing four or five hundred miles of seacoast with several good harbors; with fine forests in the north; the waters filled with fish and the plains covered with thousands of herds of cattle; blessed with a climate then which there can be no better in the world; free from all manner of diseases whether epidemic of endemic; and where the soil in which corn yields 70 to 80 fold. In the hands of an enterprising people, what a country this might be! We are ready to say. Yet how long would a people remain so in such a country? The Americans . . . and Englishmen who are fast filling up the principal towns and getting the trade into their hands are indeed more industrious and effective than the Spaniards; yet their children are brought up Spaniards, in every respect and if the 'California fever' [laziness] spares the first generation it always attacks the second.

California was described as a paradise in Alfred Robinson's *Life in California*, an 1846 account of his experiences in the 1830s and early 1840s:

Gold and silver mines have been found in upper California, from which, considerable quantities of ore have been obtained: skillful miners are only required to make them profitable. It is said that coal has recently been discovered; which if true will greatly facilitate the introduction of steam navigation in the Pacific and be the means of making California one of the most important commercial positions on the west coast of America; particularly, if ever a communication should be opened by means of a canal across the isthmus of Panama. That such an event may transpire is not improbable; the day is not far distant, perhaps when it will be realized and one may visit this fertile and interesting country and return to the United States in one-half the time now required for the long and tedious outward navigation. The resources of California, its magnificent harbors climate and abundance of naval stores would make it the rendezvous for all the steamers engaged in the trade between Europe and the East Indies as well as those from the United States; and the facilities for immigration would be such that soon the whole western coast of North America would be settled by immigrants both from this country and Europe.

Addressing the political situation, he writes,

Why not extend the area of freedom by the annexation of California? Why not plant the banner of liberty there . . . at the entrance of . . . the spacious bay of San Francisco? It requires not the far-reaching eye of the statesman nor the wisdom of a contemplative mind to know what would be the result. Soon its immense sheet of water would become enlivened with thousands of vessels and steamboats would ply between the towns which as a matter of course would spring up on its shores while on other locations along the banks of the rivers would be seen manufactories and sawmills. The whole country would be changed and instead of one being deemed wealthy by possessing such extensive tracks as are now held by the farming class he would be rich with one quarter part. Everything would improve; population would increase; consumption would be greater and industry would follow. All this may come to pass; and indeed it must come to pass for the march of immigration is to the west and not [naught] will arrest its advance but the mighty ocean.

■ Estevan Tapis was president of the missions in Alta, California, from 1803 to 1812. In a letter he wrote at the Mission of Santa Barbara on October 12, 1804, he writes, "I received your official letter . . . in which the king decreed that no Knight of the Order . . . can receive the sacrament of marriage without having received, in writing, the permission of the Council [of the Indies]. [This] will be given after having seen and approved the information, which the Knight must present, on the limpieza de sangre [purity of blood] of the woman he intends to marry."

■ The earliest printed maps of America all correctly show California as a peninsula. About 1620, however, a Carmelite friar drew a map that—probably based on reports by the Spanish navigators—depicted California as an island. The ship carrying the map to Spain was captured by the Dutch and the chart taken to Amsterdam. Soon thereafter, maps representing California as an island began to appear. This 1690 map by Justus Danckerts, titled *Recentissima Novi Orbis Sive America Septentrionalis et Meridionais Tabula,* is a reissue of one first drawn by the Dutch cartographer Claes Visscher in 1670 and copied many times afterward.

CHAPTER 11

OVERLAND TRAILS

For hundreds of thousands of Americans, the Oregon Trail was their pathway to their Western pursuit of the American Dream.

The Oregon Trail was possible because of South Pass in Wyoming. This 20-mile-wide pass is a natural gateway through the Rocky Mountains. The east and west slopes are so gradual it is difficult to realize when you are at the highest point. South Pass was discovered by Robert Stuart in 1812 as he was heading east from Astoria, at the mouth of the Columbia River.

2,000 miles .... The length of the Oregon Trail.
1843 .... The first large migration on the Oregon Trail (900 people).
1848 .... 12,000 immigrants travel the Oregon Trail.
1835–1855 .... Between 250,000 and 650,000 travel the Oregon and California trails; an estimated 10,000 die of cholera and smallpox. Approximately 400 are killed by Indians.

In 1832 Nathaniel Wyeth traveled over what would become the Oregon Trail on his way to set up a trading venture in the Pacific Northwest. Two years later he established Fort Hall, Idaho, as an important trading post on the trail, and this was the route of migration to the West. In 1836 Narcissa Whitman and Eliza Spaulding became the first white women to travel on the Oregon Trail, and during the 1840s the number of immigrants kept increasing until the discovery of gold in California set off a tidal wave of people traveling overland to California.

The Oregon Trail began in Independence, Missouri, and went across present-day Kansas and Nebraska and into present-day Wyoming. Fort Laramie was a major stop for travelers before they crossed the rest of Wyoming and proceeded through South Pass. The trail then split into two branches, one leading to the Great Salt Lake, and the other continuing west and later dividing into the California Trail to Sutter's Fort (now Sacramento) and the original route to Oregon.

It was important to leave Independence in late spring or early summer to ensure that there would be good grass near the trail (too early and there wasn't grass; too late and the earlier wagon trains would have used all the grass within easy proximity to the trail). To be among the first also meant some chance of hunting game for food. Soon into the season the game was driven far from the trail.

Companies formed at Independence because larger groups offered security from Indians. Ten wagons was the minimum. Two thousand pounds was the usual load, and east of Fort Laramie the trail side was scattered with furniture that overloaded wagon trains had to dump. The entire trail was marked with graves, an impressive number of which are still visible today.

FOR THE COLLECTOR AND HISTORIAN

Despite the number of letters and diaries quoted here from my collection, they are quite rare. They represent much of what has come onto the market in the past 40 years. Guidebooks, however, excluding the early ones, are available, and those from the mid-1850s are very reasonably priced.

Depending on the weather, the ability of a group, and luck, the trip to California averaged five months. The Gambrel brothers' letters later in this chapter describe a trip of three months, but, as the Gambrels wrote, their trip was exceptional. Twelve miles was the average distance covered in a day.

There were two alternatives to the Overland Trail. The first was to take a boat to Panama, cross the isthmus, and hope to find a ship traveling to California. The letters of S.D. King describe the hardship of this mode of transportation firsthand, as well as the costs. The other alternative was the six-month voyage from the East Coast around Cape Horn to California. Relatively speaking, this could be comfortable. Travelers didn't write of the hardships faced by those crossing Panama to California. Thomas Sherman's journal of his voyage from Boston to California from November 17, 1849, to May 26, 1850, which runs to 79 pages, is completely positive and records a pleasant journey around the Horn.

The Santa Fe Trail was almost exclusively for trade caravans, and while the Englishman who wrote the diary at the end of this chapter reached California this way, it was hardly the sensible route.

THE TRIP THAT PIONEERED THE OREGON TRAIL

Nathaniel Wyeth became interested in the proposals for a colony in Oregon, and he organized an expedition to go overland to Oregon in the summer of 1832. Separately, he sent a ship full of trade goods to meet him at the mouth of the Columbia River. Wyeth attended the 1832 fur trade rendezvous in the Rocky Mountains and then continued on to the Columbia River. It was not until nine years later that his route became the Oregon Trail as it is thought of today. In this letter written from St. Louis on April 18, 1832, he writes to his wife in Massachusetts:

> Here I am on the outskirts of Civil Soci[e]ty having advanced so far without accident and without the desertion of a single man. I leave this in company with a party of traders of 40 persons who journey with me as far as the west side of the Rocky Mountains. In the first vessell that comes out to the Columbia [River] I wish seeds of all vegetables, grains and trees sent me for which purpose be collecting them this fall. I wish only a small quantity of each. . . . I cannot receive on this side of the Mountains.

■ *The Rocky Mountains: Emigrants Crossing the Plains,* a Currier and Ives lithograph from 1866.

Wyeth wanted the seeds so that he could determine whether the same plants would grow in the Pacific Northwest that thrived in the Northeast. He had grand plans for the Oregon Country. His plan was to bring set-tlers by land and supplies by ship, and then to send back salmon on the boats so he could profit instead of wasting their return trip. However, his first ship was lost, putting an end to the venture.

Wyeth returned east in 1833 to organize another expedition to Oregon. He stopped again at the fur rendezvous in the Rocky Mountains and negotiated a contract to bring trade supplies to the 1834 rendezvous. When he arrived there in 1834 he found that his contract had been disregarded, and he was left with a caravan of trade goods. He decided to open a trading post that would compete with the Rocky Mountain Fur Company, which had broken his contract. He established Fort Hall, the first permanent U.S. post west of the Continental Divide. In this letter to his brother, written from the Columbia River, October 6, 1834, he writes:

timber, and watered by a good mill stream. The soil is beautiful. If some of the things on which the mind's eye casts a "longing lingering look" were here, I might be content to rest from my labors, and lay my bones in this remote world. I leave here in a few days on a voyage to the interior, and shall establish two more forts, one of which will be near the Great Salt Lake, if I can find any tribe of indians who can give trade enough to support it.

MESSRS. PATTIE AND SLOVER RESCUED FROM FAMISH.

■ An illustration from *The Personal Narrative of James O. Pattie . . . During an Expedition from St. Louis, Through the Vast Regions Between That Place and the Pacific Ocean, and Thence Back Through the City of Mexico to Vera Cruz,* 1833, one of the classics of Western Americana. The author wandered for six years through the Southwest, and his account of his adventures, hardships, and explorations includes 22 descriptions of California that encouraged Americans to head west.

Since my last of June 21st I have made the establishment spoken of on Snake River in Latt. 46-14N, Long. 113-30W and raised the Stars and Stripes amid the explosions of Gunpowder and whisky, according to custom, and they now wave to the wind in the naked wastes of central America, a wonderment to the simple savage, who can not conceive the meaning of so much disturbance. I have also made a farm on the Multnomah on a prairie of about 15 miles long bordering the River which is nearly as large as the Ohio, surrounded by beautiful and well assorted

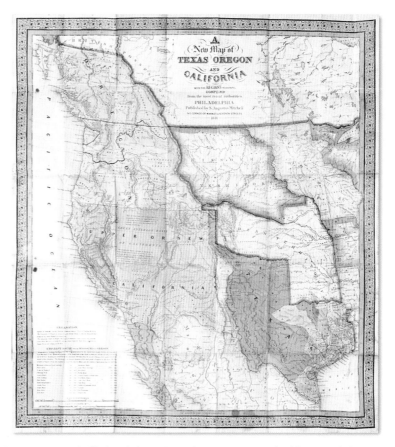

■ S. Augustus Mitchell's detailed *New Map of Texas, Oregon and California With the Regions Adjoining . . .,* from 1846, shows the western portion of the United States to the Pacific, with the Indian Territory, Missouri Territory, Iowa, and portions of the states of Missouri, Arkansas, Louisiana, and Wisconsin, as well as northern Mexico and part of British Columbia, illustrating in detail the Trans-Mississippi region just before the Mexican War. Texas is elaborately depicted, with the Rio Grande as its southern border; the Santa Fe Trail and the Oregon Trail are both detailed, the latter with a table of distances published in the lower corner of the map. The map is among the first by a commercial cartographer to utilize the recent explorations, and because of its popularity it exerted great influence.

THE FIRST GUIDE TO THE OVERLAND TRAIL

Lansford W. Hastings was an early promoter of emigration to California. His propangandistic work *A New History of Oregon and California* (earlier titled *The Emigrants' Guide to Oregon and California*) played on the hopes and ambitions of emigrants, who were lured by the promise of "as much land as you want" in California. Hastings has been blamed for contributing to the Donner Party tragedy because of his promotion of a cutoff south of Salt Lake (his error is corrected in the edition shown).

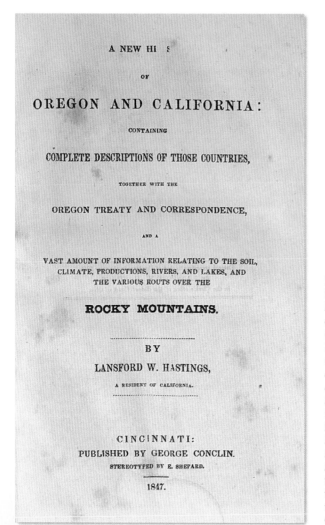

A PARTY OF EMIGRANTS CROSSING THE ROCKY MOUNTAINS.

■ Left and right: Lansford W. Hastings's *New His[tory] of Oregon and California: Containing Complete Descriptions of Those Countries, Together with the Oregon Treaty and Correspondence, and a Vast Amount of Information Relating to the Soil, Climate, Productions, Rivers, and Lakes, and the Various Routs Over the Rocky Mountains*, 1847. This is the second known and first revised edition of the first guide to the Overland Trail.

Hastings described his own party setting out in May of 1842 "for the long desired El Dorado of the west":

> [A]ll was high glee, jocular hilarity and happy anticipation as we thus darted forward into the wild expanse of the untrodden regions of the "western world." The harmony of feeling the sameness of purpose and the identity of interest which here existed seemed to indicate nothing but continued order, harmony and peace amid all the trying scenes incident to our long and wholesome journey but we had proceeded only a few days travel from our native land of order and security when the "American character" was fully exhibited. All appeared to be determined to govern but not to be governed.

Hastings's very detailed description of California and Oregon covers all aspects of life there, a life that he highly recommends: "A new Era in the improvements of California has commenced. Here as in Oregon foreigners from all countries of the most enterprising and energetic character are annually arriving selecting and improving the most favorable sights for towns and selecting and securing extensive grants of land and the most desirable portions of the country."

Another important guide, by Overton Johnson and William Winter, was *Route Across the Rocky Mountains with a Description of Oregon and Cali-*

fornia . . ., published in 1846. This was an important overland guide, one of the earliest issued, and a primary guide book of the first great overland emigrations. Both of the authors went to Oregon in 1843, returning in 1845. They write in part:

The climate in Oregon and California is far milder and more agreeable. . . . As the farmer's stock can live well all winter . . . he will here possess one advantage that he can never have east of the Rocky Mountains. . . . [H]e will not be compelled . . . to labor six months to produce grain and provender to feed out at the expense of another six months labor to his stock. . . . Another great advantage . . . paramount to all others is health. Those countries . . . are . . . very healthy. . . . They are high dry rolling mountainous and well-watered with the purest springs and streams. When this Province shall have been settled by an industrious and enterprising population disposed to avail themselves of all the advantages which Nature has so bountifully spread out over this country; it will be covered with vast multitudes of stock of all kinds; the upper country will become a manufacturing district and everywhere on and around the extents of Bay of San Francisco, the most active and extensive commercial operations will be constantly going on but no country of which we have any knowledge is so fitted by nature to become one great manufacturing region as the territory of Oregon. It has everywhere over it an abundance of never failing water power sufficient to propel machinery of any kind. . . . But little is yet known of the minerals of the country. Some lead and iron have been discovered and if an intimate acquaintance with the country shall discover an abundance of the metals then will there be nothing wanting to make Oregon one of the

greatest manufacturing countries in the world but the necessary population and capital, both of which time and enterprise of our countrymen will give.

THE DONNER PARTY

The Donner Party was organized by two wealthy brothers in Springfield, Illinois, along with Irish immigrant James F. Reed, and was plagued from the beginning by bad decisions and internal fighting. The latter was common to many immigrant parties, but the poor decisions were almost unique to the Donner Party. They had read Lansford Hastings's guidebook describing a short cut to California from Fort Bridger, across the mountains, and then across the desert south of the Great Salt Lake. At Fort Laramie they met a guide heading east who told them that this route could not be traversed by a wagon train, but they did not consider the advice and at Fort Bridger followed the Hastings route. Hastings had very repeatedly promised to personally guide them, but he was with a much smaller, more appropriately equipped, and better organized immigrant group ahead of them. At today's Weber Canyon he told them they could not make it through the mountains there and sent them on a completely unexplored route over the mountains through what is now Emigration Canyon. Enormous time was lost cutting trees to clear their way, and when they reached the Great Salt Lake they were far behind schedule.

As they crossed the desert, Reed's over-sized wagon, referred to derogatively as "the prairie palace," bogged down and had to be abandoned along with many other wagons and most of the animals. When they reached

ROUTE

ACROSS THE ROCKY MOUNTAINS,

WITH A

DESCRIPTION OF OREGON AND CALIFORNIA;

THEIR

GEOGRAPHICAL FEATURES, THEIR RESOURCES, SOIL, CLIMATE, PRODUCTIONS, &c., &c.

BY OVERTON JOHNSON AND WM. H. WINTER,
OF THE EMIGRATION OF 1843.

LAFAYETTE, IND:
JOHN B. SEMANS, PRINTER.
1846.

■ The title page of Johnson and Winter's *Route Across the Rocky Mountains.*

■ George Donner and James F. Reed were the leaders of the most ill-fated overland party. Shown here are documents signed by each, dated 1830 and 1843.

the western side they lost even more time as surviving members went back into the desert to look for their animals. They were camped just below the pass that today bears their name when an early snowstorm struck on October 28. The snow continued, and they realized they could not get over the pass. On December 16, 15 of the strongest survivors left to get to Sutter's Fort and bring back help. They had six days' rations, but the journey took them 32 days; as members died, cannibalism set in, reaching a low point when the party killed their two Indian guides for food. Cannibalism was also being practiced for survival by those who had stayed behind.

On February 19, the first of several rescue parties reached their camp, and the survivors were brought to Sutter's Fort. Of the 89 immigrants who had left Fort Bridger, only 45 reached California.

1848: SPREADING THE NEWS OF GOLD

George Brewerton was 19 when he joined the California Volunteers as a second lieutenant in 1846 and sailed from New York to California around Cape Horn, arriving in San Francisco in March 1847. In January 1848, gold was discovered at Sutter's Mill, and Brewerton was chosen for the job of carrying the news east. He sailed from San Francisco to Los Angeles, where he met Kit Carson, the legendary scout and explorer, who was to serve as his guide across the desert and Indian Country. From Los Angeles they set out with their small party on May 4, 1848, bound for Independence, Missouri, via Santa Fe. This significant journey became known as "Brewerton's Ride," which he later described in a series of three narratives published in *Harper's Monthly*: "A ride with Kit Carson" (December 1853), "Incidents of Travel in New Mexico" (April 1854), and "In the Buffalo Country" (September 1862). The three articles later appeared in book form as *Overland With Kit Carson* (published in New York by Coward-McMann in 1930).

Brewerton kept no diary of the trip, and the sketches and notes he made were lost during the party's crossing of the Colorado River. Therefore the works he wrote and sketched after the trip were done entirely from his memory, which was prodigious. His narrative sparkles with details, as do his sketches. Felled by illness after reaching Santa Fe, Brewerton was forced to remain there while Carson went ahead to Independence; Brewerton followed soon thereafter and joined his regiment in Mississippi.

His sketchbook, illustrations from which are shown here, is an important record of many of Brewerton's memories of his momentous trip of 1848. There are several scenes of California, including one of Los Ange-

■ Rocky Mts. 1848.

■ Log Cabin. S. Antonio Road. Texas. 1849.

■ Valley near 'Los Angeles,' Cala. 1848.

■ Street in 'Los Angeles', California. 1848.

■ Church. Laredo, Texas 1851.

■ The Great American Desert. 1848.

■ The Great Prairies. 1848.

■ *Westward Ho!*, an engraving by T.D. Booth after a painting by James H. Beard, 1866.

les that is one of very few views of the city from this period. The view is similar to the one illustrated in *Harper's* and shows a one-story adobe building with several figures in the foreground.

Of Los Angeles Brewerton wrote, "The Pueblo of Los Angeles has a population of several hundred souls; and boasts a church, a padre, and three or four American shops; the streets are narrow, and the houses generally not over one story high, built of adobes, the roofs flat and covered with a composition of gravel mixed with a sort of mineral pitch. . . . In most respects, the town differs but little from other Mexican villages."

There are very few views of California extant from this period. As Willard O. Waters noted in *California 1847–1852*, "Accurate and artistic contemporary drawings of scenes from the time of the American conquest to the Gold Rush are not common. There were few persons in California, during those years, who had the training or inclination to make a record, with pencil or brush, of what they saw."

In addition to the California scenes, there are 8 views of Texas, 2 of New Mexico, 13 of the Rocky Mountains, and 4 of the Great American Desert, as well as views of New England, New York, and South America. The choice views of Texas are a particularly rare form of documentation; very little artwork of Texas by trained artists in the 19th century is extant. The sketches resemble those published in *Harper's*, although, for obvious reasons, the original sketches are more detailed and highly finished. Brewerton was an inventive and talented artist; he developed a new painting medium during the 1860s in which he combined pastels with oil. His versatility and mastery of medium are evident in the sketches that combine silverpoint, ink, and watercolor. Four loose silverpoint sketches are instructive of Brewerton's technique. He most likely made a silverpoint sketch, then finished and highlighted it with ink and watercolor. The drawings in the album are rendered on a thick, glossy, coated paper, which imparts a luminous quality.

Brewerton probably presented this sketchbook, which includes scenes from all his travels from 1847 until 1860, as a Christmas gift to his father in 1860. Apart from his paintings and published drawings, this sketchbook is the only documentation of "Brewerton's Ride," and it records scenes that soon passed into memory, history, and legend.

Shown on page 107 is a selection from his album of one hundred original silverpoint, pen, ink, and watercolor finished sketches, each measuring approximately 2 1/4 x 3 3/8 inches. Each sketch in the album is identified by Brewerton in ink, indicating the location of the scene; most have a year written in ink as well. It is a remarkable collection of unpublished original artwork.

Offering a different perspective on the discovery of gold is this letter from the army paymaster at Monterey, California, who wrote to the Paymaster General in Washington on October 23, 1848:

> I arrived on the 18th inst. From San Diego; and have paid the four companies of the 1st New York Regiment in full, [Col. J.D. Stevenson commander], and they have all started for the gold mines. . . . [T]he command of Lt. Col. Burton are now here and will muster out today . . . as the residents are extremely anxious to get rid of them. . . . Nearly all the men of Co. 'F' 3d Artillery, have deserted. We have the Ohio, Warren, dale, Lexington and Southampton [U.S. war ships] in port, but they cannot land a man, as they desert as soon as they set foot on shore, the only thing the Ships could do in case of an outbreak would be to fire upon the town. . . . Treasury Notes are good for nothing now. . . . Gold dust can be purchased for eight or ten dollars the ounce and it is said to be worth $18.00 in the U. States. . . . Col. Mason and most of the Army officers are at fort Sutter. . . . THE GOLD FEVER RAGES AS BAD AS EVER and the quantity collected has not diminished but increases.

AMONG THE INDIANS

The first Western letters I acquired for my collection are a series by D.B. Christ, which begins in Independence, Missouri, on March 13, 1849:

> Independence contains from 16 to 17 hundred inhabitants is within twelve miles of the Indian Teritory, it is a business place on account of the Emigration to California and Origon, then the Sante Fe trade is carried on to a large extent. Mules cost from sixty to Eighty Dollars a piece, oxen sell from fourty to sixty Dollars pr. yoke, waggons from eighty to one hundred and twenty Dollars and with bed and bows. Every thing is high in price; Boarding one Dollar pr. day. Plenty of Indians here. They are a miserable looking set of Beings; I pity them in my soul. . . . I thought I would make a visit to the Indians; I went twenty four Miles in their Teritory and remained four days with them. I have seen many strange things among them, they wore no clothing except what we call leggings and a Blanket now and then. You see some with a few rags tied round his privet part of the body,

A letter by D.B. Christ describing his experiences.

the squaws the same. The Indian has this head ornimented with different kinds of feathers, the squaw has no covering to her head except her Long Black hair. The squaw has to do all the Laibour such as cutting and gathering wood, fetching water, carry g[r]ain. Their wigwam is made by sticking sticks in the ground and the top of them tied together and then they cover them with Buffalow skins. Their Bed consists of no more than sometimes a skin and some lay on the bare ground on account of having used up their skins for food. Being a hard winter they could get no game; some of them nearly starved. They eate any and everything they can chew and swallow—dogs, Mules, Horses, guts and all. . . .

Now I will give you an account of our state of things and arrangements. In the first place there are six of us in company.

This is followed by Christ's decription of the equipment and provisions he had bought, along with the cost of each item. He continues:

I think there will not be Less than twenty thousand people to pass through this place to California this Spring. The reason of our staying here is an account of the grass which we must depend on for food for our animals. . . . Many hardships dificulty and dangers we have to encounter before we can expect to see the promised land of gold. In the first place we have two thousand miles from this to California; nearly seven hundred miles of this is a prairie or plain where we cant get wood for fire. All we can get in this distance for to cook with is Buffalo Dung. Here it is termed Buffalo Chips. After we cross this plain we will reach the rocky mountain where we will find much dificulty in getting our waggons over many rivers and Creeks. We have to contend with whare I expect to have to Built rafts to cross on by all this I don't mind. But the greatest trouble we will find with the Indians. It is reported that the Indians have a knoledge of this emigration and allready are gethering from all parts of the forest to the route which we have to go. It is not my life that I am afraid of but of their robing us of our animals and provision and if we must starve. . . . There is not much danger in going among them if you have no property or provision, but it is for property that the[y] will kill, but if all is delivered up they will spare life at least in many cases.

Perhaps the piece of Western travel writing most familiar to modern readers is Francis Parkman's *The California and Oregon Trail: Being Sketches of Prairie and Rocky Mountain Life*, published in 1849. The narrative describes his experiences on the Oregon Trail and in Wyoming and Colorado in 1846. The exciting adventures of the young Boston Brahmin loose on the plains makes excellent reading, especially his account of life with the Sioux in the Black Hills.

■ An illustration from Francis Parkman's *The California and Oregon Trail*.

■ *On the Prairie,* an 1860 engraving by Leopold Grozelier after a painting by Charles Wiman.

A member of the Delaware Company, A.C. Moses, had gotten a very early start on the Oregon Trail and wrote from Fort Laramie on May 28, 1849,

> At the Missouri river we had rigged up a set of harness for each wagon and had driven six horses until the day we reached the Platte. . . . About a mile the other side of the ford we met the first Sioux. . . . We were surrounded by them. They are fine set of men most of them six feet in highth. They are friendly enough. . . . By thunder I thought they would hug me to death. . . . We made the chief a present of about a bushel of corn. They are the greatest lot of beggars ever I went any where. My red Coat took I had more than a hundred offers for it. . . . I was after a pony but could not wring in for want of time. . . . Several of the boys traded worne out coats for [buffalo] robes. . . . There was about fifty Squaws come up. Among them I noticed about a dozen very good looking ones and a couple of positively handsome ones.

■ This token was issued by the trading post at Fort Laramie on the Overland Trail.

From Oregon Canyon, Christ wrote this on March 14, 1850:

> I . . . am in the promised land of gold. After four month and four Days travel we reached a Land inhabited by whites. . . . Much suffering and hardships we all had to endure during this journey; I suffered most every thing but Death. Thousands have left their bones on the plains and Rockey Mountains. Many Died from that horrid dissease the Colara and some whare murdered by the Indians and many Died from hardships which were greater than they could endure. It is reported that there is over two thousand souls Died during this Journey last summer. . . .
>
> We had much trouble with the Indians. They would steal our Cattle and murder our men . . . whenever they had an oppertunity, but thank God they did not kill any of our Company as we always stuck close together. They are a cowardly and treacherous Nation; they will not attackt the whites unless they have every advantage of them.

The letter next describes an encounter with the Indians while out hunting that nearly cost him his life:

Emigrants Crossing the Plains, an engraving from 1860.

> We was in the buffalo countrey . . . [and] after traveling two or three miles I discovered five Indians all mounted on their ponys. I immediately put my spurs to my horse and steared my course for the train. They followed me until I got in sight of my Company. They got within sixty or seventy yeards of me. In this chase I injured my horse so that he was unable to travel any further so I was obliged to travel the remainder of the road afoot. This Chase took place on the south Fork of Platt River about six hundred miles from the states on the plains. . . . This was the Sioux Tribe that gave me this Chase. There were some of the whites killed by the Indians, but far more Indians were killed by the whites, as most of those wild Tribes have no other weapon than Bow and arrow and Lance. We had every advantage of them on account of our firearms as we could kill them at a further Distance and had our waggans for to fortify us while they had to take at all times the open plains. Perhaps it would be well to mention here that it is one vast plain Barren Mountains and sandy Desert from the Line of the States untill to California Mountains, with the exception of now and then a few cotten wood trees along some of the streams. But from Fort Hall to the Sink of Humbolt River which is over five hundred miles there is not the sign of a tree.

The last letter was written from Lewellyn, March 1, 1852:

> It was not gold that induced me to make my first trip across the Rocky Mountains, no it was something more noble, it was that inquiring mind which my Creator bestowed to me, and I was richly rewarded for all my sufferings in that adventure. But if I did not go for gold then it is not to be supposed, that I cannot go for gold this time, and I do think that I will bring some gold with me when I return, that is if my life is spared. . . . I think they have full confidence in me as a leader . . . or Guide . . . especially for this trip I have carefully counted the cost before I consented, for I am well aware that we have a Long journey before us, and that we have hardships sufferings and Dangers to encounter. But in all these things I shall act with a firm and determined mind to sustain the character of a man. Fear will find no hiding place in my brest, justice will be my Motto, Love and Friendship shall be my governing principles.

Fort Laramie was a major point on the Oregon Trail and an opportunity to send letters back home. David Howe wrote to his wife on June 5, 1850, from there:

> There has past thirty five hundred wagons past this fort up to this date. I dont think that is one third that will pas but I am keen to swear that there wont one half the horses get to the mines that is on the road. . . . [T]his is the porest cuntry I ever seen in time. No grass the bufalo has used the botams so much they have kild the grass out. We seen a company this day right from the mines which give us som incuragement for to procede on. The[y] said they had money enough to doo them and that there was plenty for all So dont think that I am sick of my trip yet. I expect to bee in Sacrimento city by the first day of august.

THE HARDSHIPS OF CROSSING THE COUNTRY

Crossing the desert between Salt Lake and the Sierras was the worst part of the journey in the heat of summer, as Jessie Mason wrote his parents on September 15, 1850:

> From St Joseph to the Rocky Mountains we met with no serious diffculties excepting from poisonout springs and alkali water the latter of which was very plentiful. Cattle and horse both would drink this if they had been long without water and causing instant death. The 1st of July we were in the city of the great Salt Lake settled by Mormons.
>
> They have plenty of cattle horses &c and raisde large crops of grain and that to where there is not a particle of rain for four or five months. There are thousands of streams running from the mountains however which are made to run over the fields. . . . The cattle and horses are the fattest that I ever saw. On the 5th we left and on the 12th of Aug we were on the top of the Sierra Nevada mountains at the height of 9,538 feet 3,000 higher than the top of the White Mountains. . . . These troubles however were nothing to what we encountered in the Humbolt River. . . . [I will provide] a short description of the country. Bounded on the North East South & West by high mountains covered with a perpetual Snow the Great Basin as this country is called is entirely shut out from [the] World and [ha]s rivers and lakes of its own. It is 600 miles East and West & about the same North & South. Salt Lake city is on the Eastern side of the Basin. The Springs in this Basin are generally impregnated with sulphur and iron frequently boiling hot. The ground contains much salt and Alkali. It never rains here and the ground is parched the greater part of the year so that nothing except a few insignificant shrubs grow except on the Rivers and creeks which run from the mountains and continually grow smaller until they lose themselves in the sand. It is inhabited by a hostile race of Indians the most degraded perhaps that exists in the world but are not very dangerous as they are extremely cowardly and will run when discovered. They sometimes shoot cattle & horses so that they are obliged to leave them. On the Humbolt River they stole many horses and killed one or two men with arrows. They took two horses f[rom] us.

At about the same time, Charles Treadwell wrote to his sister describing his terrible overland trip:

> [We encountered] the angel of death in the shape of the cholera in its form terrific, following us for 700 miles. Out of 160 of us, 6 weeks after reaching California, every 4th man was dead. . . . It is said that all men in crossing the plains are more or less insane. We were in constant danger of being attacked by Indians or having our mules stampeded. . . . For 300 miles west of the Missouri to this place, the country may be considered one vast waste. I could tell you of Scotts Bluffs, of the soda springs of ash hollow, the terrible Humboldt valley, winter river mountain cover'd with eternal snows, of the hot springs, of the saleratus ponds, of the Canons of the platte & sweet water Rivers pronounced canyon, of the [sink] of the Humboldt. . . . California is pretty much moonshine, & those that have started lately will wish such a country never existed.

The personal toll of the overland journey is described in a series of letters by Alden Putnam to his wife. The earliest letters were written on the Oregon Trail and described the daily difficulties. When he arrived at Sutter's fort he wrote to her on December 3, 1849:

I find most all the Origon peapol are willing to return when they make a fortion. . . . They call it very helthy and a fine farming cuntry. . . I shall not leave you to go to California again. . . . If I had known the feelings from being from my family, Origon and the gold in California would not hav seperated me from you. . . . You rite you do not know but I think more of gold that I do you or I would not gon to California. . . . I asure you . . . I would not swap you for your heft in gold. I would like to make anough to make us in easy sercamstance in life.

William Gambrel wrote the first in a series of letters to his mother, "Near St. Joseph," Missouri, May 8, 1849. "[T]here are more than two thousand persons in this place . . . bound for California. . . . I consider our chance for crossing the plains equal to that of any other."

He next wrote from "On Big Platte 80 miles from Ft. Chile," June 4, 184[9].

We left the mother company on day after our separation and are I suppose 20 miles ahead of them at this time, as the majority of them are too lazy to go to California. For a man who is at all afflicted with laziness, had better change it for the most <u>persevering industry</u>. . . . [A] lazy man could not place himself more out of his element than by starting on a trip of this kind. My almost entire thoughts are on California and its gold. . . . [W]e generally travel three miles before any one else leaves camp.

He reached Fort Lamamie on June 17, 1849: "[I] am getting along . . . better than any other ox train that I have see on the route, as we have passed since we left our compay near 1500 wagons & 12000 head of stock. . . . I think we will make the trip in 3 1/2 months."

He made excellent time across the Overland Trail. He writes from Upper California, October 12, 1849: "[W]e arrived on the 7th Sept . . . after a travel of one hundred and sixteen days. Some of the first waggons

■ An immigrant's trunk covered with horsehide that has been encased in a buffalo hide by Indians. The trunk contains various animal skins, leaves, and other articles associated with the Pebble Society. There are also lesson books and letters from the Carlisle Indian School and the Omaha Agency.

however came in in the short space of 90 days. . . . Well the reports which we heard in regard to the quantity of gold in this country were not at all exagerated, though the rapidity with which is obtained, was slightly incorrect. We worked about three weeks and made near seven hundred dollars."

He convinced his brothers to head to California, and both brothers wrote from Fort Laramie on June 9, 1850:

[The] 1200 [miles] from California the longest and most difficult end of the road yet before us. . . . The only Fear we have about getting though is a sufficiency of grass. . . . When we first started the Horses teems drove by us so fast that I sometimes wished I had have started with Horses but I am of a different opinion now. Any man could have made an independent Fortune by coming out here and have purchased all the waggons that have been left here & at other places for Sale. I saw waggons sell here for $6 that in the States would command 100 very Readily. I am becoming better satisfied with oxen every day. We are beginning to pass mules & Horses already and we did not expect to outtravel them until we got near the mountains. We have been much troubled about wood for several days. We frequently have to go 4 or 5 miles and then get nothing but cedar shrubs. Notwithstanding our little troubles & inconveniences none of us have thought we have seen any hard times yet. We are all prepared for the worst & will not be disappointed when it comes. An express from Weston overtook us yesterday . . . [and] told us they had passed 8000 waggons since they left Westport.

The most unusual overland diary in my collection is that of an anonymous Englishman who began his journal on March 1, 1849, as he was departing Liverpool for New York, and it is not initially clear that he knew what his final destination would be. "Irresolute and undecided as to my future movements chance decided it. . . . A fellow passenger decided upon starting with an organized party for California. Always possessing a spirit for adventure and new places and new scenes I at once determined upon accompanying him—we . . . started a party of sixteen persons on the 9th of April."

The roads and canals got them to Pittsburgh, where they boarded an Ohio River steamer. The party encountered many difficulties after crossing the Mississippi, including the death of their leader, who was drowned while crossing the Arkansas River. He described passing through Indian villages: "[I] visited some of their dwellings and was agreeable surprised to find them so intelligent, well-informed and civilized. The young men

tall, good-looking, well-proportioned as are the women. I am told there are more handsome Indians between this and the Pacific." While the diarist continued to mention the goal of getting to California, his party continued on a southerly route: "July 1, we have this day entered upon what we consider the first marked accent to the base of the mountains leaving what we at present imagine to be the Great American Desert. The passage across has naturally been uninteresting and worrisome in the extreme. We fully trust the green mountains will soon appear in sight."

They were running short on food: "Our biscuits have been divided and perhaps like our days number few. Still I despair not yet." On August 14 he wrote, "We have seen a white man, a poor shepard who informs us we

LIFE ON THE PRAIRIE.
The 'Buffalo Hunt'

■ *Life on the Prairie: The Buffalo Hunt,* a lithograph by Currier & Ives, 1862.

have but two or three days journey to Santa Fe. This is joyful intelligence to us poor hungry souls." They continued on, staying at a Mexican village:

> Encamped within twenty-five miles of Santa Fe where many small companies lay preparing for a final start for San Francisco. The rest will lay down to San Diego on the Pacific Coast. The accounts of Santa Fe are horrible. It appears to be a den of theives and gamblers. Desolation stalks around it. . . . All kinds of provisions are extraordinarily high-priced. 24th. Started for Santa Fe, arrived early next morning. The accounts concerning this place for me were not at all exaggerated. . . . The Plaza which is certainly spacious is decorated with sundry pieces of cannon, the American flag being raised in its center. But as to the inhabitants of the place . . . dozens of unfortunate Californians, who might be said to have gotten themselves into a tarnation fix having proceeded so far on their weary and dangerous pilgrimage without the means of going further might be seen lounging and milling around the . . . Plaza . . . looking for someone to employ them. In a few days the detestable company to which I belonged was scattered in all directions very much to my relief. . . . The season was now becoming too far advanced to attempt the northern route; to travel four or five months more . . . on the southern route . . . I was determined not to do.

September was spent in dealing with raids and skirmishes by the Navajos, and then an October 12 entry notes,

> Capt. Brent . . . offered to take me with him to the States. I was nothing but loth to accept it and give up the idea of going to California. My opinion of that country is that the chances of success and safe arrival there are exceedingly doubtful and precarious; should mineral wealth abound as richly as is confidentially reported, California must prove a point of attraction for the whole world during many years to come. It will doubtless improve rapidly in civilization and good institutions.

The route to California via the Isthmus of Panama is described in S.D. King's account. King left from New York in May 1851 and wrote his cousin a 32-page letter:

Pacific Ocean, June 4, 1851:

We came off the mouth of Chargres [Panama] . . . having made the passage in 8 days & 8 hours. . . . The River is very crooked and its width varied from 100 to 300 feet. . . . Every kind of tropical tree, plant & vine formed an impervious mass of vegetable matter. From the tallest trees, vines descended like ropes to the ground. . . . This part of the trip was extremely unpleasant to such of us as were aware of what might be the consequences. . . . [W]e landed about 9 oclock at the great city of Gorgana. . . . The Hotel we stopped at was one of the best in the place. . . . Every place was crowded with dirty cots, sometimes a hundred in one long shed. Late as it was, we made some of the arrangements about having mules to start soon the next morning. . . . [A]fter dinner I started in a hammock, with 3 Indians and one half breed Negro as bearers. . . . Picture to yourself a reed or cane as thick as one's leg about 12 ft. long with a Hammock containing his "Honor" swinging between, with an umbrella to give shade to the face. . . . [A]bout 2 hours after dark . . . we reached the place we contemplated remaining at for the night called the "Ranche Americano." Owing to the rain, darkness, muddy slippery road this part of the trip was extremely unpleasant. . . .

Of the beauty of the entire land route, winding down ravines, & over hills it is impossible to attempt any account. . . . [W]e intersected, at 6 miles from Panama, the old Spanish paved road . . . now most lamentably out of order, being frequently entirely washed away or destroyed for hundreds of feet together. . . . originally . . . Deep cuts were made through it on the sides of the hills, & bridges, placed over the permanent streams. The road itself was originally generally 8 ft. wide well paved with good stones. . . . I arrived at the "Orleans Hotel" but in such a plight that I took are not to let the ladies see me, not having shaved or changed since the day before leaving the "Empire City." I looked more like a grizzly Bear, drawn through a Horse pond than anything else. . . . [E]very place & hole is occupied, and the main street is obstructed & every house covered with American signs. Hotels, taverns, Restaurants and stores fill every nook, and hundreds upon hundreds of Americans, Jews, mules &c. block up the narrow streets and passages.

CHAPTER 12

NORTHWESTERN SETTLEMENTS

The American history of the Northwest is the pursuit of the cultivation of the soil and of souls.

During the peace negotiations ending the War of 1812, Britain and the United States could not agree on the ownership of Oregon. In 1818, the two countries agreed that citizens of the United States and Great Britain would have equal rights to trade and settlement for 10 years. Hall Kelley's efforts to promote American settlement had an effect, and despite the British domination of trade, American emigrants—farmers and missionaries to the Indians—overwhelmed the British traders and Oregon became part of the United States in 1846. By the later 1840s, the Indians had had enough of the missionaries and white men's diseases and went on the warpath. The early settlers Marcus Whitman and his wife were killed along with 11 others in the Whitman Massacre, and as can be seen in the letters in this chapter, Indian warfare continued well into the 1850s.

1846.............................Britain cedes Oregon to the United States.
1859.............................Oregon becomes a state.
1889.............................Washington becomes a state.

■ *Mount Rainier From the South Part of Admiralty Inlet,* from Vancouver's *Voyage of Discovery,* 1798.

■ Henry Humphrys's original watercolor, *View in the Gulph of Georgia NWest America, the Distant Land Being the South Side of Ye Straits of de Fuca. Aboard HMS* Discovery, *San Juan Islands, June 1792*. This watercolor is believed to be the only original piece of art created on the Vancouver voyage (1790–1795) remaining in private hands. Its dating has been established by the identifying landmarks it portrays (Mount Baker and Guemes Channel in Washington State) and from the entries in the Vancouver (and Humphrys) journals for the time the expedition was in the location depicted.

British naval officer George Vancouver commanded an expedition to the Northwest Coast to determine England's rights under the Nootka convention of 1790. The ships of the expedition reached the Northwest Coast in 1792 and spent two years in surveying the coastline, resulting in the most precise maps of the Northwest for many years. This is the most important of the 18th-century English voyages to the Northwest because of its superb cartography.

Nathaniel Wyeth, one of the earliest pioneers in Oregon and the Oregon Trail, wrote a very detailed letter from Fort Vancouver on the Columbia River on January 16, 1833, to a friend in Cambridge, Massachusetts. The letter was carried by the Hudson's Bay Company express up the Columbia River, then via pack horses across the Rocky Mountain, and by rivers and the Great Lakes in canoes to Montreal. Wyeth writes:

A

VOYAGE of DISCOVERY

TO THE

NORTH PACIFIC OCEAN,

AND

ROUND THE WORLD;

IN WHICH THE COAST OF NORTH-WEST AMERICA HAS BEEN CAREFULLY
EXAMINED AND ACCURATELY SURVEYED.

Undertaken by HIS MAJESTY's Command,

PRINCIPALLY WITH A VIEW TO ASCERTAIN THE EXISTENCE OF ANY
NAVIGABLE COMMUNICATION BETWEEN THE

North Pacific and North Atlantic Oceans;

AND PERFORMED IN THE YEARS

1790, 1791, 1792, 1793, 1794, and 1795,

IN THE

DISCOVERY SLOOP OF WAR, AND ARMED TENDER CHATHAM,

UNDER THE COMMAND OF

CAPTAIN GEORGE VANCOUVER.

IN THREE VOLUMES.

VOL. I.

LONDON:
PRINTED FOR G. G. AND J. ROBINSON, PATERNOSTER-ROW;
AND J. EDWARDS, PALL-MALL.

1798.

■ The title page of George Vancouver's *A Voyage of Discovery to the North Pacific Ocean, and round the world . . . Principally With a View to Ascertain the Existence of Any Navigable Communication Between the North Pacific and North Atlantic Oceans . . . in the Years 1790 [to] 1795 . . . ,* London, 1798.

A GEOGRAPHICAL SKETCH

OF THAT

PART OF NORTH AMERICA,

CALLED

OREGON:

CONTAINING

AN ACCOUNT OF THE INDIAN TITLE;—THE NATURE OF A RIGHT
OF SOVEREIGNTY;—THE FIRST DISCOVERIES;—CLIMATE AND
SEASONS;—FACE OF THE COUNTRY AND MOUNTAINS—NATUR-
AL DIVISIONS, PHYSICAL APPEARANCE AND SOIL OF EACH;—
FORESTS AND VEGETABLE PRODUCTIONS;—RIVERS, BAYS, &c.;
ISLANDS, &c.;—ANIMALS;—THE DISPOSITION OF THE INDIANS,
AND THE NUMBER AND SITUATION OF THEIR TRIBES;—TO-
GETHER WITH AN ESSAY ON THE ADVANTAGES RESULTING
FROM A SETTLEMENT OF THE TERRITORY.

TO WHICH IS ATTACHED

A NEW MAP OF THE COUNTRY.

BY HALL J. KELLEY, A. M.

Boston:
PRINTED AND PUBLISHED BY J. HOWE, MERCHANTS ROW.
SOLD BY LINCOLN & EDMANDS, 59, WASHINGTON STREET; A. B. PARKER,
46, NORTH MARKET STREET; AND BY A. BROWN AND
THE PUBLISHER, CHARLESTOWN.

1830.

■ The title page from Hall J. Kelley's *A Geographical Sketch of That Part of North America Called Oregon . . . ,* Boston, 1830. Kelley was a one-man organizing office for immigration to Oregon. This is his first work, describing Oregon and promoting American settlement there.

I am about commencing my return home, and if I am not very unfortunate I shall arrive in Oct. next, I have now but two men, and therefore can only travel when I can get company of whites or friendly Indians. I return by a different route from that by which this will reach you in order to raise some deposits of valuables which I have near the mountains [most likely a cache of beaver pelts]. My men proved worse than none, they would starve amid the greatest plenty of game, and their leaving was rather a benefit than otherwise in this there is so much room for disappointment that it need occasion surprise if I do not reach home for a year after the time above stated. Having traveled almost constantly since I last saw you, sometimes on

FOR THE COLLECTOR AND HISTORIAN

Almost all Oregon- and Northwestern-related material is very rare. Vancouver's *Voyage of Discovery* is one of the most available works, and, relative to other works seen here, not expensive.

No. 78

This certifies that

has paid Twenty Dollars to the AMERICAN SOCIETY FOR ENCOURAGING THE SETTLEMENT OF THE OREGON TERRITORY, *as a pledge for the faithful performance of obligations, to be stipulated and defined by Covenant between him and the said Society.*

_____ President.

_____ Secretary.

N. B. The following are the principal conditions and stipulations of the Covenant, viz : that the emigrant shall give oath or affirmation to obey and support all just and equal laws and regulations made and provided for the settlement by the Society, the same not being repugnant to the Constitution and Laws of the United States of America.

That all the common and public property and revenues of the settlement shall be held liable to the payment of all debts that may be incurred on account of said settlement; and that, in all other respects he shall truly and faithfully demean himself a peaceable and worthy member of the Oregon community.

That the Society shall defray all expenses of the first expedition from St. Louis, excepting arms, knapsacks, clothing and blankets, which are to be supplyed by the emigrants respectively.

That the Society allow to each emigrant, agreeable to the terms of their first Circular, a lot of seaport land, or 200 acres of farming land, *provided* he or his assigns continues to occupy it, two years from the time of receiving said lot; the Society will guarantee and maintain his or her right to a free enjoyment of religious and civil freedom, and an equal participation in all the privileges and immunities of a member of the Oregon settlement.

■ This unissued certificate from the American Society for Encouraging the Settlement of Oregon Territory is signed by the president and the secretary in 1831.

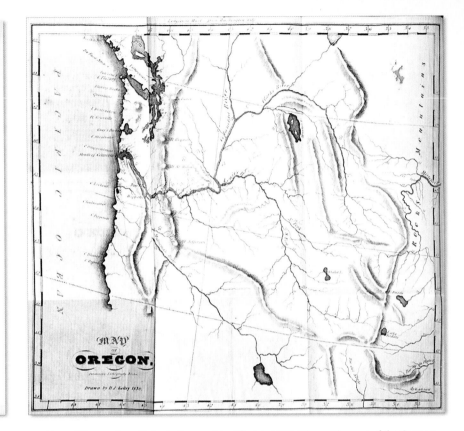

■ Map of Oregon from Kelley's *Geographical Sketch,* 1830. "The settlement of the Oregon country has been as long contemplated as its paramount advantages of climate and soil and its local opportunities for trade and commerce have been known. . . . No portion of the globe presents a more fruitful soil or a milder climate or equal facilities for carrying into effect the great purpose of a free and enlightened nation, a country so full of those natural means which best contribute to the comforts and conveniences of life is worthy the occupation of a people disposed to support a free representative government and to establish civil scientific and religious institutions energized by the mild and vital principles of our republic. . . . Life in that country may be made easy with comparatively little effort; but it can not be long sustained anywhere without some suffering and laborious industry. A place where the full sustenance of man is spontaneously produced would not be desirable for a settlement as it would encourage a propensity for idleness and idleness is in the soil in which vice can best flourish and produce its pestiferous fruit."

foot, sometimes on horse back, and sometimes by boats, you will imagine I am tired of a way passing life, nevertheless like all kinds of life it has some stresses, it has been a great relief to me, the blue clouds do not trouble me quite so much as formerly, on the other hand I have some more real troubles, these latest are always more easily borne. I shall make a great loss in this first part of the undertaking. . . . I shall escape with the skin of my teeth. You will expect to have a little off the face of the country, in two fill up the paper I will ratify you the plan of my route is to leave this in company with a party of the Hudsons Bay cos. People, with whom I get to the Flatheads or Ponderays, take their return convoy home. From the rocky mountains to within 200 miles of the sea the country is open, Barren, and in its summit level far from mountainous but in this space areas ranges mountains, and the rivers seem to follow in enormous

cracks, their banks perpindicilar mostly without bottom lands, and their beds filled with great stones, rapids and falls, the days are intensely hot, and the nights equally cold, in August I have observed the ther[mometer] at 18 at night and the following day at 85 this circumstance alone without the barreness of the soil, or want of communications and impossibility of making them,

would forever render this section of the country what it is now a den. The country within 200 miles of the coast is more mountainous covered with perhaps as heavy timber as the world produces chiefly of the pine, there is one kind of good oak, similar to the white oak of N.E. . . . There are almost no bottom lands on the Columbia that are not annually flooded, the only good country that I have seen is on the Multnomah or Wallammet (rivers) there the country consists of moderate dry prairies surrounded with Ward among which there is much oak and maple, the soil is deep and muddy. . . . There being but one fall between this and the sea, in this country there are plenty of deer. I am told there is good land on the Columbia River and at Puget Sound but these places I have not seen.

Jason Lee and his brother led the first mission to the Indians "beyond the Rocky Mountains." In 1839 he wrote from New York giving advice on what to take on a voyage that would begin in October and cover 22,000 miles, via Cape Horn and Hawaii, arriving at the mouth of the Columbia River on May 21, 1840:

Individuals must furnish their own saddles, bridles, stoves &c. and the society will pay the freight to Oregon, of any thing they need to furnish their houses, or make them comfortable. All will be furnished by the Society, with the Tools necessary for their work. Money is of little use. . . . The Settlers want goods, tools &c for whatever they have to sell. We shall take out a supply of goods. . . . Bro. Perkins who went around Cape Horn says, "each person should have 25 changes of rainment, for to wash is out of the question". It may be well to have 25 shirts but I shall not have 25 changes of other rainment. The say "light matirial such as duck is best for the voyage, and that all clothing should be changed once a week".

■ Wyeth writes from Oregon describing his overland trip in 1832 and his intended trip east in 1833: "Until I fall in with some Am. Trapping party, with the east to their rendezvous."

The conflict with the natives seems to have dominated life in Oregon in the 1850s, at least as reflected in my collection. Robert Atherton wrote from Scots Valley in 1853:

> I arrived here a few days ago from the Klammuth River, the Indians having commenced killing the whites in the vicinity has brought on a general war between them, and renders it dangerous for small parties to be out. The whites have all assembled at Rogues River Valley and built a Fort for protection.

All the farms in that vicinity have been abandoned as well as the mines. The Indians have declared their intention of driving the whites from that section of the country; expresses are daily arriving from them for aid, but the[re] are hardly people enough here to protect themselves and are very poorly armed; about two hundred Indians have assembled within ten miles of us, all well armed but have said that they do not intend to fight unless attacked—we place very little faith in what they say and expect them to make a break on us.

■ Miners' cabin, Oregon.

MINERS CABIN, OREGON

■ Snowshoes from the Northwest Coast, late 19th century.

The following year, A.P. Thayer wrote from Corvallis:

We succeeded in reaching Salem the Capital of this Territory on the 1st day of September . . . 1853. . . . We both enjoyed good health . . . but we were unfortunate in loosing our Cattle. . . . My farm consists of about 250 acres of good dry prairie & the balance timer, it is well watered with a running stream running acrost it. . . . [T]he grass grows green & fresh all winter hence it must be the best grazing country in the world. . . . The soil is very productive & natural for wheat. Our prairie here can be broken with a pair of horses. The first time, oats potatoes & barley together with all kinds of vegetables grow in abundance here. . . . Were I to cross the plains again I would take mules & bring no freight whatever except what clothing I wanted on the road & 100 lbs of provision to a person. But it is far better to come by water, it costs less & far safer. The Indians have been very hostile to the Immigrants this last summer. A good many have been killed, I crossed the Cascade Mts this fall with a neighbor who had heard that his brother had been killd. We did not know but that he had been left wounded. We found when we met the train that he was with at the time, that he had been shot dead.

■ *Fort Vancouver.*

■ Henry Warre's *Sketches in North America and the Oregon Territory,* published in London in 1848, is one of the rarest and most beautiful of Western books. In 1845, Captain Warre was sent by the British government to the Oregon Territory, at the height of the dispute with the United States over its ownership, to scout out the country in case British troops were brought into Oregon. He traveled overland across Canada to the Pacific Northwest, visiting present-day Oregon, Washington, and British Columbia. By the time he returned, the political crisis had been resolved. Warre, an accomplished artist, executed these illustrations on the spot, and published them upon his return to London.

■ *Source of the Columbia River.*

■ *The American Village.*

■ *Valley of the Willamette River.*

CHAPTER 13 THE MORMONS

The Mormon migration to the Great Salt Lake is, along with the California gold rush, the clearest and most focused example of the Western pursuit of the American Dream. Harassed and persecuted in the East, the Mormons after the murder of Joseph Smith carefully considered different areas to which they could relocate from Nauvoo, Illinois. An initial group led by Brigham Young in 1847 founded Salt Lake City based on the power of religious belief, combined with hard work and ingenuity. The letters of Brigham Young in the collection quoted here tell the Mormon story firsthand.

April 5, 1847.................The first Mormon migration leaves Omaha, led by Brigham Young, 143 men, 3 black settlers, 3 women, and 2 children. They reach the Great Salt Lake in July.

1896.............................Utah becomes a state.

THE PROPHET

Joseph Smith, the founder of the Mormon church, and his followers arrived in Nauvoo in the summer of 1839 after they were forced out of Missouri by religious persecution. Within three years, Nauvoo had become the tenth-largest city in the United States. In 1844, Joseph Smith and his brother were assassinated and the Mormons were forced to evacuate the city in 1846. The Mormon temple was burned that year.

BRIGHAM YOUNG BEGINS THE JOURNEY TO THE GREAT SALT LAKE

The following is the text of one of the letters that Brigham Young wrote seeking a new home for the Mormons less than a year after the murder of Joseph Smith. Young would be president of the Mormon church from 1847 to 1877. The letter was written from Nauvoo, Illinois, to the governor of an unnamed state and was also signed by Mormon trustees N.K. Whitney and George Miller.

> Suffer us . . . in behalf of a disfranchised and long afflicted people to pr[of]fer a few suggestions for your serious consideration in hope of a friendly and unequivocal re[s]ponse. . . . It is not our

FOR THE
COLLECTOR
AND HISTORIAN

The history and personalities of the Mormon church have always been avidly collected, beginning with the church itself. Letters by pioneers on the Mormon Trail are rarely seen on the market. Anything signed by Joseph Smith is very rare and in great demand. Letters and documents signed by Brigham Young, because of his long life span and the positions he held, are much more commonly available. Coins and currency are both very rare but occasionally available. First editions of *The Book of Mormon* are both rare and expensive, other books much less so.

■ Joseph Smith signed this document in Nauvoo, Illinois, on April 1, 1840: a contract for the sale of "a lot in the town of Nauvoo."

THE

BOOK OF MORMON:

AN ACCOUNT WRITTEN BY THE HAND OF MOR-
MON, UPON PLATES TAKEN FROM
THE PLATES OF NEPHI.

Wherefore it is an abridgment of the Record of the People of Nephi; and also of the Lamanites; written to the Lamanites, which are a remnant of the House of Israel; and also to Jew and Gentile; written by way of commandment, and also by the spirit of Prophecy and of Revelation. Written, and sealed up, and hid up unto the LORD, that they might not be destroyed; to come forth by the gift and power of God unto the interpretation thereof; sealed by the hand of Moroni, and hid up unto the LORD, to come forth in due time by the way of Gentile; the interpretation thereof by the gift of God; an abridgment taken from the Book of Ether.

Also, which is a Record of the People of Jared, which were scattered at the time the LORD confounded the language of the people when they were building a tower to get to Heaven; which is to shew unto the remnant of the House of Israel how great things the LORD hath done for their fathers; and that they may know the covenants of the LORD, that they are not cast off forever; and also to the convincing of the Jew and Gentile that JESUS is the CHRIST, the ETERNAL GOD, manifesting Himself unto all nations. And now if there be fault, it be the mistake of men; wherefore condemn not the things of God, that ye may be found spotless at the judgment seat of CHRIST.

BY JOSEPH SMITH, JUNIOR,
AUTHOR AND PROPRIETOR.

PALMYRA:

PRINTED BY E. B. GRANDIN, FOR THE AUTHOR.

1830.

■ Title page of the first edition of *The Book of Mormon: An Account Written by the Hand of Mormon, Upon Plates Taken From the Plates of Nephi . . .*, Palmyra, New York. Printed by E.B. Grandin for the author in 1830. This is one of the most influential publications issued in America in the 19th century and the founding work of the most important religious sect in the American West.

■ A Mormon family is shown outside their house in the Great Salt Lake Valley.

present design to detail the multiplied and aggravated wrongs that we have received in the midst of a nation that gave us birth. . . . [W]e are a disfranchised people. We are privately told by the highest authorities of this state, that it is neither prudent or safe for us. . . . [T]he blood of our best men has been shed, both in Missouri, and the state of Illinois with impunity. . . .

But . . . the startling attitude recently assumed by the state of Illinois . . . has already used the military of the State . . . to coerce and surrender up our best men to unparallelled murder. . . . [T]he murderers of Joseph Smith are suffered to roam at large, watching for further prey. . . . [I]f we continue passive and nonresistant, we much certainly expect to perish, for our enemies have sworn it. . . .

[W]ill you express your views concerning what is called the Great Western Measure, of colonising the Latter Day Saints in Oregon, the Northwestern Territory, or some location remote from the states, where the hand of oppression shall not crush every noble principle and extinguish every patriotic feeling?

In an 1847 letter to church elder J.C. Little, Young describes the great Mormon migration:

I expect to start for the mountains before you arrive, as it is necessary for a Pioneer Company to be on the way, as early as possible, to ensure crops a-head, and I know of no better way than for me to go with the Company: and if the Brethren love me as I them, they will not be long behind. I feel like a father with a great family of children around me in a winter storm, and I am looking with calmness, confidence, and patience for the clouds to break, and the sun to shine, so that I can run out and plant and sow and gather in the corn, and wheat, and say children, Come home. Winter is approaching again and I have houses, and wood, and flour and meal, and meat, and potatoes, and squashes, and onions, and cabbages, and all things in abundance, and I am ready to kill the fatted calf, and make a joyful feast, so all who will come and partake: come on then Bro Little; you need not stop at Washington to transact any business for the Camp, for we have made all necessary arrangements with our friend, Colonel Kane, through Bro. Grant, and if you do not arrive at Winter Quarters before I leave, We will say, all is right, We shall only loose each other's society for a few days: you will come on in the next company, and a taste of the mountain air together will be sweet to us.

Set the churches in order, and leave everything just as it should be: and if you are meek and lowly in heart, and watch continually the whisperings of the Spirit: —the still small voice, you will not look for wisdom and knowledge, and you will prosper in all you put your hands unto, and the Saints will be blessed by your labors. You will select some good efficient Elder on whom you will confer your local office and calling, to seek the best interest of the children of the kingdom, and counsel them with a fathers care.

We now have a survey of 41 Blocks, of 820 Lots, 700 Houses, 22 Woods, with Bishop & Counsellors and municipal high Council all happy & prosperous. A good flouring mill, and the whole camp organized into companies of hundreds, fifties, and Tens, all of which are comprised in two divisions: —preparatory to removal from hence to our final destination, as fast as circumstances will permit.

About 170 of the Battalion including Laundresses, are at Ft. Pueblo, on the Arkansas, and the remainder about 300 miles West or South of Santa fe at Alpasso, at the latest dates, except about 16 that have died.

Bishop Miller and family have returned from Punea, where are about 100 families, ready to pass on and join us on our route. The Indians have killed many of our cattle, and stolen several horses, —And the Siouxs have killed 43 Omahas this Winter. Loss of cattle and horses we think little of. We have done all we could, and are satisfied it will all be right, in the end for we are sure our father, will do all that is necessary to be done, when the strength of his children fails. God bless and prosper you is the wish and prayer of your Brother in Christ Jesus.

■ Brigham Young.

GURNEY & SON,   FIFTH AVE. N. Y.

■ In this signed letter by Brigham Young, from Winter Quarters (Nebraska), February 26, 1847, he writes to Elder J.C. Little, describing the great Mormon migration.

■ James Marshall, who discovered gold at Sutter's Mill, was a Mormon, as were many of the original miners. When gold dust was brought back to Salt Lake City, Brigham Young conceived the idea of producing Mormon coins. The obverse depicts the emblem of the Mormon priesthood, the three-pointed Phrygian crown above the all-seeing eye. HOLINESS TO THE LORD appears around the edge. The reverse is engraved with clasped hands representing friendship, and GSLCPG (Great Salt Lake City Pure Gold)—though the gold was from California and the coins overvalued by fifteen percent. Issued in $2 1/2, $5, and $10, as well as in the $20 shown here—all were mass melted because of the overvaluation.

THE WESTWARD MOVEMENT

Mormon pioneer Martha Haven described to her mother the hardships of the Westward journey from Winter Quarters in January 1848:

> Our little black cow could not stand the journey. She laid down and refused to travel before we got to the last settlement. Mr. Haven went back and made out to get her to the settlement where he got 4 dollars for her. I can tell you, Mother, these Western moves are hard on cattle as well as on the people. You can have but a faint idea of it. . . . I begin to think that I have had about my share of sickness, but the God of all the earth will do right. . . . We can never know how to value any thing until we are once deprived of it. . . . We now expect to leave this place in May or June for the mountains. There is a plenty of sale there. . . . Our pioneers brought back considerable. . . . [Mr. Haven] is toiling hard to make a fit out for the mountains. We shall probably have to go without many things that would add greatly to our comfort, but if I can have health I can stand hardships very well. You know but little, Mother of a Western life. This place has got to be vacated in the coming summer. I expect the missionaries are at the bottom of it. They will have their reward. We have

■ The Mormons issued a different coin—made from Colorado gold and worth $5—in 1860. The Lion of Judah is depicted on one side. The beehive, the symbol of Mormon productivity, is depicted on the other side and is protected by an American eagle.

■ Letter from Martha Haven to her mother from Winter Quarters, Omaha Nation, January 3, 1848.

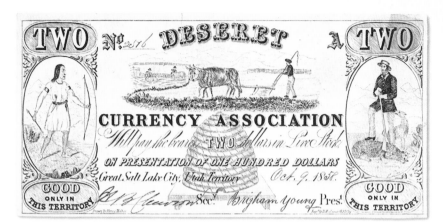

■ Currency issued by the Mormons, 1858. Payable in livestock and "Good only in this territory."

done a great many thousand dollars worth of work here, which will be of great service to them, such as digging wells, fencing and breaking the ground. . . . Truly we have no abiding city. The ensign is to be reared upon the mountains and all nations to flow unto it. We are not going to a remote corner of the earth to hide ourselves. Far from it.

Another Mormon pioneer, Washington Mousley, described to his family the Mormon Miracle—the Mormon pioneers' journey to, and successful settlement of, Salt Lake City. In November 1857 Mousley wrote:

It is a pleasure . . . to inform you of our good health and prosperous Journey to these peaceful vales of the mountains of Eaphrem . . . over 1300 miles with ox team. I have sawe & converse with the red man of the forest I have slept where wolf howled & buffalo roam I have saw the red antelope and deer in his native air & all was a pleasure to me. . . . I never saw so handsome a site as is presented to our view when emergine from the canion to Salt Lake Valey. . . . The farmes are not so scattered as they are in the

■ Four printed bills in the amounts of 50¢, $1, $2, and $3, signed by Heber C. Kimball, Thomas Bullock, and Brigham Young. The bills bear the inscription "G.S.L. City, Jan. 20, 1849," and the embossed seal with the miter-and-eye device.
The burgeoning Mormon settlements in the Salt Lake Valley soon felt the need for a convenient medium of exchange. Gold dust was used at first, but the loss resulting from repeated weighings led Brigham Young to order the printing of paper currency in 1849. Using a small handpress, which had been brought overland in a covered wagon, the Mormon leaders issued bills that are the earliest known specimens of Utah printing.

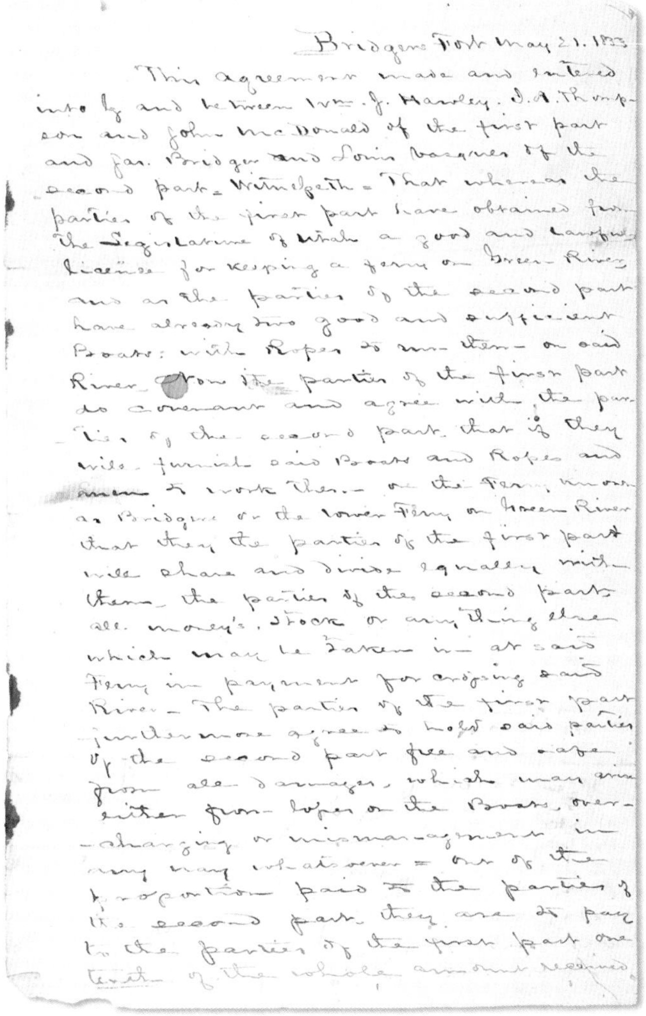
Bridgers Fort May 21. 1853
This agreement made and entered into by and between Wm. J. Hawley, I.A. Thompson and John McDonald of the first part and Jas. Bridger and Louis Vasquez of the second part. Witnesseth — That whereas the parties of the first part have obtained from the Legislature of Utah a good and lawful license for keeping a ferry on Green River and as the parties of the second part have already two good and sufficient Boats with Ropes to run them on said River. Now the parties of the first part do covenant and agree with the parties of the second part that if they will furnish said Boats and Ropes and men to work them on the Ferry known as Bridgers or the lower Ferry on Green River that they the parties of the first part will share and divide equally with them the parties of the second part all money's, stock or any thing else which may be taken in at said Ferry in payment for crossing said River. The parties of the first part furthermore agree to hold said parties of the second part free and safe from all damages, which may arise either from ropes or the Boats, over-charging or mismanagement in any way whatsoever. Out of the proportion paid to the parties of the second part they are to pay to the parties of the first part one tenth of the whole amount received

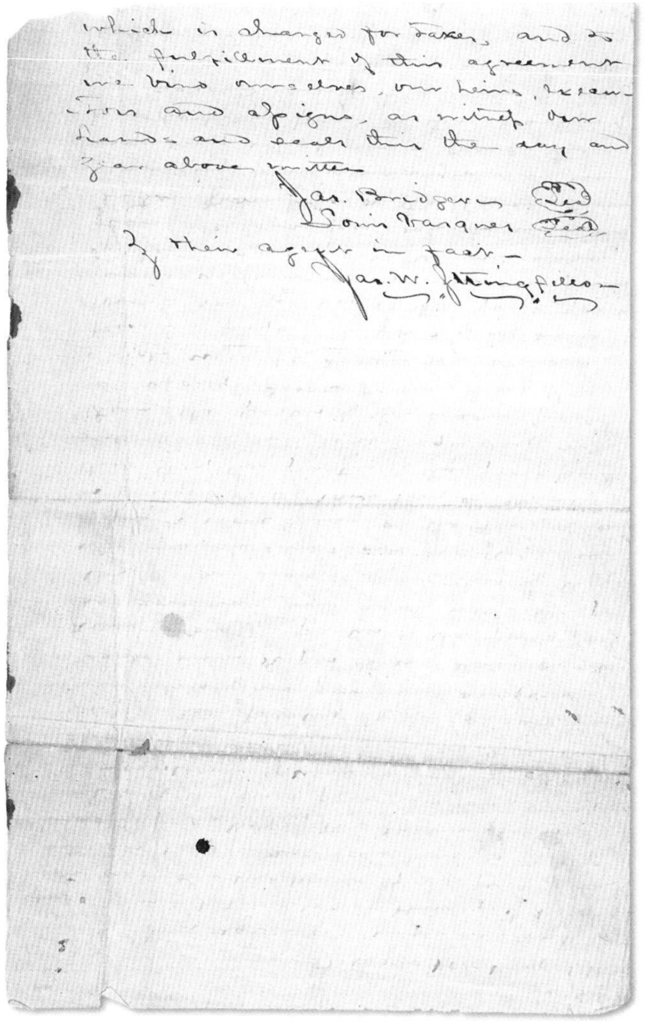
which is charged for taxes, and to the fulfillment of this agreement we bind ourselves, our heirs, executors and assigns, as witness our hands and seals this the day and year above written

Jas. Bridger (Seal)
Louis Vasquez (Seal)
by their agent in fact —
Jas. W. Stringfellow

■ Jim Bridger was forced to sell his Green River ferry to Mormon interests as a prelude to their takeover of Fort Bridger and establishment of a monopoly of the emigrants' business. This document specifying the details of the ferry sale dates from May 21, 1853.

> states. . . . I have been some 60 or 70 miles from the city and I believe I never pasd through a country that there was one quarter as much wheat raised in one year. There is enough grain in Utah to serve the population for 3 years. . . . I can accumulate more property in this country in 5 years under present prospects, than I could in the east in 25 years.

BRIGHAM YOUNG'S WORK CONTINUES

In 1852, Brigham Young petitioned the U.S. Congress for an appropriation for a fledgling school system. His petition also discusses the problem of land given to Utah by the United States—land that was unusable because it was under Indian title.

> Your memorialists [are] feeling a deep interest in the promotion of a general system of education and the general diffusion of knowledge among all classes, and laboring under the difficulties incident to the settlement of all new territories, & especially

those so far removed from the confines of civilization, and feeling grateful to the general government for the valuable library furnished our territory, as also for the appropriation of two sections of land in each township when the same shall have been surveyed & brought into market, & which lands will eventually, in some cases, prove beneficial in promoting the object for which they are granted, but, at present, they are wholly unavailable . . . as your honorable body must readily perceive, owing to the fact that the Indian title has, in no instance, been extinguished in any part of said territory . . . & having no resources on which to base the establishment of a school fund.

In a lengthy letter signed from Salt Lake City on May 29, 1857, Brigham Young informed Horace Eldredge:

On Friday 24th April I left this City in company with . . . over 150 male & female, in 54 carriages & waggons, for Salmon River and other settlements north; distance 381 1/2 miles . . . , returning to this city on Tuesday 26th May, found peace, health and a goodly measure of contentment prevailing on our return. . . . [W]e are encouraged in the belief, that we shall have abundance and prosperity this season, and that "There is a good time coming to them who will wait a little longer."

Some few have grown weary of their continued privations, disappointed hopes, and the stern realities connected with living as saints should live, and building up the Kingdom of God. They could not build themselves up, and a tenth of their substance and labor, shook them, but the consecration of their all, they could not endure. And we realize that our atmosphere is purer, and but little if at all tainted with gentile putrefaction, or apostate discontent. The earth seems to revolve as formerly, all these affairs notwithstanding, for we found on our return from the north, as we rounded the hill south of the hot springs and east of the lake, our eyes feasting on the city of white houses, peaceful homes and verdant gardens, here still it stands, lovely when seen by the clear beams of silver light now shed nightly upon it from the fair moon. Where is its equal? Where do the cooling streams of melted snow water every tree-shaded street as here? Here the same am[oun]t of peace, faith, power? Nowhere at present, not even in Washington! And most assuredly neither in St. Louis nor New Orleans!!! . . .

■ The retained draft of Brigham Young's 1852 petition to Congress.

I perceive the saints are scattered for 9 miles in . . . your city, and as there are many hordes of apostates, and dens of iniquity much vigilance and the constant labors of a faithful priesthood will be necessary to purify your flock, and measurably the atmosphere in which they live. Morally and physically the saints had better be removed to the mountains, or to the settlements on the way than remain in St. Louis. It is an unhealthy place, morally & physically, & I desire you to remember that I said to you of your own person, habits & health while there, & practice bathing &c. as I suggested.

[The] . . . offer of Kearney Gov[ernmen]t lands—if these are not beyond the reach of your counsel and influence, let them be peopled, if not already occupied, as circumstances & wisdom shall direct. A portion of Deer Creek we learn has been taken up, and built upon. Let our brethren be taught, at all times to concilliate the favor of the Indians, and bear themselves respectfully towards the Gov[enmen]t officers, without being over servile. . . .

I perceive that your predecessor has labored abundantly to awaken the drowsy, trim the vine & to inspire energy and life among the saints by re-baptism, confessing and forsaking sin.

Brigham Young wrote in December 1856 to the president of the British and Scandinavian missions:

The last train of hand carts arrived on last Sunday—many of them with frozen feet but greatly improving in health since they were met by the assisting companies. They were met at the upper crossing of the Plate where they had been encamped in a storm which they could not travel in for nine days. The ox trains, or so called 'Independent companies,' . . . have not yet arrived. . . . [T]hey are probably at Bridger by this time where they will also receive sufficient assistance to bring them in. We learn that they are generally well. We wrote you last mail that no company must hereafter leave the Missouri later than the first day of August, [but] upon further consideration we have fixed upon the first of July as the latest that any emigrating company should be permitted to leave the Missouri River.

The wagons are good this year and we suggest that they hereafter be of the same kind with the following exceptions—let them be made to track five feet, shoulder boxes 4 1/4 and point boxes 3 inches in diameter in the clear, . . . hub 1 inch thicker— the braces that go from the hind axle to the reach should be 12 inches longer and be set one inch nearer to the forward hubs than they now do, the iron strap on the tongue should be straight & be as heavy again as it now is; wagon boxes or beds should be enlarged in proportion to the increased width of track; in other respects they will answer as heretofore made, except that all the timber must be of the very best quality, or we do not want them.

■ *Great Salt Lake City in 1853* in James Linforth's *Route from Liverpool to Great Salt Lake Valley . . . Together With a Geographical and Historical Description of Utah . . . Also, an Authentic History of the Latter-Day Saints' Emigration from Europe . . .* , 1855. One of the most important publications devoted to the Mormon emigration to Utah, this book was a landmark in the artistic depiction of Western scenes. On one level it is a guidebook for Mormon emigrants, following the usual formula of overland guides except with elaborate illustrations. Beyond this, it depicts many of the significant places of Mormon history.

14

THE CALIFORNIA GOLD RUSH

The riches that gold would provide were the American Dream for tens of thousands of men after its discovery in California in 1848. The letters of the forty-niners and later prospectors describe life during the California gold rush very eloquently, if phonetically, and tell the story firsthand. It began when James Marshall, who was in charge of building a sawmill for John Sutter, discovered gold on January 19, 1848. Neither he nor Sutter benefited—in fact, Sutter was ruined by the wave of gold seekers who occupied his land and paid no attention to the legal niceties of ownership. It is ironic and tragic that this Swiss émigré, whose interest was in building the infrastructure for settlement, was ruined by the stampede.

PRICES IN SAN FRANCISCO, JANUARY 15, 1850

Cigars, common	$10–12
Cigars, Havana	$25–35
Opium	$7 per pound
Morphine	$8 per ounce
Fruits—preserves	$6 per pint
Prime pork	$9 per barrel
Mackerel	$9 per half barrel
Butter	25–45 cents per pound
Cotton shirts	$12–24 per dozen
Linen shirts	$30–50 per dozen
Gold dust	$16.25 per ounce

Others, like Collis Huntington and Mark Hopkins, quickly saw that the best chance of making money was not in pursuing gold directly in the rivers and mines but in selling the prospectors the tools they needed. The two partners were in the hardware business and went on to finance the Central Pacific Railroad with Charles Crocker and Leland Stanford. In all but a few areas of California, the days of panning for gold in the rivers and streams were over quickly and were replaced by the rocker or sluice, which would process more gravel and could sometimes be handled by one man but was usually run by a small group. By 1853, this method had been superseded by the practice of digging mine shafts to follow the veins of gold underground and shooting high-pressure jets of water that would tear apart mountainsides to get at gold. Several of the later letters describe the destruction of the landscape that came about because of this practice.

■ The autograph of James W. Marshall, who discovered gold in California.

THE DISCOVERY OF GOLD

John Sutter was a pioneer in California who founded his colony on the site of what is now Sacramento; after gold was discovered on his property in 1848, he went bankrupt, as his workmen deserted him, his sheep and cattle were stolen, and his land was occupied by squatters. In a letter of April 5, 1866, to Edward E. Dunbar, who was soon to publish *The Romance of the Age: or, the Discovery of Gold in California*, he corrects one account of the momentous discovery:

> [Your] narration . . . attending the Discovery of Gold by Marshall at my saw mill in February 1848 . . . is . . . correct. . . . The account of this great discovery in . . . the "Encyclopedia Americana," is quite incorrect . . . especially where it states that the first gold was picked up by a little daughter of Marshall's . . . Feb. 9, 1848. Marshall never had a daughter. . . . The account is also incorrect when it states that a party of three Americans, two of them Mormons, collected in January 1848 a large amount of gold on Mormon Island, Sacramento. Gold diggings were not discovered at the Saw Mill by Marshall. I never heard of Mormons connected with the Army or of Mexicans & Indians having gathered gold on the banks of the streams in California during the years of the Mexican war.

■ Letter from John Sutter to Edward Dunbar, April 5, 1866.

Article of Agreement made and entered into this 20th day of July 1849 By and between David Croomer Sen. of the the County of Daviss & State of Missouri of the one part, & Addison Powel of the County & State aforesaid of the second part Witnesseth; That David Groomer hath this day Agreed & Bound himself to Fit & Furnish The out fit for me the sd. A. Powel to go to California, there to dig for Gold, sd. Groomer furnishes the full out fit specified in the Pattonsburg article, For which I bind myself to go & dig Gold to the best of my abilities & strength and after taking out the Expences thay accrue, when I return home to sd. Groomers house (or the States) there to make an equae divide Giving sd. Groomer half of all my Earnings; also obligating myself in Failure to go (with the Pattonsburg Company) to pay to Groomer all the Expences he may be at & pay him for his trouble Given under my hand & seal this day & year first above written

Test— J, M, Nicholas   Addison X Powel (Seal)
                              his
                              mark

~~D, David Groomer is to pay the whole out fit from the time of Starting untill the said A, Powel return home~~ The above Powell is to have half of his own earnings exclusive of the Pattonsburg out fit

■ Contract in which a forty-niner agrees to share equally what gold he finds with his backer, who is staking him to his trip to California from Missouri, 1849.

Gen. Sutter

■ John Sutter, one of California's pioneers.

■ A scale styling itself a "miners improved gold scale manufactured expressely for California."

■ Knife with blade inscribed "California / gold seeker protector."

Many gold rush ventures started with reading a guide to the California gold fields, such as J.E. Sherwood's *Pocket Guide to California: A Sea and Land Route Book*, published in 1849. The preface is certainly encouraging:

> To assist the increase of those preparing to immigrate to the rich and inviting regions of California—to embody in a condensed form all the valuable and trustworthy information in regard to the location extent and character of its mineral wealth, particularly its gold whether in mines or scattered upon the varied surface of its soil or intermingled with the sands of its rivers—to furnish a clear succinct and full account of its climate, its native and immigrant population, its agricultural resources, its commercial prospects and advantages—and also aid to supply facts—facts in regard to the best cheapest and most expedious modes of reaching this newly opened and richly developing country is the design of this pamphlet.

It also contains more than 25 pages of very interesting advertisements addressed "To California gold diggers, exploring parties and other," offering everything necessary for the overland voyage and the finding of gold in comfort.

Many groups formed companies in which each argonaut had a share, or in which financial backers who stayed home shared ownership with the miners. In the papers of Samuel Allen there is a printed charter for a mutual aid corporation in which the members could pool resources in order to get to the mines. Signed by all 15 members of the company, the agreement required the men to act jointly in the interest of the whole, stating they would not "engage in, or be concerned with, any game of chance or skill, by which money may be lost or won; neither shall he use intoxicating liquors . . . neither shall any work be engaged in on the Sabbath."

In the diggings, Allen's early optimism quickly became informed skepticism:

> I find that it is all a lottery in the diggings, some make thousands in a week but they are rare while others make but a bare living. . . . Dollars here take the place of cents at home, a man wont look at any thing less than a dollar. . . . Those of us who work steady can make 6 dollars a day in the best of the season. Our living, pork, bread, and flour costs about $1.50 a day a man and if we should go into the luxurys . . . such as onions and potatoes . . . would take all to live. . . . I would not advise any one to come here.

FOR THE
COLLECTOR
AND HISTORIAN

The California gold rush is one of the most collectible areas of the American West. Letters and guidebooks are frequently available and, less often, illustrated letter sheets.

SAN FRANCISCO DURING THE GOLD RUSH

San Francisco in 1849 was described by one George Payne in terms of property values:

> A large fire occurred last week, by which a large amount of property was destroyed . . . but in order to understand the loss which parties have sustained it is necessary to know something about the amount for which the buildings rented. . . . The largest building—a hotel, rented for $14,000 per month, the house originally cost $100,000. The next two—occupied as eating houses and gambling houses—rented for $10,000 per month each. Then there were about twenty five small buildings & stores that rented for about $2,000 per month each—& must have cost an average of $5,000 each to build them.

Another fire is briefly mentioned by one Edward Allyn in a letter in June, 1850: "A fire the Friday before we came in I should think it burnt one third of the Citty. [T]here is nearly as many folks live in tents as there is in houses." Allyn then turns to a general description of San Francisco:

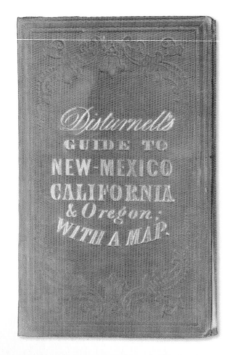

The best buildings are used for the lowest and mos wanton purposes, the first floor of such house is for gambling, they are furnished in the most costly style. . . . [T]he Churches are about the poores buildings in the City Women attract about as much attention when they promenade the Streets as a Carrivan would to home. Murder is only an honorable

■ John Disturnell, *The Emigrant's Guide to New Mexico, California, and Oregon; Giving the Different Overland and Sea Routes . . .*, 1849. One of the best guides generally available at the beginning of the gold rush.

■ The inscription on the back of this painting reads, "This painting is the likeness of Daniel Trip, and Henry Eldridge, Taken in California, at the gold mines in 1849." It is signed by C.T. Allen.

way of Settling disputes. . . . [T]he Streetes are full to a jam with human beings of all collers, and Countrys under heaven. . . . Pork 30 cents a pund Chees .50 to one dollar Butter one dollar Onions one dollar Coffee .60 fresh beef. 18 Tea one dollar . . . molasses two dollar a gallon. . . . [A] rugged woman can make fifty dollars a week washing . . . if she can git the water herself without buying it. [W] ater is .25 bts a pail full . . . pails two to 3 dollars each, brooms two dollars apice. . . . [I]t was not an uncommon thing for a person to get stuck in the mud, so he could not git out without helpe, which would cost him two dollars, with regard to crime. . . . Stealing and the punishment is quite severe. If a person steals the smallest thing and is catchd it is a job on the chain gang for thirty days, that is he has to work with a large iron ball chained to his leg, but if a large amount their life is the forfeit. . . . [T]here is some five hundred buildings now in progress and it is possible that before this letter reaches you they may be in ashes.

■ Studio ferrotype of three miners wearing sourdough hats and dressed in work clothes, the first holding a double barrel shotgun.

that river; the people live in tents principlely as in San Francisco, and business is carried on in the same bustling go ahead stile; there are a few vessels lying in the river, which are used as boarding, store houses, & offices; and are a source of great profit to the owners.

I have now been in the country almost 4 months, and can safely say that I can do a great deal better (as far as money goes) than I can at home. Perhaps you will say that is not very definite, well it is not; neither can I be, for as report says, it is a kind of lottery. Some make their tens of thousands in a single day while others toil all summer for as many hundred—but . . . I want to try the experiment one season and I will promise you that next thanksgiving shall find me in Old Connecticut, come what will if I am able to get there and the means are never wanting at this end of the route for at present, high water (under which are the richest deposits) and these short days I could go to work and earn enough in two weeks, beside paying my board, which is dear enough, to take me home in the first steamer.

SUCCESS STORIES AND FAILURES

Prospector John Kiskham wrote from the "green river camp, 40 miles above Sacramento city," January 5, 1852, to his father and mother:

The 18 of Oct ten of us . . . started for the mines: we took a deck passage at $14.00 apiece on a small schooner bound up the Sacramento, and in five days reached Sacramento city. The variety of scenery on such a trip, through such a beautiful country, and in such a delightful season was anything but disagreeable to a six month's voyage round Cape Horn. Sacramento city is much pleasanter situated than San Francisco, being on the east-bank of the Sacramento, just below the junction of the American, with

■ Theodore T. Johnson's *Sights in the Gold Region and Scenes by the Way*, from 1849, is one of the earliest published accounts of the gold fields and one of the most popular descriptions of the gold rush.

139

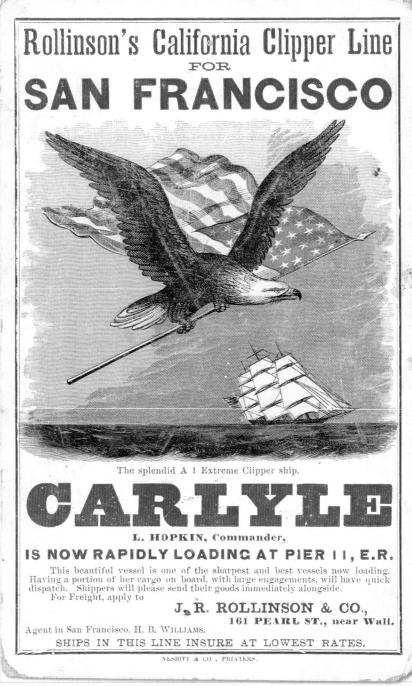

■ Clipper ship advertising cards for ships sailing to San Francisco from Boston or New York.

■ Watercolor, *The Golden Gate and San Francisco in 1849.*

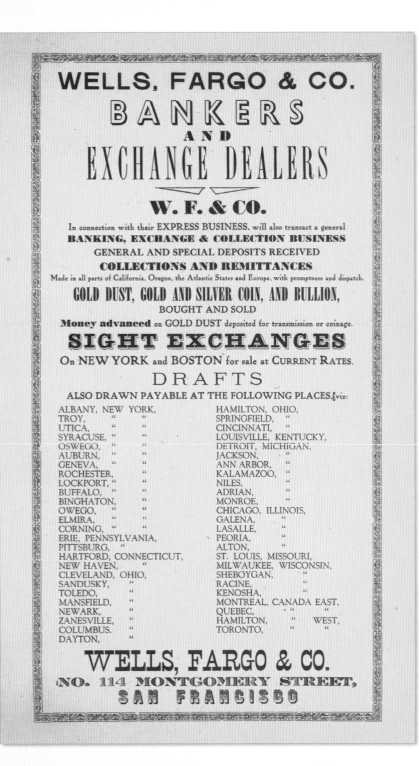

M.S. Gookin, another prospector, told his sister in a letter from September 1850 that "having spent the summer in the mountains prospecting . . . for gold . . . but not being one of the fortunate kind [I] did not succeed . . . & have come to the very wise conclusion that I do not know anything about the business." He turned instead to freighting supplies and was successful. He then discussed something other than the hardships of prospecting:

> The larger valleys near the Pacific are the most Beautiful I ever saw, Mexican Ranches with emmense droves of Horses & Cattle, Grapes, Pears, Oranges, &c in abundance, last February the Clover & oats were a foot high & in March the Hills & valleys presented a most Beautiful view being covered with a great variety of Flowers. . . . When one is in the valleys among Flowers turn to the East and snow covered mountains are only to be seen. . . . I came to this Country as Thousands others have done to make money, if I should be fortunate you may see me again.

Just like their letters on the Overland Trail, the Gambrel brothers' letters from California provided their family with interesting observations about life in California. The first, dated November 30, 1849, notes:

> We have realised nearly 1000$ since, laid in our winter provision and are comfortably fixed in a . . . log cabin of our

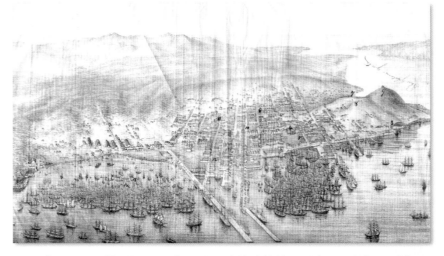

■ Bird's-eye view of San Francisco from *Miriam's Model & Nature July 1852*. Lithograph by Cookes Le Count, with contemporary annotations.

■ This gold pan holds a large gold concretion of irregular form, recovered from the SS *Central America*, containing a mixture of various types of placer gold: flour gold, dust, nuggets, grains, and flakes. The bottom of the formation contains fragments of wood, apparently from the box originally containing the gold. Several large nuggets found in California during the gold rush are at left.

■ SS *Central America* treasure. This ship was carrying both passengers and gold from San Francisco to New York when it was struck by a hurricane in the Atlantic, September 12, 1857. Of the 578 passengers and crew, 153 survived; all of the gold was lost. In 1986 modern technology led to the recovery, in 8,000 feet of water, of much of the gold. These gold bars and placer nuggets were among those recovered.

■ In 1848 the military governor of California sent 230 ounces of gold bullion to the secretary of war, who instructed the Philadelphia Mint to have the gold coined into specially marked $2.50 gold coins (a total of 1,389), each with CAL above the eagle.

■ This large gold amalgam ball is the result of one of the oldest means of separating gold dust from the surrounding detritus. Mercury was mixed with the gold-bearing materials, attracting the gold dust. After the detritus was washed away, the gold and mercury were formed into a ball and the mercury was burned off, leaving a concentrated ball of gold. One method frequently used by prospectors was to halve a potato, scoop a hollow out of the center, place the ball within, rejoin the halves, and "bake" it for three quarters of an hour in the campfire. This removed the remaining mercury, leaving a ball of nearly pure gold. Recovered from the SS *Central America*.

■ Private coinage firms met the demand for lower-denomination coins by merchants, but there was always the question of whether they contained their face value in bullion. The first firm whose members' names are known was Norris, Gregg & Norris. They minted this $5 coin in 1849.

■ Private coiners were constantly accused of minting coins whose bullion value was less than the face value. Some coins were 25 percent overvalued. Moffat & Co. was the great exception, and its reputation was unimpeachable. This $16 ingot was produced in 1849; its weight corresponds to that of a Latin American doubloon.

■ Wass, Molitor & Co. shared a reputation similar to Moffat's for honesty. The delay in opening the San Francisco branch mint caused a severe coin shortage, as private coiners had stopped operating and most coins had been melted down in anticipation of the federal coins. Local bankers convinced Wass, Molitor to resume minting, and in 1855 they produced $10 and $20 coins as well as this $50 coin. All private coinage ended in 1856, when the new branch mint was fully operational.

■ Baldwin & Co. started in San Francisco as jewelers and watchmakers. In 1850, they added private coining and produced this horseman design. When the coin was found to be 3 percent overvalued, the company was forced out of California and their coins melted down for bullion.

■ The 1851 $5 coin produced by Schultz and Co. is known only in 10 to 12 examples because when assayed they contained only $4.87 in gold. This was sufficient reason for the public to reject them, and they were melted into bullion.

■ Less than a year after the discovery of gold, miners who were being flagrantly underpaid for their ore, merchants who were desperate for an accurate medium of money, and the general public all petitioned the military governor for a state assay office. In September 1850, a federal assay office was approved by Congress. In 1851, $50 gold coins were minted and, in 1852 and 1853, both $20 and $10 coins were added.

California pictorial letter sheets provide the best visual chronicle of the California gold rush. Imprinted on sheets of writing paper were views of mining camps, argonauts panning for gold, pioneers pushing their way across the continent, terrifying city fires, vigilance committees in San Francisco streets, and California's spectacular natural wonders.

Most were double sheets, 8 1/2 by 10 1/2 inches when folded, and gave the writer two-plus pages for writing (when folded smaller they required no envelope as the final space left by the writer was the address panel). While historians have called them forerunners of picture postcards, they may also be compared to printed greeting cards—it was easier to have someone else tell the story of your everyday life. Few surviving examples, however, were used for letter writing; instead, most were saved for their pictorial qualities. They are a unique record of lives and scenes from the gold rush.

■ *Crossing the Plains to California.*

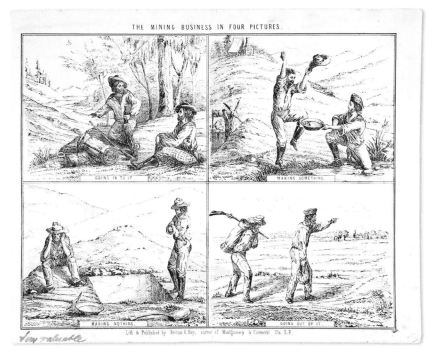

■ *The Mining Business in Four Pictures: Going in to It, Making Something, Making Nothing, Going Out of It.*

■ Pepperbox revolver by Allen and Thurber, popular in the gold fields.

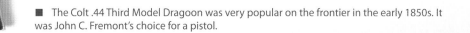

■ The Colt .44 Third Model Dragoon was very popular on the frontier in the early 1850s. It was John C. Fremont's choice for a pistol.

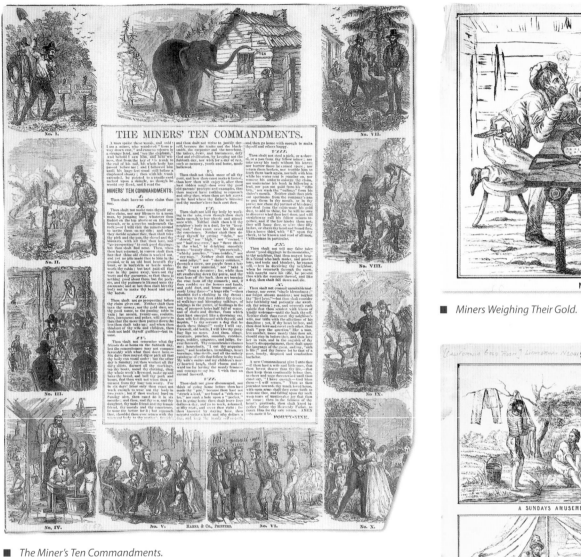

The Miner's Ten Commandments.

Miners Weighing Their Gold.

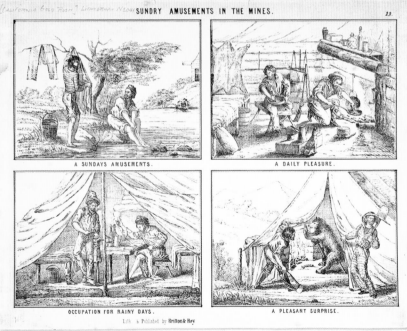

Sundry Amusements in the Mines: A Sundays Amusements, A Daily Pleasure, Occupation for Rainy Days, A Pleasant Surprise.

own manufacture. Our . . . dining Table is constructed of a pine puncheon, the surface of which has been hewn with a hatchet. . . . Our chairs are all three legged stall, as our floor is quite uneven. . . . The last though not least that I will mention are our Bedsteads & Bedding . . . a repose on them is far more luxurious than on the best Feather bed in Missouri.

Our fare with some would not be considered of the most dainty kind, meat & bread & bread & meat are daily cooked up by we cooks, Jno and myself, [and] sometimes we indulge in the luxury of Coffee. . . . [W]e have become thoroughly accustomed to this way of living. . . . [W]e put out for the diggings and work hard all day, and return home at night, as our diggings are about one mile from camp—all as merry as larks being conscious of having made from 20$ to 60$ a piece that day, all cash in hand and no Credit. This is what renders a life of this kind so agreeable. Hard work and a change of climate has wrought quite a change in the appearance of my corporeal frame. . . . I have become more avaricious since my arrival here than I had ever before been. I want 25 or 30,000$ before I start home, which amt I can accumulate. . . .

This is also one of the most enjoyable climates in America and I have no doubt as healthy as any part of the Globe.

A letter from October 25, 1850, reads in part:

There are thousands just arrived who are working for just enough to take them home, having become utterly disgusted with the country, already particularly men who have left families behind. They are realizing all those feelings which I predicted to you and a thousand others—nearly all the married men from Randolph intend returning this fall & winter—those who have enough money will leave immediately, the balance this winter & next spring.

The Situation of California has undergone a complete Revolution. Several of the most important Streams in C[alifornia] have almost proved a most complete failure & thousands have lost every cent realize by the hardest labour last fall. The little spot selected by us last fall for our opportunity is completely overrun by people. There is a town building up in the diggings— which will excel in population Glasgow & Huntsville combined. All the emigrants from Randolph flocked directly here—those who are working are making from 2$ to 12$ pr day. They are nearly all dissatisfied and wish themselves back home. . . .

Though notwithstanding all this a young man can [earn] two or three times as much as he can at home. During my last trip to Sacramento City I was offered 150$ pr month to Clerk.

December 9, 1850:

Last year . . . every Body seemed to be satisfied but men who had left families—but this year it is every Body & I expect there is no country in the world where there are so many dissatisfied People congregated

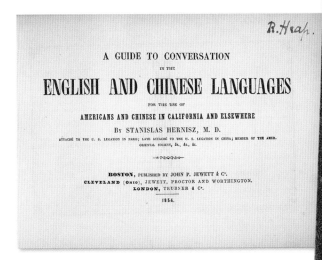

A Guide to Conversation in the English and Chinese Languages . . . , by Stanislas Hernisz, 1854. The words *please* and *thanks* don't appear in the dictionary.

■ The Chinese population of California was unable to file many claims because of the widespread discrimination against them but became invaluable when the Central Pacific Railroad began to employ Chinese workers in large numbers to build the railroad across the Sierra Nevada. The work ethic of the extraordinarily industrious Chinese was the key element in the success of Stanford's, Crocker's, and Huntington's efforts to get their track laid over the mountains.

together & no Prospect to become Reconciled but it will be a lesson learned by experience long to be Remembered by young & old Rich & poor When they are doing tolerably well to let first rate alone.

July 17, 1851:

Things are coming to a [frightful mess] in California at present so far as crime of every description is concerned as we are daily apprised of the perpetration of some murder or robbery. The people are commencing to take the law in their own hands, as the civil law seems to be perfectly disregarded. If a man is caught stealing the slightest thing he is immediately taken out and swung on the nearest tree. There have been four men condemned to death in the last 3 or 4 days for robbing our mare. . . . Notwithstanding there seems to be no abatement of crime. Two or three men have been stopped lately in the public roads not one mile from our House and robbed of large am[oun]ts of money, and what is worse many who have been detected in committing thefts &c were recognized as being men of respectability and good standing at home. Such are the affects of Cal[ifornia] on poor Human nature.

This is no doubt the most contaminating Country in its influence on the character of youngmen of any other in the known world, here every species of vice and immorality is practiced openly and above board and in such a manner as to decoy young men, who have naturally, a disposition to morality and virtue, but who are in a measure devoid of self government.

April 16, 1859:

I am getting very tired of California life, and that of an old Bachelor, although there are many more inducements at present

■ This double barrel shotgun was made by A.J. Plate in San Francisco during the 1850s.

in this country for one to remain than in former times, yet I cannot reconcile myself to its customs yet. We have many young Ladies and many Grass widows in our new and flourishing place, the latter particularly, are very numerous.

December 25, 1860:

Los Angeles was the capitol of California under Mexican Government, and is yet quite a novel city. It yet has its ancient churches and Forts, erected more than 200 years ago, and the country generally contains relics of old missions, which are great curiosities to an American. The climate is unsurpassed, and while you are now almost freezing with severe cold, oranges, Figs, & Grapes are ripening, and are quite cheap and abundant in the market.

THE CONSTITUTION OF THE COMMITTEE OF VIGILANCE

The discovery of gold attracted not only men who were willing to work but also those who intended to make their fortunes at the expense of others. The mining camps that sprang up overnight were soon confronted with incidents of lawlessness, and miners' courts organized by committees of vigilance were set up in many camps to administer justice. Most observers were impressed by the fairness of the miners' courts. Bayard Taylor, whose travel narrative, *Eldorado* (1850), did much to popularize California and who spent six months touring the mining camps as correspondent for the *New York Tribune*, wrote, "Regulations [were] established as near as possible in accordance with the existing laws of the country. . . . Nothing in California seemed more miraculous to me than this spontaneous evolution of social order from the worst elements of anarchy." It was a lesson worth even more than the gold.

In 1856 the Constitution of the Committee of Vigilance was published:

Whereas it has become apparent to the citizens of San Francisco, that there is no security for life and property, either under the regulations of society as it at present exists, or under the laws as now administered, and that by the association together of bad characters, our ballot-boxes have been stolen . . . or stuffed with votes that were never polled . . . our dearest rights violated, and no other method left by which the will of the people can be manifested: Therefore, the citizens whose names are . . . attached . . . unite themselves into an association for the maintenance of the peace and good order of society—the prevention and punishment of crime—the preservation of our lives and property, and to ensure that our ballot boxes shall hereafter express the actual and unforged will of the majority of our citizens. . . . We are determined that no thief, burglar, incendiary, assassin, ballot-box stuffer, or other disturbers of the peace, shall escape punishment. . . . The name . . . of this association shall be the Committee of Vigilance.

Great public emergencies demand prompt and vigorous remedies. The People—long suffering under an organized despotism which has invaded their liberties . . . have . . . arisen in virtue of their inherent right and power. . . . For years they have patiently waited and striven, in a peaceable manner . . . to reform the abuses which have made our city a by-word. Fraud and violence have foiled every effort, and the laws to which the people looked for protection . . . have been used as a powerful engine to fasten upon us tyranny and misrule. . . . Organized gangs of bad men . . . have parceled out . . . offices among themselves, or sold them to the highest bidders [and] have employed bullies and professional fighters to destroy tally-lists by force, and prevent peaceable citizens from ascertaining . . . the true number of votes polled at our elections and have used cunningly contrived ballot-boxes, with false sides and bottoms. . . . Felons . . . and unconvicted criminals . . . have thus controlled public funds and property. . . . The Jury-box has been tampered with . . . to shield the hundreds of murderers whose red hands have cemented this tyranny, and silenced with the Bowie-knife and the pistol, not only the free

voice of an indignant press, but the shuddering rebuke of the outraged citizen. . . . Our single, heartfelt aim is the public good. . . . We . . . shall spare no effort to avoid bloodshed or civil war; but undeterred by threats or opposing organizations, shall continue peaceably if we can, forcibly, if we must, this work of reform, to which we have pledged our lives, our fortunes and our sacred honor.

THE GOLD RUSH FIVE YEARS LATER

By 1854, there were few if any opportunities for individuals, and letters are usually pessimistic. Josiah Boucher did not encourage his brother:

I say to all yong men who have no intrest in that country and would like to stay here five years, and not care wheather they ever got away they will do well by comeing. Men who have familing and interests at home and wishing to come to this country and make A fortune and return home withen A year. I say they had better cut there throts. Then theyr friends can attribute the act to inanity and honor them with A decent burial. It is not the man who works but the man who manoevers he gets the money and the man who econemises he saves it.

Underground mining was not what those who went to California had in mind, but by the mid-1850s a large number of those who went to California could find

■ A very ornate certificate of membership in the Committee of Vigilance of San Francisco, which was "reorganized . . . 1856 for the mutual protection of life and property." Signed by William Coleman as president and other officials, and bearing the embossed blind seal of the Committee, "Be Just and Fear Not . . . Self-Preservation, The First Law."

149

work only in these mines. P.J. Norton wrote to his son Charles on July 13, 1856:

> We have Ben having Some Sony warm weather for the Laste Month but it has not Afected Me Much for I have Ben Working in A Tunnel Nigh[t]s and Sleeping Day times and it is very harde worke for it is al vary hard Rock and I have to Blaste it all and to give you Some eideas of how hard it is take two of us Aboute three Hours steady Drilling to Sink A hole one foot Deape and working Day and nigh[t] we are Able to Make from 2 to 4 ft A weake in Length of tunnel.

Despite the grueling nature of the new mining methods, there was still hope that one could strike it rich. In early 1858, a letter from Drytown signed "Dan" and addressed to "Jane" reads in part:

> It is dangerous for a person to venture out of town at night, from the fact that the miners have lit[er]ally gutted the Earth, and co[n]sequently left holes sticking out all over the count[r]y —some of them a hundred feet deep. . . . Men sometimes work for a whole month on a claim, which does not pay their bord— others make a fortune in a day, thus uncertain is Gold digging.

Eight years after the gold rush had started, Joseph Seavy described a very different California. He wrote from Mission Dolores in 1857:

> California is an excellent state. Vegetable productions attain the highest degree of perfection both in size and flavour. Here is a field for obtaining wealth for young active enterprising men. Yet all do not get rich here. Many destroy themselves by intemperance. In San Francisco there are but a very few persons that were there six years ago—many are dead—many have left the state. It is a great city for one only about seven years old, containing 60 or 70 thousand inhabitants. I live three miles from the city but it is thickly settled all the way and two lines of omnibuses are constantly running starting once in about 20 minutes—fare to the city eight cents.

In a manuscript entitled "California Sketches, from Crane's Flat, Head of Yosemite Trail," written for the *Republican Journal* of Lawrence, Kansas, E.Z. Gore gives a fascinating report of a stagecoach traveler following the Yosemite Trail in the period after the California gold rush. He describes his journey through deserted mining camps:

> Everywhere we saw where the "whirlwind" had passed over— the ground all turned over or deeply dug into deep quarries or pits—all vestiges of the original surface lost and oftentimes for miles on our path nothing left but a desolate wilderness of rocks below us on either side, probably now showing very much the appearance they originally presented . . . before the sand, gravel and gold had been washed and filtered.

He notes that the towns are "melancholy to look upon—so weather-beaten and dilapidated" with the "loafers lounging around the liquor saloons." He finds it "difficult to imagine the noisy activity, the dashing, reckless prosperity which must have pervaded them in the 'flush' days of California gold digging." He pities a "gang of Chinamen, perhaps washing over the gravel that had been washed a dozen times already and making two to four bits a day from it and a good living for them at that, except when they try a faster method of getting gold by robbing their neighbors sluices at night."

■ *Kinney, Goodridge and Ingram's Steam Saw Mill, Eureka, Sierra Col[ony], California 1857.*

CHAPTER 15

CROSSING THE CONTINENT

STAGECOACHES

Crossing the continent was the western pursuit of the American Dream. The start of stagecoach service from St. Louis to San Francisco via Tucson and Los Angeles on September 15, 1858, inaugurated a dramatic ability to cross the continent. This much longer southern route was forced on the stage line by Southern politicians who controlled the mail subsidy that the stage line needed in order to operate. This route averaged 25 days and cost $200. The Concord Coaches cost $1,500, featured leather springs that created a rocking effect, and weighed more than 2,000 pounds. They carried up to 20 passengers (crammed inside and on the roof) on a first-come, first-served basis. These expensive coaches were initially used only on the better roads.

April 1860......................The Pony Express begins service; a letter costs $5 and is delivered in 10 days.

October 1861................A letter costs $1; the Pony Express ceases operation.

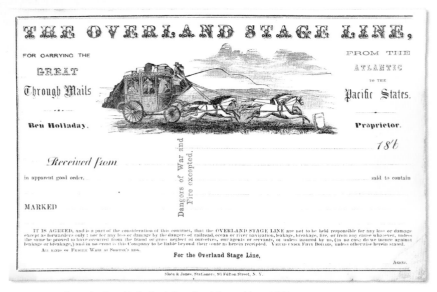

■ Receipt form for Ben Holladay's Overland Stage Line, 1860s.

■ In this manuscript, President James Buchanan called the establishment of the Overland Mail "a glorious triump[h] for civilisation & the Union" and predicted that "settlements will soon follow the course of the road & the East & the West will be bound together by a chain of living Americans which can never be broken." On the verso, A.R. Corbin, Ulysses S. Grant's brother-in-law, wrote an explanation for Buchanan's statement: "The within draft of the reply to the telegraphic dispatch from John Butterfield (announcing the arrival of the first Overland Mail delivery at St. Louis from San Francisco in 23 days and four hours) was written . . . October 9, 1858."

FOR THE COLLECTOR AND HISTORIAN

Almost everything relating to crossing the country by stagecoach is rare. Passengers must have written letters describing the experience, but these have not come onto the market. Envelopes of philatelic interest can be very attractive—and expensive. Envelopes carried by the Pony Express bearing their very distinctive stamps and postmarks are avidly collected and costly. Pamphlets and envelopes urging the building of the transcontinental railroad are fairly available, as are stereoptic slides of scenes along the completed railroad. Advertisements in the form of broadsides for the new transcontinental railroad are virtually unobtainable, but later advertisements are much more available. Pamphlets giving information about the railroad are the most available and least costly.

■ *Clipper Ship Sweepstakes* is an 1853 lithograph by N. Currier. Clipper ships regularly competed for the fastest times from New York to San Francisco around Cape Horn. The establishment of regular stagecoach service across the country took away the clipper ships' passenger traffic.

■ Classic Concord Western stagecoach made by Abbot & Downing in 1874. This stagecoach was made for Sealy and Wright, who ran the route between Tucson and San Diego. It was then sold to Pioneer Stage Line and ran between Los Angeles and San Francisco. Virtually all of the stagecoach parts are original and have not been replaced or restored. The "red plush" upholstery over horsehair specified in the original order (in the Abbot & Downing Archives) is tattered but present. Of the approximately 15 Western Concord stagecoaches surviving, it is one of the few that has not been restored.

California State Telegraph Company.

The Public are requested to report, by letter, to the Superintendent, at San Francisco, any cause of dissatisfaction.

Austin, July 13, 1866

Rec'd San Francisco July 13, 1866, 11 a.m.

To Gov. H.G. Blasdell

Indians at the South East are murdering all unprotected parties that pass through the Country. I dare not go through alone as I intended, give me authority to quiet them and you will not regret it.

Henry Butterfield

■ Henry Butterfield sent this telegram from Austin, Texas, to governor H.G. Blasdell in San Francisco on July 13, 1866: "Indians at the south East are murdering all unprotected parties that pass through the country. I dare not go through alone as I intended, give me authority to quiet them and you will not regret it."

■ Steamboats with flat bottoms were the major means of transportation into the West before stagecoach routes were established. This illustration of the Yellowstone River is by Karl Bodmer and dates from 1833.

[Agents of WELLS, FARGO & CO. will please place this in the hands of local Officers and Business Men, and preserve a copy in Office. ☞ DO NOT POST. ☜]

$1200 REWARD.

ARREST STAGE ROBBERS.

The stage from Sonora, Tuolumne Co., to Milton, Calaveras Co., was stopped by two men, armed with shot guns, about 5 o'clock Monday morning, February 2nd, 1885, at a point about four miles east from Copperopolis. They broke open the iron safe in the stage, and rifled Wells, Fargo & Co's Express of Coin and Gold Dust, valued at about $2,000. Both men are believed to be Americans; the taller one speaks fair Spanish.

There is a liberal reward offered by the State and Wells, Fargo & Co., for the arrest and conviction of each offender. For particulars, see Wells, Fargo & Co's "Standing Reward" poster of March 1st, 1877.

Among the Treasure taken are the following described articles:

1 Sealed Bag, addressed D. Meyer, San Francisco, containing one lot of 2oz. and $2. amalgam, value $17.50; one lot 5oz. Gold pounded out of quartz, value $18 per oz; one lot 1oz. and $11.25 Placer Gold; one lot 12oz. Gold pounded out of quartz, value $18.50 per oz.; and about $18 in mixed Gold.

1 Sealed Bag, addressed to Selby Smelting & L. Co., San Francisco, containing one piece Retorted Gold, 38 oz.

1 Sealed Bag, addressed to Wells Fargo & Co's Bank, San Francisco, value $160.—No other description.

1 Sealed Bag, addressed to Bank of California, S. F., value $20.—No other description.

Also, Sundry Packages, etc., of Coin, aggregating $694.20, and $35 Currency.

Parties making arrest of, or obtaining clue to said robbers, will please communicate by wire with B. K. Thorne, Sheriff Calaveras County, San Andreas, or with the undersigned, at San Francisco.

Gold Dust Buyers, Bankers and Assayers are especially requested to keep a sharp lookout. Any person giving the undersigned information that leads to the arrest and conviction of robber or recovery of treasure will be suitably rewarded.

JAMES B. HUME,
Special Officer W. F. & Co.

SAN FRANCISCO, February 11, 1885.

■ San Francisco, February 11, 1885.

■ This double barrel shotgun's inlaid badge reads, "Wells Fargo & Co Stage Depot."

My dear Judge

I must have $2,500 Monday morning for 30 or 60 days. I can look to no one but you to help me...

■ Wells Fargo strong box in original condition with the original padlock.

■ Ben Holladay, pioneer of the Overland express business, wrote this letter on June 15, 1861, to J. B. Judge: "I must have $2,500 Monday morning for 30 or 60 days. I can look to no one but you to help me."

■ This stock certificate of the American Express Company is signed by the two founders, Henry Wells and William Fargo, and dates to 1855.

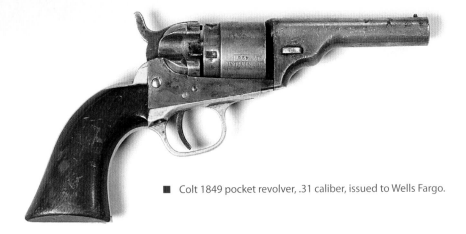

■ Colt 1849 pocket revolver, .31 caliber, issued to Wells Fargo.

Stage Robbed!

The up stage from Milton to Sonora was robbed at 2 P. M., Friday, August 3d, 1877, by three masked men, and Wells, Fargo & Co.'s box robbed of about $600 in silver coin and $200 in gold coin. Two of the robbers were armed with shot guns, and the other with a six shooter. A passenger gives the following description:

No. 1.—A stout, well built man; 5 feet 8 or 10 inches high; weight probably 160 pounds; short, thick hands; nails stubby and short; did not look like a working man's hands; one eye blue, the other white with a film over it, may be blind; spoke good English; wore an old dark coat; dark pants; black hat; common every-day boots; probably a middle aged man; black mask.

No. 2.—Slim man; weight probably 130 to 140 pounds; very small, delicate hands; the left hand covered with a nice fitting blue cotton glove, with border around the wrist; long slim fingers and nails; small feet; fine, very high heeled boots; heels standing well under; blue eyes; wore rust colored pants or overalls; blue cotton jumper; did considerable talking; voice smooth and pleasant; used good English and no profanity.

No. 3.—Did not speak; smallest man of the three; fine high heeled boots; foot short and stubby; hands dark, as a Mexican; wore rather high black hat with black cord and two small tassels. Armed with pistol.

☞ There is a liberal reward offered by the State and Wells, Fargo & Co. for such offenders. For particulars see Wells, Fargo & Co.'s

"STANDING REWARD"

Posters of March 1st, 1876.

J. B. HUME,

Special Officer Wells, Fargo & Co.

Stockton, August 15th, 1877.

[Don't post this but hand to officers.]

■ This report of a stage robbery originates from Stockton, California, on August 15, 1877.

THE PONY EXPRESS

The Pony Express was romantic from the first day riders headed east from San Francisco and west from St. Joseph, Missouri: April 3, 1860. Crowds in both cities realized the historical significance of the start of this 10-day mail service across the central route of the continent, which was 15 days faster than the Overland stagecoach, which went by a much longer southern route.

The approximately 1,800-mile route had way stations about every 10 miles, where riders changed horses. In its 18 months of operation, before staggering costs, lack of a government subsidy, and the telegraph put it out of business, the Pony Express carried 34,753 pieces of mail.

A former Pony Express rider, Walter Crowninshield, wrote from Dayton, Nevada, in 1885:

> To give you a history of the Pony Express from its inception with its incidents, accidents and adventures, even those only with which I was acquainted would fill a book. . . . Yet it is well worth preserving. If you should attempt it I hope you will do it in a more reliable manner than was done some years ago in a sketch that I saw in 'Harper's Monthly.' The author made us ride each

■ The one-dollar Pony Express stamp appears on this letter sent from San Francisco on August 15, 1861, to New York City.

■ A two-dollar Pony Express stamp appears on the envelope from a letter sent from San Francisco on May 25, 1860, which arrived in St. Joseph, Missouri, on June 6. The oval Pony Express cancellation is in the upper center.

■ This letter was sent from San Francisco via Pony Express to New York. Shown here is the original printed envelope of Wells Fargo & Co. with a 10-cent U.S. postage seal and one-dollar Pony Express stamp. It has cancellations at San Francisco, on September 5, 1861, and Atchison, Kansas, on October 9, 1861. The long time it took this letter to arrive is explained by the "MISSENT & FORWARDED" stamp.

■ Undated woodcut showing a Pony Express rider, circa late 19th century.

horse sixty miles without changing. I did not care for myself but sympathized with the poor horses.

In 1858, Buchanan, then president, sent an army to Salt Lake. General Floyd was Secretary of War and gave a contract to forward army supplies to Messrs. Russel and Majors, one of them being the relative of the Secretary. Of course they made a few millions out of the contract and as the war proved a fiasco they made a few more by buying the army equipment for little or nothing and selling to the 'saints' at a high figure. . . . What has that to do with the Pony Express? A great deal. In 1858 a daily mail contract was lett by the superintendent to take the mail overland by stage. It was taken by the so-called 'ox bow' route—down through lower California, Arizona, etc. and took something over thirty days. . . . Russell and Majors saw at once that the time could be beaten by at least ten days on this central route but the 'powers that be' in Washington did not believe it could get over the mountains in winter. To prove that it could, they . . . started the Pony Express as their own venture in the spring of 1860. Showing beyond a doubt that ten days could be saved on this route, summer or winter. Meanwhile Lincoln was elected letting out Mr. Floyd and his friends but the fact had

been demonstrated and the Overland Stage was removed from the southern to the central route.

The 'pony' had become too great a pet on the Pacific Coast to be dropped and with some assistance from the government was continued until the telegraph was finished in the fall of 1861 when the famous 'little horse' was killed by its lightening. The riders rode from 50 to 70 miles each four trips a week, two each way, using from four to six horses each—that is changing every ten or fifteen miles according to stations, water, etc. On Lincoln's election, 1860 we made the trip between the telegraph at St. Jo, Mississippi and Carson City, Nevada in five days, eighteen hours. Our quickest trip having double relief, that is an extra horse midway between stations. . . . We truly saw some rough times between the Indians and the jealous Mormons.

THE TELEGRAPH

In New York on September 2, 1837, Alfred Vail saw Professor Samuel Morse give a demonstration of his "electronic telegraph" over one third of a mile of wire coiled around a room. Fascinated, he

persuaded his father and brother at Speedwell to help him provide Morse with all the necessary assistance . . . advice, a workshop with tools and the money to perfect the telegraph. . . . On September 23 . . . an agreement was signed between Morse and Alfred in which the latter promised to construct by January 1, 1838, 'at his own proper cost and expense' a model of the telegraph to exhibit before officials in Washington. The Vails were also to pay for all incidental expenses including the cost of the patent. In return Alfred [and his brother George, as silent partner] would receive one fourth of the rights. At about the same time, Dr. Leonard Gale became a partner with another one-fourth interest. That left Morse with one-half rights and an agreement that legally entitled him to the major share of the credit.

At the start of the Civil War, there was a strong commercial incentive to construct a telegraph line across the western plains, linking the two coasts. Many companies, however, believed the line would be impossible to build and maintain. In June 1860, Congress passed and President James

Shown here is a section of the copper wire from Morse's first telegraph line, seven inches in length, about five inches of it wrapped in cotton insulation, together with an explanatory note by William Penn Vail: "Piece of the wire used by Prof. Morse and Alfred Vail, in the 1st trial of the Magnetic telegraph, over a long wire, on Jan. 6th, 1838, at Speedwell, Morris County, New Jersey. Length of wire used was three miles."

Buchanan signed an act to "Facilitate Communication Between the Atlantic and Pacific States by Electric Telegraph" and authorized the secretary of the treasury to advertise for builders of the line, which was to be completed within two years. Hiram Sibley, the only bidder, then undertook the construction of the line on his own, running it from Missouri to San Francisco, and completing it to the government's satisfaction in 1861. The Pacific Telegraph Company had been organized for the purpose of building the eastern section of the line from Omaha to Salt Lake City. Sibley sent Jeptha H. Wade to California, where he consolidated the small local companies into the California State Telegraph Company. This entity then organized the Overland Telegraph Company, which handled construction eastward from Carson City, Nevada, joining the existing California lines to the Pacific Telegraph Compay.

The federal government approved the building of the telegraph "Between the Atlantic and Pacific States" on November 11, 1861. The historic document to this effect was signed by U.S. secretary of the Treasury Salmon P. Chase and Hiram Sibley, the leading American promoter of the telegraph industry. In this document dated shortly after the completion of the line, the federal government upheld its end of the deal, promising to pay Sibley $40,000 a year for the priority use of the line for 10 years, with the proviso that the same line would be available to all citizens at a regular telegraph charge. The agreement also contained provisions for connecting military bases and for complimentary service to the Smithsonian Institution and the National Observatory for their scientific communication needs. The government also capped the rate that could be charged to private citizens who wished to send a telegraph at not more than $3 per dispatch of 10 words, and set guidelines for prioritizing requests by corporations sending business communications.

After Hiram Sibley formed an association with Ezra Cornell to found the Western Union Telegraph Company, chartered in 1856, with Sibley as president for 10 years, he advocated a transcontinental telegraph line. When it was completed, the telegraph became one of the most important factors in the development of the social and commercial life of America. It not only ended the usefulness of the Pony Express but also facilitated communication with the army's western forces and generally opened the western frontier to huge potential growth.

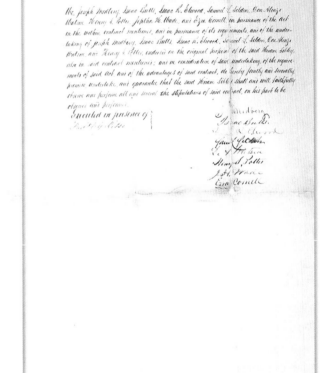

■ The agreement between the federal government, represented by Secretary Chase, and Hiram Sibley, dated November 11, 1861, for the transcontinental telegraph.

THE TRANSCONTINENTAL RAILROAD

The dream of a transcontinental railroad stirred the imaginations of many Americans during the early part of the 19th century. Merchants interested in Pacific trade, gold seekers, and people simply seeking a new home in the West all yearned for a better way of reaching the Pacific Coast. As early as 1838, the daguerreotypist John Plumbe had petitioned Congress to fund a transcontinental railroad route survey, but to no avail.

The first proposal for a transcontinental railroad was Asa Whitney's *Project for a Railroad to the Pacific*, published in 1849. He addressed the preface "To the people of the United States," urging

For yourselves, for your children, for your country, for the destitute over population of Europe without food and without homes—for the heathen, the barbarian and the savage on who the blessings and lights of civilization and Christianity have never shown—for the Chinese who for the want of food must destroy their offspring—for the aged and infirmed who deliberately go out and die because custom, education and duty will not permit them to consume the food required to sustain the more youthful vigorous and useful—and for all the human family and not for myself do I ask you to examine this subject, read and examine it. . . . I do consider this subject of vast and vital importance to the many interests and objects I have enumerated and I do hope for those interests, for the glory of our country and for

Transcontinental Railroad Facts and Figures

January 18, 1863	Date construction started eastward from Sacramento. 4,000 workers, mostly Chinese, built the Western portion.
$1	Daily wage; Chinese workers were paid less.
$16,000	Sum paid by the government to the railroads for each mile of track laid on flat terrain.
$48,000	Sum paid by the government per mile of track laid in the mountains.
10 square miles	Size of land grant, including 400-foot right of way, for every mile of track laid.
10 miles	Record for length of track laid in one day.
May 10, 1869	Date when the Central Pacific Railroad and the Union Pacific met in Promontory, Utah.
6 days	Travel time from the East Coast to the West Coast.
$25	Cost of a ticket from the Mississippi Valley to California during an early fare war.

■ Putt's envelope urges the building of a railroad and satirizes the problems of delivery by horse or mule.

the preservation of our union to the Pacific that the whole subject may be examined by the people. There is no time for delay for the land the only means will soon be no longer available.... Will you allow me to take these wastelands and from their settlement build this great thoroughfare for all mankind, the construction of which can not under any plan advance faster than the settlement of the country on its line? By connecting the two together the facilities which the road would afford for settlement would furnish means and facilities for the advancement of the work quite as rapidly as is possible from any other source or means.

Three surveying parties were sent out by the government in 1853 and 1854 to determine the best route to the Pacific. Each of the proposed routes—the northern, the central, and the southern—had the strong support of the politicians representing the eastern starting points. Stephen

■ Asa Whitney's *Project for a Railroad to the Pacific...*, New York, 1849.

A

PROJECT

FOR

A RAILROAD TO THE PACIFIC.

BY ASA WHITNEY, OF NEW YORK.

WITH REPORTS OF COMMITTEES OF CONGRESS, RESOLUTIONS OF STATE
LEGISLATURES, ETC., WITH OTHER FACTS RELATING THERETO.

NEW YORK:
PRINTED BY GEORGE W. WOOD, NO. 18 SPRUCE STREET.
1849.

A. Douglas of Illinois favored the northern route, Thomas Hart Benton of Missouri the central, and Jefferson Davis, then the secretary of war, the southern. It became a purely sectional issue.

The Civil War settled the selection process, and in 1862 Lincoln signed the Pacific Railway Act, the first step toward a central transcontinental railroad.

Work began in the West by the Central Pacific Railroad, which had discovered the work ethic of the large population of Chinese immigrants in San Francisco and hired them to build the railroad across the Sierras. In the east the Union Pacific hired mostly Civil War veterans, many of them Irish, to build the route across the plains.

On May 10, 1869, the two lines met at Promontory, Utah. Two years later it was possible to cross the continent in six days.

The three competing railroad surveys of northern, central, and southern routes were published in 1855 to 1860 in 13 volumes. Profusely illustrated with maps, colored lithographed plates, profiles, and drawings, they are the most important and massive compilation of exploration reports and data about the Transmississippi West published in the era of exploration. The Pacific Railroad survey in two years increased the contemporary knowledge of the geography, topography, geology, and natural history of the West by a quantum leap. The illustrative material (engraved and lithographed views, specimens of birds, fish, and other animals, etc.) is of the high-

Leland Stanford certifies that the Central Pacific Railroad has completed the first 92 miles of track in its historic journey to meet the Union Pacific at Ogden, Utah, in this document originating from Sacramento on December 18, 1866: "In accordance with . . . the Act of Congress, entitled 'An Act to aid in the Construction of a railroad and telegraph line from the Missouri River to the Pacific Ocean . . .' [s]aid Company is authorised to issue its bonds to the extent of One hundred miles in advance of a continuous completed line of construction . . . ($8,422.000)."

■ Jack Casement, chief of construction for the Union Pacific Railroad, wrote this letter to his wife from Cheyenne on April 29, 1868. "I came from the end of track this evening.... We have got the track clear over the Black Hills and hope now to push along three miles per day. The Indians shot two conductors at Sidney today. They scalped one of them; they will probably both die."

■ Buffalo hunters were employed by the railroad as it advanced west to feed the work crews. Typical equipment, illustrated against a large buffalo hide, included skinning knives, sled, snowshoes, buffalo-skin winter mittens, and Sharps, Spencer, and Winchester rifles.

■ "Supply Trains," from Andrew J. Russell's *The Great West Illustrated in a Series of Photographic Views Across the Continent; Taken Along the Line of the Union Pacific Railroad, West from Omaha, Nebraska*, published in New York "by the authority of the Union Pacific Railroad Company," 1869. The book comprises 50 original albumen photographs depicting scenes along the railroad.

■ "Citadel Rock, Green River Valley," from Ferdinand Hayden's *Sun Pictures of Rocky Mountain Scenery ... Containing ... Photographic Views Along the Line of the Pacific Railroad,* 1870. This photograph by Andrew J. Russell illustrates the Union Pacific Railroad's method of erecting temporary bridges out of timber, shown on the right with the locomotive crossing it, while on the left the time-consuming job of building a permanent bridge of stone goes on.

■ "Dale Creek Bridge, From Above," is from Russell's *The Great West Illustrated*.

■ The Golden Spike ceremony joined the Central Pacific and the Union Pacific Railroads in Promontory, Utah, in 1869. Photograph by Savage & Ottinger, Salt Lake City.

■ Executives of the Union Pacific gather at Promontory, Utah, for the joining of the east and west rails in 1869. Photo by A.J. Russell.

est quality. The project represents the greatest printing of illustrative material undertaken in the United States up to that time.

One of the signs of the fading frontier was the approach of the transcontinental railroad. When Brigham Young signed a contract in 1868 with the Union Pacific Railroad to construct the transcontinental railroad around Salt Lake, his Mormon domain was shrinking. Newell Bringhurst discusses Young's role in the railroad's development in *Brigham Young and the Expanding American Frontier:*

As with mining, Young viewed this development with mixed feelings of hope and anxiety. On the one hand, he welcomed the railroad. As early as 1853, he had petitioned Congress for the construction of a transcontinental railroad to link the Great Basin with the East Coast, making it easier for East Coast–

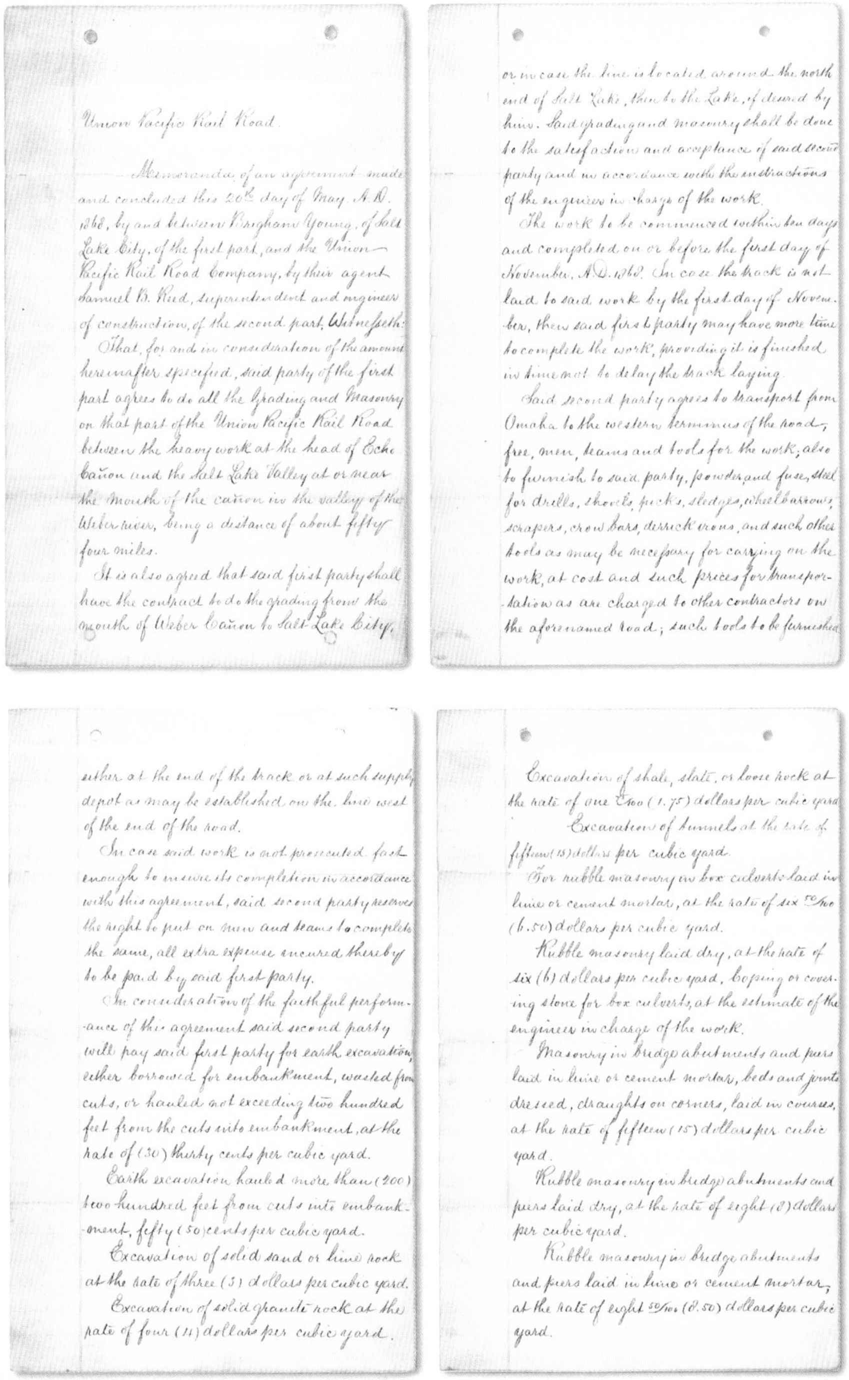

Union Pacific Rail Road.

Memoranda of an agreement made and concluded this 20th day of May A.D. 1868, by and between Brigham Young, of Salt Lake City, of the first part, and the Union Pacific Rail Road Company, by their agent Samuel B. Reed, superintendent and engineer of construction, of the second part, Witnesseth:

That, for and in consideration of the amount hereinafter specified, said party of the first part agrees to do all the Grading and Masonry on that part of the Union Pacific Rail Road between the heavy work at the head of Echo Cañon and the Salt Lake Valley at or near the mouth of the cañon in the valley of the Weber river, being a distance of about fifty four miles.

It is also agreed that said first party shall have the contract to do the grading from the mouth of Weber Cañon to Salt Lake City, or in case the line is located around the north end of Salt Lake, then to the Lake, if desired by him. Said grading and masonry shall be done to the satisfaction and acceptance of said second party and in accordance with the instructions of the engineer in charge of the work.

The work to be commenced within ten days and completed on or before the first day of November, A.D. 1868. In case the track is not laid to said work by the first day of November, then said first party may have more time to complete the work, providing it is finished in time not to delay the track laying.

Said second party agrees to transport from Omaha to the western terminus of the road, free, men, teams and tools for the work; also to furnish to said party, powder and fuse, steel for drills, shovels, picks, sledges, wheelbarrows, scrapers, crow bars, derrick irons, and such other tools as may be necessary for carrying on the work, at cost and such prices for transportation as are charged to other contractors on the aforenamed road; such tools to be furnished either at the end of the track or at such supply depot as may be established on the line west of the end of the road.

In case said work is not prosecuted fast enough to insure its completion in accordance with this agreement, said second party reserves the right to put on men and teams to complete the same, all extra expense incurred thereby to be paid by said first party.

In consideration of the faithful performance of this agreement said second party will pay said first party for earth excavation, either borrowed for embankment, wasted from cuts, or hauled not exceeding two hundred feet from the cuts into embankment, at the rate of (30) thirty cents per cubic yard.

Earth excavation hauled more than (200) two hundred feet from cuts into embankment, fifty (50) cents per cubic yard.

Excavation of solid sand or lime rock at the rate of three (3) dollars per cubic yard.

Excavation of solid granite rock at the rate of four (4) dollars per cubic yard.

Excavation of shale, slate, or loose rock at the rate of one 75/100 (1.75) dollars per cubic yard.

Excavation of tunnels at the rate of fifteen (15) dollars per cubic yard.

For rubble masonry in box culverts laid in lime or cement mortar, at the rate of six 50/100 (6.50) dollars per cubic yard.

Rubble masonry laid dry, at the rate of six (6) dollars per cubic yard, coping or covering stone for box culverts, at the estimate of the engineer in charge of the work.

Masonry in bridge abutments and piers laid in lime or cement mortar, beds and joints dressed, draughts on corners, laid in courses, at the rate of fifteen (15) dollars per cubic yard.

Rubble masonry in bridge abutments and piers laid dry, at the rate of eight (8) dollars per cubic yard.

Rubble masonry in bridge abutments and piers laid in lime or cement mortar, at the rate of eight 50/100 (8.50) dollars per cubic yard.

■ Brigham Young's contract with Union Pacific Railroad, Salt Lake City, May 20, 1868.

■ "East End of Tunnel, Weber Canon."

European Mormons to migrate west. Young was so anxious for a transcontinental railroad that he had paid the entire cost of the first two-year survey made by the Union Pacific Railroad prior to actual construction. And he attempted to influence the proposed route by recommending its construction along the North Platte, over the hills to the Sweetwater, to South Pass, and from that point to the Green River, and ultimately to Echo Canyon down the Weber River into the Great Basin. In the end, Young's proposal was almost identical to the actual route followed by the Union Pacific. By 1868, as the railroad reached present-day Wyoming, Young secured a contract to grade, bridge, and tunnel for the Union Pacific and enlisted the services of several thousand Mormon workers. The Mormon leader viewed the contract a godsend for helping to pull the region out of a severe economic slump. . . .

Finally, on May 10, 1869, construction on the transcontinental railroad was completed. . . . Brigham Young wasted little time utilizing the railroad for the benefit of himself and his followers. He organized his own enterprise, the Utah Central Railroad

■ "Central Pacific Railroad, Cape Horn."

■ This Currier & Ives lithograph from 1871 depicts the route to California by way of the Truckee River in Sierra Nevada.

Company, which connected Salt Lake City with Ogden and the transcontinental route. Completion of this line in January, 1870, meant that the days of Mormon pioneer travel across the plains by wagon, horseback, or on foot were over forever. . . . Young also pushed the building of additional railroad lines, running both south of Salt Lake and north of Ogden, designed to establish closer transportation links throughout the territory. Although the transcontinental railroad benefited the Mormons, Young worried about its negative effects. There was an increased influx of non-Mormons into the Great Basin, which forced the Mormons to confront more and more a non-Mormon population whose practices and beliefs ran counter to their own. The railroad also contributed to increased dissension within the ranks of Mormonism itself.

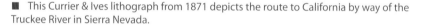

■ The transcontinental route of the Northern Pacific Railroad opened settlement on the northern prairies, bringing European emigrants to buy the railroad's land and use its rails.

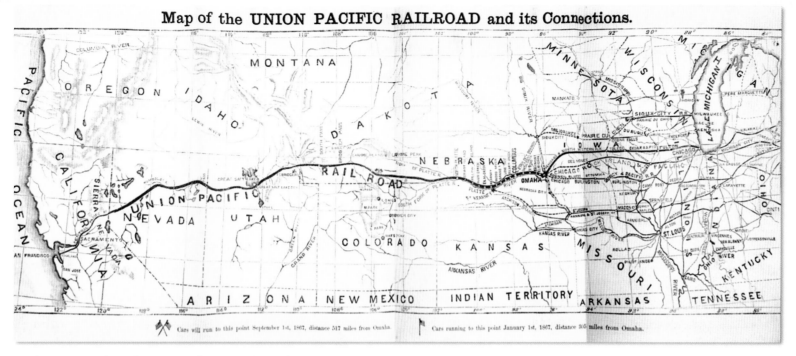

This 1867 map shows the Union Pacific route to the Pacific.

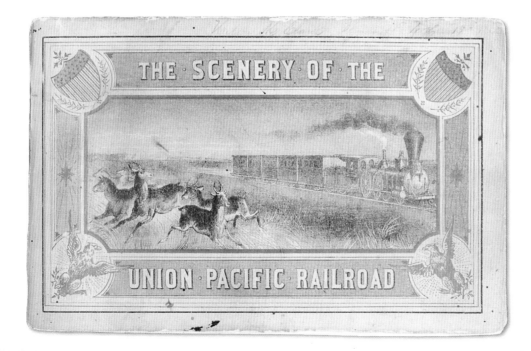

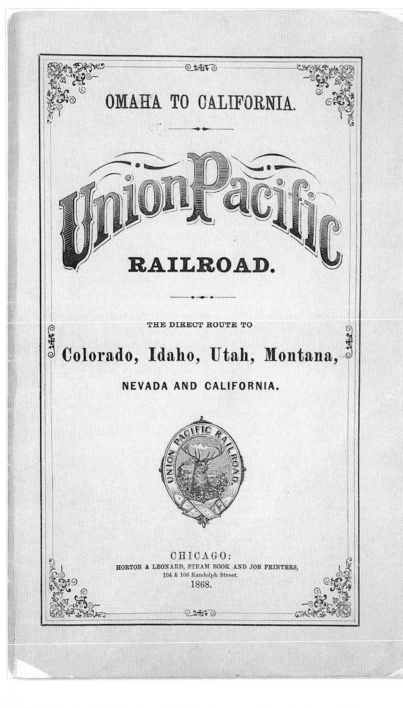

■ The Union Pacific Railroad's schedule for the journey from Omaha to California, 1868.

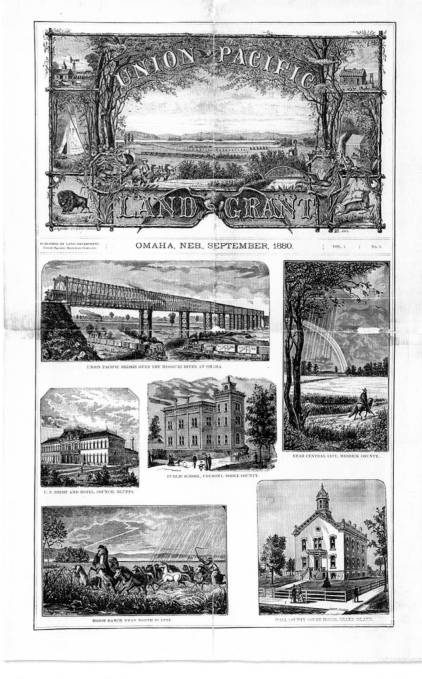

■ An 1880 Union Pacific advertisement extols the opportunities for new settlers of the railroad's land grants.

CHAPTER 16
PROSPECTING, SETTLING, AND WONDERMENT

The pursuit of gold, the dream of a new life in a new settlement, and the wonder of the Western landscape are major parts of the magnetism of the West. That these dreams were realized by hundreds of thousands of people is a testament to the opportunities provided by both the natural resources of the West and the character of those who followed their dreams.

DATES OF STATEHOOD

Missouri	1821
Iowa	1846
Kansas	1861
Nebraska	1867
North Dakota	1889
South Dakota	1889
Oklahoma	1907
New Mexico	1912
Arizona	1912

■ The Colorado gold rush began slowly in 1859 with the discovery of gold in what would become Denver. As in California, there was an immediate demand for coinage to eliminate arguments over the fineness and quality of gold; in 1860 Clark, Gruber & Co. minted this $10 coin.

PROSPECTING

Prospectors scoured the West hoping to find another California gold field. Discoveries from Colorado, Idaho, Montana, Nevada, South Dakota, and, finally, Alaska and the Klondike spurred the settlement of the West as the suppliers to the prospectors moved to the areas of new discoveries, along with merchants, farmers, and all the other people needed to form communities.

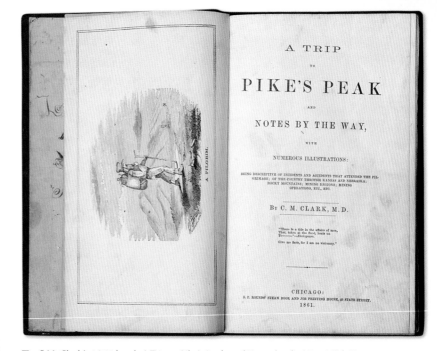

■ C.M. Clark's 1861 book *A Trip to Pike's Peak and Notes by the Way, With Numerous Illustrations* gives an account of the Colorado gold rush. In 1860, Clark became part of the gold rush but prospected there without success. In this book he describes in detail the frontier towns, which he found distastefully full of gambling, crime, and bad language. His narrative is considered to be an authentic and truthful account of life and travel in Colorado of the day.

FOR THE COLLECTOR AND HISTORIAN

Most of the artifacts, letters, documents, and ephemera relating to the settling and prospecting of the West are easily found and inexpensive. The same is true of the firearms commonly used. People saved guns. Prints, photographs, pamphlets and books relating to the natural wonders of the West are generally available and inexpensive, with notable exceptions such as Hayden's *Yellowstone*, illustrated by Thomas Moran.

■ The photograph "Prospecting Outfit," by C.-S. Fly, was taken in Tombstone during the 1880s.

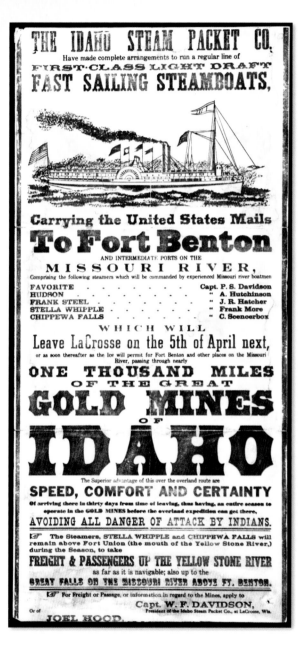

■ This poster advertises the Idaho Steam Packet Company's service to Fort Benton on the Missouri, circa 1865. The discovery of gold in Montana and Idaho in the mid-1860s greatly stimulated steamboating on the Missouri River. Steamboats were able to proceed as far up the river as Fort Benton, Montana, some 2,300 miles from St. Louis.

■ A large map of the Comstock Lode and Sutro Tunnel, illustrating the complex Nevada silver mine, dating from October 1878. The map shows more than 50 mining properties generally running from north to south over a span of about eight miles. At the top is a cross-section of the Sutro Tunnel, which was built to drain water from the mines. Virginia City stood on the mine sites concentrated at the center of the right side of the chart; Ophir, the original bonanza mine, was sunk in the very middle of the town. The Comstock Lode was the single greatest find in the country.

■ Adolph Sutro proposed to solve the problem of flooding in the Comstock Mines by digging a tunnel four miles from the Carson River to the Comstock Mines, 1,650 feet below the surface. The tunnel took seven years to complete, and by that time, 1878, the Comstock was much deeper than 1,650 feet. Nevertheless, Sutro's project did mean that pumps had to raise water only to the level of the tunnel, and from there it would pour downhill to the river.

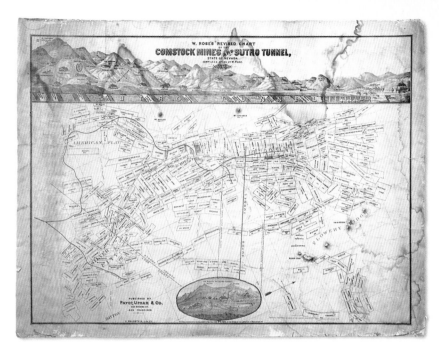

By 1862, Denver had witnessed the mass migration to Colorado of some 100,000 people between 1858 and 1860, a movement triggered by the discovery of gold at the confluence of Cherry Creek and the South Platte River, followed by a dramatic exodus. Only one out of three stayed, as reflected in the census of 1860, which recorded 34,277 residents. Although the population had dropped precipitously, it was by no means snuffed out. Denver in 1862, as described by "Harry" in his letters, was a lively city at its incipience, bubbling with political, judicial, and social intrigue, coping with law and order, and dealing with dispossessed Arapaho and Cheyenne.

"Harry" was a young lawyer who had come to Denver with his father, a judge traveling the circuit, holding court in Boulder and Colorado City. He wrote about many aspects of life in Colorado:

> Ladies, in such a country as this, unless they keep house, have very little to do, unless it is to gossip. They say Denver is famous for that. Ladies at the hotel seem to be pretty well ennui-ed. There is one beautiful virgin, i.e., mantrap, —of forty summers, who sits at dinner at the next table to us, who is perfectly and bewitchingly excruciating. . . . I might have fallen in love by this time, but unfortunately I sit with my back to her. . . . A great many trains are arriving from the States, and they have curious mottoes on their wagon covers. Sometimes they write on it 'Pikes Peak or bust' and if they fail when they go back they put the 'ed' on and make it 'busted'. . . . Times are brightening, emigration is coming in, families are moving here to remain, business is increasing. I have commenced to earn something, and everybody seems to be in good spirits generally. . . .
>
> A party of Arapahoes came in and encamped on the Platte. I walked down there in the afternoon and examined their lodges, which are of skins. I did not enter them, although they would have considered it an honor, for very good reasons. The little youngsters are generally in a state of nudity. One of them who could just toddle had an old piece of calico, which he used to wrap around him Indian style. He had not quite learnt the knack, but he managed to get it around him with all the grace . . . of a big Injun. . . . Mr. Colly, the Indian agent has returned from the Reservation of the Arapahoes and Cheyennes. This war party that is here, he says are Blackfeet, and not Arapahoes. The

people begin to fear trouble from the Utes, for these war parties of Arapahoes, every time they have a fight with the Utes, whether they are victorious or not, make straight for some village or city of the whites, and virtually place themselves under our protection. As we have nothing to do with their wars, this running back to us, makes the Utes think us as enemies, and as a consequence trouble is expected. . . . The citizens are complaining of the city tax now, which is double that of the county. But we need as many improvements that it is necessary. A bridge over the Platte that was swept away last spring, is to be rebuilt, [and] a fire engine is to be bought.

SETTLING THE WEST

Settlements followed the westward movement, though not in geographic sequence, as the West Coast had many settlements before the prairies attracted homesteaders. Communities were important, and as soon as possible churches and schools were established, as well as businesses to support local activities. Politicians developed out of the communities to bring order and planning for the future.

The Homestead Act of 1862 allowed any adult citizen to claim 160 acres of public land for $10. At the end of five years, if he had not left it for more than six months, it was his.

■ The Currier & Ives lithograph *The Pioneer's Home on the Western Frontier* dates from 1867.

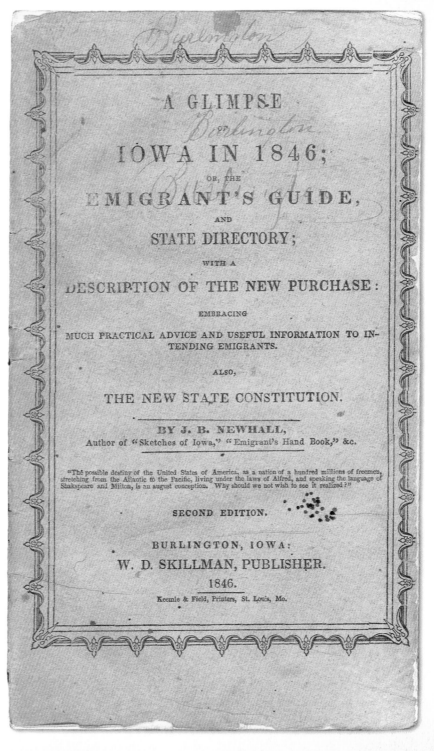

■ This grant of land in "Lands of the United States" in the territory northwest of the Ohio and above the mouth of the Kentucky River was signed in 1806 by Thomas Jefferson as president and James Madison as secretary of state.

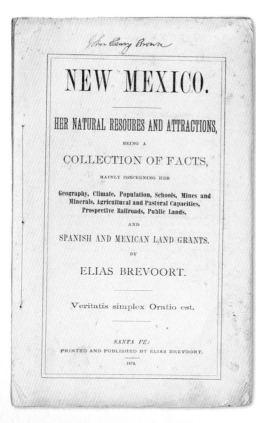

■ *New Mexico: Her Natural Resoures [sic] and Attractions, Being a Collection of Facts, Mainly Concerning Her Geography, Climate, Population, Schools, Mines and Minerals, Agricultural and Pastoral Capacities, Prospective Railroads, Public Lands, and Spanish and Mexican Land Grants* was written by Elias Brevoort and published in Santa Fe in 1874.

■ John B. Newhall's book *A Glimpse of Iowa in 1846; or, the Emigrants Guide, and State Directory; With a Description of the New Purchase: Embracing Much Practical Advice and Useful Information to Intending Emigrants* appeared in 1846.

■ John Haddock set out with a few friends in September 1870 and spent several years traveling on the frontier. His *Journal of Life on the Frontier* contains hundreds of full-page pencil sketches recording his observations and experiences roaming the plains, ranging from a sketch of the town of Golden, Colorado, to scenes of buffalo hunting, roping and branding cattle, and fighting Indians. Many sketches of the interiors of frontier cabins as well as drawings of saloons and seemingly every other aspect of life on the frontier (see below and lower right) are also included.

■ The illustrated cover of Haddock's journal.

THE

KANZAS REGION:

Forest, Prairie, Desert, Mountain, Vale, and River.

DESCRIPTIONS OF

SCENERY, CLIMATE, WILD PRODUCTIONS, CAPABILITIES OF
SOIL, AND COMMERCIAL RESOURCES;

INTERSPERSED WITH

INCIDENTS OF TRAVEL,

AND ANECDOTES ILLUSTRATIVE OF THE CHARACTER OF THE TRADERS AND
RED MEN; TO WHICH ARE ADDED

DIRECTIONS AS TO ROUTES, OUTFIT FOR THE PIONEER, AND
SKETCHES OF DESIRABLE LOCALITIES FOR
PRESENT SETTLEMENT.

BY MAX. GREENE.

"FOLLOW LOVE'S FOLDING STAR TO THE EVENING LAND."

NEW YORK:
FOWLER AND WELLS, PUBLISHERS,
308 BROADWAY.
1856.

Boston: 142 Washington Street. } { Philadelphia: No. 231 Arch Street.

■ Max Greene's book *The Kanzas Region: Forest, Prairie, Desert, Mountain, Vale, and River...*, published in 1856, is an extensive work written at the beginning of the settlement of Kansas.

■ *Home Sweet Home.*

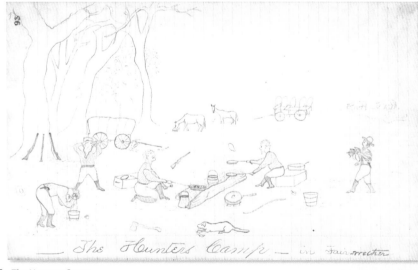

■ *The Hunters Camp.*

■ This buffalo hide coat dates from about 1875 to 1880. After 1880, these coats became prohibitively expensive due to the dwindling number of buffalo. They were replaced by canvas coats with blanket liners.

■ The proprietors of frontier business "Bolles & Bradshaw Horsehoers and General Blacksmiths" pose proudly.

■ Colt 1873 Frontier Six Shooter, single action, Winchester 44-40 center fire. The classic Western pistol.

■ Colt's first double action revolver, the Model 1877, .38 caliber Lightning.

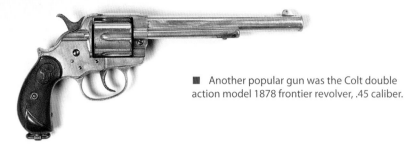

■ Another popular gun was the Colt double action model 1878 frontier revolver, .45 caliber.

■ The Winchester Henry Rifle was revolutionary with its 15-round magazine, lever action, and reliability. The .44 caliber Henry competed with the much larger-caliber Spencer rifle.

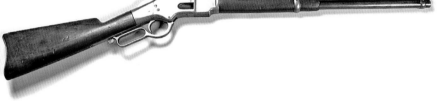

■ The Winchester model 1866 saddle ring carbine solved the problem of the Henry rifle's fragile magazine tube and allowed easy loading through the side of the receiver.

■ Winchester 1873 Rifle, .38 caliber.

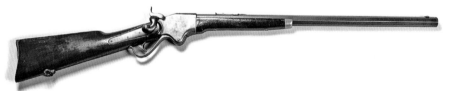

■ The Spencer buffalo rifle, dating from the 1870s, was created by many frontier gunsmiths from surplus Civil War Spencer rifles. They installed longer and heavier octagon barrels and made other improvements for hunting on the plains.

■ The Sharps model 1874 military rifle was reworked by Freund. A 45/70 smooth bore or forager, it has a front sight made from an old coin.

STOCK Sale!

I will offer for sale at public auction at the farm of L. C. Wilbur on the territory line near Tar creek, six miles west of Baxter, on

SATURDAY, JUNE 23d, '88,

BEGINNING AT 10 O'CLOCK SHARP,

50 COWS WITH CALVES!

These are considered the finest lot of cows in this section of country, and are nearly all broke to milk. The calves are all out of thoroughbred bulls.

2 Thoro'bred Shorthorn Bulls!

Two Work Horses!

Three Brood Mares

Two Mowing Machines in Good Running Order!

ONE LUMBER WAGON!

NINE FINE BROOD SOWS WITH PIGS!

ONE THOROUGHB'D BERKSHIRE BOAR!

TERMS.---Seven months credit without interest, on notes with approved security, or 6 per cent discount for cash.

J. P. HARTLEY, Auctioneer.

F. N. MOORE.

M. H. Gardner, Printer, Baxter Springs.

■ A Kansas stock sale in 1888 advertised "Terms—Seven Months Credit."

■ This large advertising board contains original cartridges made by Winchester.

In 1889, under tremendous pressure from would-be settlers, the government opened two million acres of what had been Indian Territory in Oklahoma. By 1907, millions more acres had been opened, and settlers then occupied all of the United States.

William Marin, an Irish immigrant, wrote from Washington County, Iowa, on July 19, 1849, to a friend back home,

> I . . . am well pleased with the country and think that it is the [best] place for a free man that I have seen. . . . [Y]ou can suit yourselves in land of any kind either with improvements or no improvements can be for six dollars an acre and there is any quantity of unimproved land which can be had for one dollar and 25 cents per acre. There is thousands of acres of this last sort here covered with the best pasture from 8 to 36 inches long. It can soon make good hay and stock gets fat in summer. If a man is not able to buy this land he can go and improve on it till he is able to pay for it without any rent or tax and a man can get three bushels of corn for a day's work or one bushel and one half of wheat.
>
> The State of Society here is good and a man of almost any profession can be suited.

The Plan of Operations of the Immigrant Aid Company, 1854, encouraged immigrants to come to the Kansas Territory, declaring in its preface that

> its duty is to organize immigration to the west and bring it into a system. . . . The immigrant suffers whenever he goes along into his new home. . . . All accounts agree that the region of Kansas is the most desirable part of America now open to the immigrant. It is accessible in seven days continuous travel from Boston. Its crops are very bountiful—its soil being well-adapted to the staples of Virginia and Kentucky and especially to the growth of hemp. In its eastern section the woodland and prairie land intermix in proportions very well adapted for the purposes of the settler. Its mineral resources, especially its coal in central and western parts are inexhaustible. A steamboat is already plying on the Kansas River and the territory has uninterrupted steamboat communication with New Orleans. . . . All the overland immigration in California and Oregon by any of the easier routes passes of necessity through its limits. Whatever roads are built westward must begin in this territory for it is here that the immigrant leaves the Missouri River. The demands for provisions and breadstuff made by immigrants proceeding to California [h]as given to the inhabitants of the neighboring parts of Missouri a market at as good rates as they could have found in the Union. It is impossible that such a region should not fill up rapidly. The immigrant aid company proposes to give confidence to settlers by giving system to immigration.

One writer sent the following to the children and members of the Sabbath school from Fort Dodge, Iowa, in 1864:

> There is more intelligence here than I expected to find in the west. Fort Dodge is remarkable for the refinement of its society. There are quite a number of liberally educated men in business here & some of the ladies are equal to any I ever saw in the east for refinement. Yet the place is young. The schools are not very good and the people are making haste to get rich. There is not much money in the place & the wealth of the people consists chiefly in real estate. It is very difficult to get a house. . . . Every thing . . . house keeping clothing & all eastern & imported goods all very high. There are trains of waggons going thro this place

every day, bound for the gold regions in Idahoe, perhaps 800 or 1000 miles from here. They are generally drawn by oxen from one to two pair to a wagon. These waggons all covered with quilts or cotton sheeting. They contain a cooking stove & all the personal property of the travellers.

William Tecumseh Sherman, the Union's famous Civil War general, had a practical military attitude toward those heading west. In January 1866, he wrote to Colonel Bowen in Washington:

> I am . . . in receipt of the letter . . . endorsed by you . . . by the State of Minnesota for the establishment of a Line of Military Posts to Walla Walla Oregon. . . . [It] is judged both impracticable and unnecessary to guard the Whole Road by costly military posts, but rather to confine travel to one Road, and require emigrants to go in bodies sufficient for self protection. There will be no real danger in travelling from Minnesota to Fort Pierce but there to Virginia City some protection will be necessary. Were we to grant one half the regiments of the Territories, the National Congress would have to increase the Army far beyond any present estimate, and the cost would be beyond all estimates. The People on our Frontiers must conform to the national interests, instead of forcing us to cover them in their wandering propensities.

In a postscript, Sherman wrote, "Petition re-enclosed."

As commissioner of the General Land Office Thomas A. Hendricks wrote in 1856, "All the public lands which may be in market and subject to private entry at $1.25 on which there may be no settlement, may be located by any party with military bounty warrants. Second—Ample notice through the public prints will be given when the United States reserved sections, or railroad lands, will be offered at public sale. Third—No lands in the Territory of Nebraska have as yet been offered at public sale."

Fort Dodge, Iowa, is described in a letter from 1864:

> Ten years ago there were no buildings in Fort Dodge except the Barracks that were occupied by soldiers, who held a garrison to defend the frontier against the Indians. Civilization has swept the frontier one or two hundred miles further west, & there is no garrison here now. . . . There are about 800 inhabitants in the village now & 1500 in the town. . . . Fort Dodge is destined, however, to be one of the largest places in N Western Iowa.

Joseph C. Miller wrote to his cousin Anna from Topeka in 1855 and 1858. Miller's first letter chides Anna for "toiling and driveling" at a Providence factory when she might be living in "a land flowing with milk and honey." He extols the "richness of the country" and concludes that "soon the east will be emptied of all the wise, and nothing but fools will be left." Miller mentions that the Constitutional Convention in Topeka is in "great hopes" of making it the state capitol. In 1858 Miller still urges his cousin to emigrate, promising her that there is a surplus of marriageable young men. He says the town has grown and that it is probable that a railroad line from St. Joseph will be built. There is no paper money in Kansas, but people have refrained from putting pressure on each other for payments. "We have peaceable times now . . . so far as a conflict of arms is concerned, but there is a war of words between the different elements. . . . It seems that Kansas, Utah and Nickeraugan affairs are acting like bombshells thrown into Congress."

NATURAL WONDERS

The pioneer environmentalist John Muir was a vital figure in the growth of environmental consciousness. Muir's writings about the mountains of California and other wild parts of the West were instrumental in the movement for national parks and an appreciation of the value of preserving wilderness. In 1903 he wrote in *Our National Parks:*

> The tendency nowadays to wander in wildernesses is delightful to see. Thousands of tired, nerve-shaken, over-civilized people are beginning to find out that going to the mountains is going home, that wildness is a necessity and that mountain parks and reservations are useful not only as fountains of timber and irrigating rivers but as fountains of life. Awakening from the stupefying effects of the vice of over-industry and the deadly apathy of luxury they are trying as best they can to mix and enrich their own little ongoings with those of Nature and to get rid of rust and disease. . . .
>
> All the western mountains are still rich in wildness and by means of good roads are being brought nearer to civilization every year. To the sane and free it will hardly seem necessary to cross the continent in search of wild beauty, however easy

■ Colored engraving by J. Smillie of Albert Bierstadt's painting *The Rocky Mountains*, 1866.

the way, for they find it in abundance wherever they chance to be. Like Thoreau they see forests and orchards in patches of huckleberry brush and oceans in ponds and drops of dew. Few in these hot, dim, strenuous times are quite sane or free; choked with care like clocks full of dust, laboriously doing so much good and making so much money, —or so little, they are no longer good for themselves.

John Muir
Sep. 15th 1896.

Going to the Mountains
is going home

■ John Muir penned this sentiment in 1896: "Going to the Mountains is going home."

■ *Yellowstone National Park,* a 1904 chromolithograph, offers a bird's-eye view of the park.

■ *The Vernal Fall.*

■ This painting of a classic vista, titled *Yosemite Valley Scene,* from circa 1880, is unsigned.

■ Josiah Whitney's *The Yosemite Book; A Description of the Yosemite Valley and the Adjacent Region of the Sierra Nevada, and of the Big Trees of California...*, published in 1868, is an important photographically illustrated work, containing 28 original albumen photographs originally produced by Carleton T. Watkins in 1866. Shown here is "El Capitan and Cathedral Rock."

17 OUTLAWS AND LAWMEN

The American Dream was pursued by outlaws in a unique way: as they pursued their dreams, others—sheriffs, marshalls, posses—pursued them. They were dependent on the hard work of others, who dreamed of new settlements—with banks—of new businesses that flourished in the West and transported their money and bullion on the railroad trains. Their exploits were chronicled in newspapers and their lives in pamphlets and books. Outlaws were feared and fascinating at the same time.

OUTLAWS, LAWMEN, AND THEIR FATES

NAME	FATE	AGE AT DEATH (YEARS)
Jesse James	Shot to death	35
Frank James	Retired	72
Bob Dalton	Shot to death	23
Emmett Dalton	14 years in prison	86
Cole Younger	25 years in prison	72
Jim Younger	Suicide after 25 years in prison	54
Bob Younger	Died in prison	35
Wild Bill Hickok	Shot to death	39
Wyatt Earp	Retired	81
Bat Masterson	Became a sports reporter	68
Black Bart	Served six years in prison	87

The media and public interest continues to this day. Their brief lives—cut short by bullets or prison—live on in the public fascination. Present-day movies and books can make it difficult to distinguish historical facts from popular entertainment. The reality was certainly very violent, and human life was cheap to those who sought out gunfights and robberies.

Many of the outlaws and gunfighters began their careers during the Civil War, often as part of the Confederate guerrilla forces. As outlaws, the James brothers, as well as Cole Younger, employed tactics similar to those they'd used as guerilla fighters with Quentrell's Raiders: intelligence missions scouting robberies, establishing hideouts in advance, and maintaining the support of farmers. To many they represented the lost Confederate cause.

While cattle towns in Kansas attracted many gunfighters, and local businessmen hired other gunfighters as sheriffs and marshals, the mining camps and districts attracted those seeking to get rich quick with their guns rather than with picks and shovels.

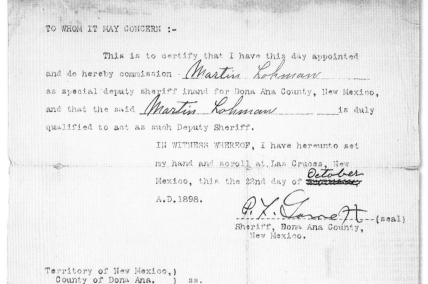

■ Pat Garrett appointed Martin Lohman "as special deputy sheriff in and for Dona Ana County, New Mexico" in this document signed in Las Cruces, New Mexico, on October 22, 1898.

BILLY THE KID.—[From a Photograph.]

■ Pat Garrett, the man who killed Billy the Kid, published *The Authentic Life of Billy the Kid, the Noted Desperado of the Southwest, Whose Deeds of Daring and Blood Made His Name a Terror in New Mexico, Arizona, and Northern Mexico . . .*, in 1882. This, the most famous outlaw book, was the beginning of a vast outpouring of literature on the outlaw. Shown here is the frontispiece illustration.

■ The Model 1873 Colt single action .45 caliber revolver was very popular with both the military and civilian markets because of its reliability and handling. This model was used by lawmen and outlaws alike, including Wyatt Earp, Jesse James, Bat Masterson, and Billy the Kid, as well as by Pat Garrett to shoot Billy the Kid.

FOR THE
COLLECTOR
AND HISTORIAN

Collecting this area is fairly difficult. Letters by the famous gunfighters and outlaws are, with few exceptions, very rare, as are the reward posters for the major outlaws. The pistols of this period can be obtained quickly and for relatively reasonable costs. Although difficult to find, the newspapers chronicling the gunfighters' and outlaws' exploits are the most reasonably priced artifacts of all.

On this .45 caliber Colt single action army revolver, the hammer screw has been replaced with a large screw for a fast-draw rig. This consists of a slotted spring steel clasp riveted to a large rectangular steel plate riveted to a brown leather belt. In addition to the manufacturer's name, PAT'D JAN 17 1882 is marked on this steel clasp. The gun was manufactured and shipped in 1887.

JESSE JAMES'S AMERICAN DREAM: BUYING A FARM

Jesse James at 35 years old knew that his career as an outlaw was drawing to a close. Six years earlier, he and his brother Frank had joined with the Younger brothers' gang to rob the bank in Northfield, Minnesota. They had not counted on the fierceness of the townspeople; in the confrontation, three were killed, the Youngers were captured, and Jesse and Frank James barely escaped. They lay low for three years before robbing a train in Missouri, and two years later they murdered two men. In 1881 the governor of Missouri offered a reward of $5,000 for the capture or death of each. Jesse decided to retire under the assumed name "Thomas Howard."

On March 2, 1882, he responded to an advertisement in the newspaper by J.D. Calhoun offering for sale "a very fine 160 acres, adjoining the town of Franklin . . . Corners with depot grounds. Living springs; beautiful creek runs

FOR SALE—A very fine 160 acres, adjoining the town of Franklin, Franklin Co. Corners with depot grounds. Living springs; beautiful creek runs through it. 90 acres in body of finest bottom land: balance natural young timber. Mill within a mile. As good educational, religious, railroad and other facilities as any point in western Nebraska. $10 per acre. Address or call on J.D. Calhoun, Lincoln, Neb. feb15d6&w1t

This ad by J.D. Calhoun attracted Jesse James's interest.

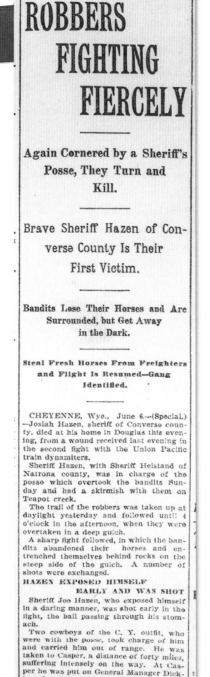

ROBBERS FIGHTING FIERCELY

Again Cornered by a Sheriff's Posse, They Turn and Kill.

Brave Sheriff Hazen of Converse County Is Their First Victim.

Bandits Lose Their Horses and Are Surrounded, but Get Away in the Dark.

Steal Fresh Horses From Freighters and Flight Is Resumed—Gang Identified.

CHEYENNE, Wyo., June 6.--(Special.) --Josiah Hazen, sheriff of Converse county, died at his home in Douglas this evening, from a wound received last evening in the second fight with the Union Pacific train dynamiters.

Sheriff Hazen, with Sheriff Helstand of Natrona county, was in charge of the posse which overtook the bandits Sunday and had a skirmish with them on Teapot creek.

The trail of the robbers was taken up at daylight yesterday and followed until 4 o'clock in the afternoon, when they were overtaken in a deep gulch.

A sharp fight followed, in which the bandits abandoned their horses and entrenched themselves behind rocks on the steep side of the gulch. A number of shots were exchanged.

HAZEN EXPOSED HIMSELF EARLY AND WAS SHOT

Sheriff Joe Hazen, who exposed himself in a daring manner, was shot early in the fight, the ball passing through his stomach.

Two cowboys of the C. Y. outfit, who were with the posse, took charge of him and carried him out of range. He was taken to Casper, a distance of forty miles, suffering intensely on the way. At Casper he was put on General Manager Dickinson's private car and taken to his home at Douglas, where he died from the effects of the wound at 5:00 o'clock this morning.

through it. 90 acres in body of finest bottom land: balance natural young timber. Mill within a mile. As good educational, religious, railroad and other facilities as any point in western Nebraska. $10 per acre."

In a handwritten letter to Calhoun (facing page), Jesse James writes from 1818 Lafayette Street, St. Joseph, Missouri:

I have noted that you have 160 acres of land advertised for sale in Franklin Neb. Please write at once and let me know the lowest cash price that will buy your land. Give me a full description of the land etc.

I want to purchase a farm of that size provided I can find one to suit. I will not buy a farm unless the soil is good. I will start on a trip in about eight days to northern . . . Nebraska and if the description of your land suits me I will look at it and if it suits me I will buy it from the advertisement in Lincoln Journal. I suppose your land can be made a great farm. . . . Please answer at once.

While Jesse James was looking for his retirement farm, one of the members of his outlaw gang had made a deal with the governor of Missouri to kill him. One month after writing this letter, on April 3, 1882, Robert Ford shot Jesse James as James was standing on a chair to straighten a picture on the wall.

Frank James spent several years in jail and had two trials, one for murder, the other for robbery, but managed to be acquitted in both cases. While awaiting his first trial he wrote to his wife from Gallaston, Missouri, in 1883: "I think my Attys are taking things rather easy, perhaps if their precious time were in any danger they would be a little more hasty to act."

"Robbers Fighting Fiercely" is the headline of this news article from the *Denver Republic* issue of Wednesday morning, June 7, 1899.

Mr. J D Calhoun
Lincoln Neb
        Dear Sir
            I have noticed
that you have 160 acres
of land advertised for
sale in Franklin co. neb
please write at once
and let me know the
lowest cash price that
will buy your land.
give me a full descripti
on of the land &c.
        I want to purchase
a farm of that size
provided I can find one
to suit. I will not
buy a farm unless the

soil is no. 1
I will start on a trip
in about 8 days, to
northern Kan & South
Nebraska and if the descript
ion of your land suits
me. I will look at it
& if it suits me. I will
buy it from the adverti
sement in Lincoln Journal.
I suppose your land can
be made a good farm
for stock & grain
please answer at once
                Respectfully.
                    Thos Howard
        No 1318 Lafayette St.
                St Joseph
                    Mo

■ In this letter, James expresses interest in Calhoun's land and speaks of his wish to buy a farm.

■ This Remington model 1875 single action army frontier revolver, .44–40 Winchester center fire, is the model Frank James used.

The Life and Tragic Death of
JESSE JAMES.

The Western Desperado.

■ This 1882 biography of James boasts the impressive title *Jesse James: The Life and Daring Adventures of This Bold Highwayman and Bank Robber, and His No Less Celebrated Brother, Frank James. Together with the Thrilling Exploits of the Younger Boys. Written by . . . (One Who Dare Not Now Disclose His Identity.) The Only Book Containing the Romantic Life of Jesse James and His Pretty Wife, Who Clung to Him to the Last!* The chapters include "Life and Startling Adventures," "Jesse in Love—His Marriage," "Frank James Gets Married," "A Seventeen Thousand Dollar Haul," "Escape of Frank and Jesse James," "The Class of People Who Befriended the Outlaws," "The Last Great Train Robbery," "The Younger Family," "The Tragic Death of Jesse James," "The Wife of Jesse James Tells Her Own Story," "Relics of Jesse James . . . ," and "A Terror to His Followers as Well as to the Public at Large."

■ The Schofield Smith & Wesson .45 caliber revolver was an improvement on the American model in reliability as well as features and was adopted by the army in 1875. This model was used by both Virgil Earp and Jesse James.

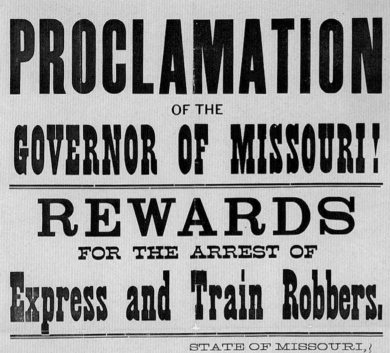

■ This Colt round barrel conversion .38 rimfire caliber revolver is believed to have been used by Jesse James in the historic James gang holdup of the First National Bank of Northfield, Minnesota. It is accompanied by a letter of provenance dated 1929: "This genuine old Colt revolver was picked up on the floor of the First National bank of Northfield Minn. when it was robbed in 1875 by the James Gang. Both Cole and Bob Younger identified this revolver as the property of Jessy [sic] James. It is in perfect condition and was made during the Civil War as the engraving on the cylinder shows. This arm was picked up by Gil Whittier who was Deputy Sheriff of Dakota County at the time of the robbery. As to the validity of all this, the heirs of Mr. Whittier who still are in Minneapolis Minn. will be pleased to corroborate. Further, the present owner who was Junior Warden of Minnesota State Penitentiary at Stillwater Minn. from 1875 until 1883 will be glad to verify the above information. John Ryan."

■ The most famous reward poster: the governor of Missouri offers $20,000 for the capture and conviction of Frank and Jesse James, July 28, 1881.

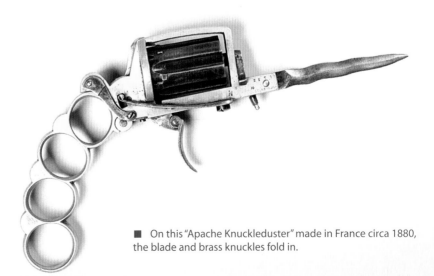

■ On this "Apache Knuckleduster" made in France circa 1880, the blade and brass knuckles fold in.

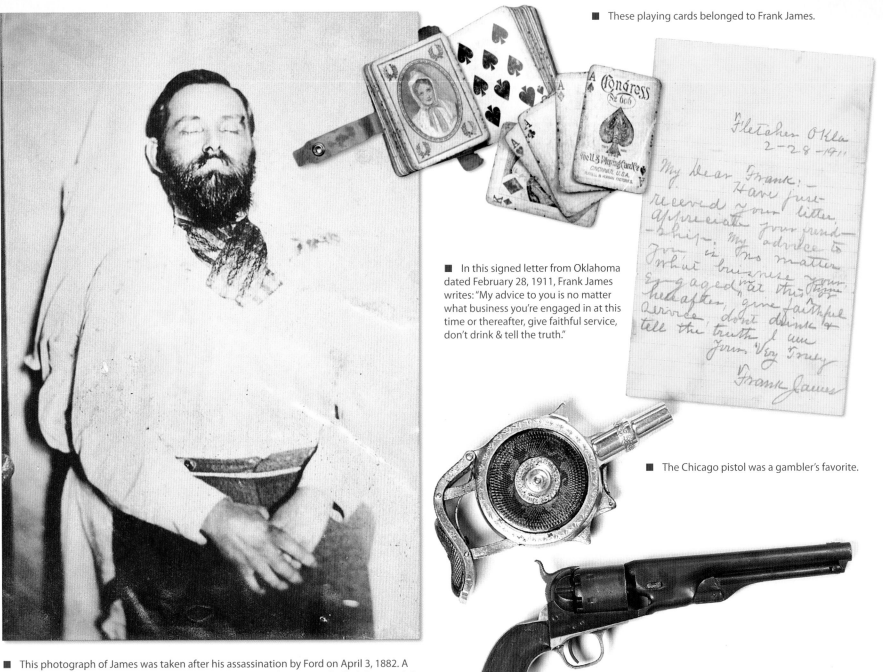

■ These playing cards belonged to Frank James.

■ In this signed letter from Oklahoma dated February 28, 1911, Frank James writes: "My advice to you is no matter what business you're engaged in at this time or thereafter, give faithful service, don't drink & tell the truth."

■ The Chicago pistol was a gambler's favorite.

■ This photograph of James was taken after his assassination by Ford on April 3, 1882. A label affixed to the lower margin reads, "Jesse James/Born Feb. 1845, and Killed, St. Joseph." The photograph was taken by local photographer R.G. Smith after James had been killed by a member of his own gang for the $10,000 reward offered by the governor of Missouri.

■ Both Wild Bill Hickok and Cole Younger used this model gun: a Colt model 1851 navy .36 caliber.

Carano—this might be of Service to you Some day—by way of Identification In a Strang place.

Jim.

■ Jim Younger, with his three brothers, joined forces with Jesse and Frank James. The Younger brothers met their downfall in the raid on the banks in Northfield, Minnesota.

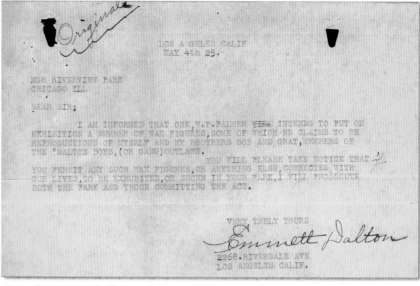

LOS ANGELES CALIF
MAY 4th 25.

MGR RIVERVIEW PARK
CHICAGO ILL

DEAR SIR;

I AM INFORMED THAT ONE W.F. PALMER INTENDS TO PUT ON EXHIBITION A NUMBER OF WAX FIGURES, SOME OF WHICH HE CLAIMS TO BE REPRODUCTIONS OF MYSELF AND MY BROTHERS BOB AND GRAT, MEMBERS OF THE "DALTON BOYS,(OR GANG)OUTLAWS.

YOU WILL PLEASE TAKE NOTICE THAT YOU PERMIT ANY SUCH WAX FIGURES, OR ANYTHING ELSE, CONNECTED WITH OUR LIVES, TO BE EXHIBITED, OR SHOWN IN YOUR PARK, I WILL PROSECUTE BOTH THE PARK AND THOSE COMMITTING THE ACT.

VERY TRULY YOURS

Emmett Dalton

2268 RIVERDALE AVE
LOS ANGELES CALIF.

■ In a letter signed by Emmett Dalton on May 4, 1925, the surviving member of the Dalton Gang acted to block an exhibition of wax figures of the "Dalton Boys (or Gang) Outlaws."

SAFE IN THE SADDLE.

The Train Robbers Baffle Their Pursuers.

Not the Slightest Trace of the Scoundrels.

The Story Told by One of Their Victims.

An Old Man Beaten and Robbed by Tramps.

New Jersey's Sensation---The Criminal Calendar.

Special Dispatch to the Globe-Democrat.

INDEPENDENCE, Mo., October 10.—There have been no new developments of interest in the Glendale express and train robbery to-day. Officers in large numbers are still scouring the country, and strong hopes of the speedy capture of the thieves are still entertained. The opinion that the gang was under the leadership of the notorious Jesse James is still very strong in this part of the county, as is also the suspicion that the entire gang were former chums of the James and Younger brothers, of this (Clay) and Lafayette Counties. The United States Express Company officials state that they have so far only discovered a loss of about $6,000. The search for the robbers will be diligently kept up, as the officers, as well as the people, are determined that this outrage shall not go unpunished.

■ "Safe in the Saddle," declares the headline of the *St. Louis Globe-Democrat* in its Saturday morning issue of October 11, 1879.

Cole. Younger

■ Cole Younger and his brother Bob, as well as Jesse and Frank James, were Confederate guerrillas who became outlaws after the Civil War.

WESTERN DISTRICT OF ARKANSAS,
April 27 1887

I hereby certify that I have been employed and have acted 2 days, as a Guard over

James Shaw   , a United States prisoner in charge of
Frank Dalton   Deputy Marshal, from Muskogee I.T.
Fort Smith ark   being a distance of 80 miles.

Bob Dalton
Fort Smith
ark

■ Bob Dalton and his brothers, cousins of the Youngers, tried after a number of unspectacular train robberies to simultaneously rob two banks in Coffeyville, Kansas. Only Emmett, though badly wounded, survived.

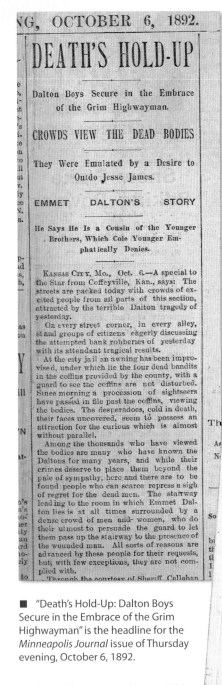

DEATH'S HOLD-UP

Dalton Boys Secure in the Embrace
of the Grim Highwayman.

CROWDS VIEW THE DEAD BODIES

They Were Emulated by a Desire to
Outdo Jesse James.

EMMET DALTON'S STORY

He Says He Is a Cousin of the Younger
Brothers, Which Cole Younger Em-
phatically Denies.

KANSAS CITY, Mo., Oct. 6.—A special to
the Star from Coffeyville, Kan., says: The
streets are packed today with crowds of ex-
cited people from all parts of this section,
attracted by the terrible Dalton tragedy of
yesterday.

On every street corner, in every alley,
stand groups of citizens eagerly discussing
the attempted bank robberies of yesterday
with its attendant tragical results.

At the city jail an awning has been impro-
vised, under which lie the four dead bandits
in the coffins provided by the county, with a
guard to see the coffins are not disturbed.
Since morning a procession of sightseers
have passed in file past the coffins, viewing
the bodies. The desperadoes, cold in death,
their faces uncovered, seem to possess an
attraction for the curious which is almost
without parallel.

Among the thousands who have viewed
the bodies are many who have known the
Daltons for many years, and while their
crimes deserve to place them beyond the
pale of sympathy, here and there are to be
found people who can scarce repress a sigh
of regret for the dead men. The stairway
leading to the room in which Emmet Dalton lies is at all times surrounded by a
dense crowd of men and women, who do
their utmost to persuade the guard to let
them pass up the stairway to the presence of
the wounded man. All sorts of reasons are
advanced by these people for their requests,
but, with few exceptions, they are not com-
plied with.

Through the courtesy of Sheriff Callahan

■ "Death's Hold-Up: Dalton Boys
Secure in the Embrace of the Grim
Highwayman" is the headline for the
Minneapolis Journal issue of Thursday
evening, October 6, 1892.

■ "Homelier than ever" is how Wild
Bill Hickok described himself in 1858.
This photograph shows him in his prime.

WILD BILL AND OTHERS

"Wild Bill" Hickok led a colorful life as a gunfighter and was a favorite of the newspapers. He was sheriff of Abilene, Texas, where he was usually found at his poker table in the town's wildest saloon, the Alamo. In 1876, he was shot in the back while playing poker in a saloon in Deadwood, Dakota. In this handwritten letter, signed "James Butler Hickok," he writes to his sister on April 22, 1858, from Monticello, Kansas, the day after being elected a town constable:

■ Hickok's letter to his sister of April 22, 1858, urged, "wright to me often."

If I yoused you bad some times when I was angry you must forget it . . . you did not think that I was in earnest when I spoak of marrying did you[?] . . . I was only joking[.] I could not get a wife if was to try. . . . I am homelier than ever now days and you no that the wiman don't Love homly men. . . . Waner was here the other day and I sent a letter home by him[.] [H]im and myself drank some Lager together. . . . [Y]ou ought to see me fishing on my Clame[.] I Can ketch any kind of fish that I was to.

I have fed my fish till they are all tame[.] [T]he girls Comes to my Clame a fishing some times and that I don't like[.] [B]ut I Cant help my self[.] [T]his is a free country[.] [E]vry one dze as he pleases.

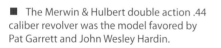

■ The Merwin & Hulbert double action .44 caliber revolver was the model favored by Pat Garrett and John Wesley Hardin.

■ This marshall's badge of the era is the type that Hickok would have worn.

➤ Agents of W., F. & Co. will *not* post this circular, but place them in the hands of your local and county officers, and reliable citizens in your region. Officers and citizens receiving them are respectfully requested to preserve them for future reference.

Agents WILL PRESERVE a copy on file in their office.

$800.00 Reward!
ARREST STAGE ROBBER!

1.

On the 3d of August, 1877, the stage from Fort Ross to Russian River was stopped by one man, who took from the Express box about $300, coin, and a check for $305.52, on Grangers' Bank of San Francisco, in favor of Fisk Bros. The Mail was also robbed. On one of the Way Bills left with the box the Robber wrote as follows:—

"I've labored long and hard for bread—
For honor and for riches—
But on my corns too long you've trod,
You fine haired sons of bitches.
BLACK BART, the P o 8.

Driver, give my respects to our friend, the other driver; but I really had a notion to hang my old disguise hat on his weather eye." (*fac simile.*)

Respectfully B. B.

It is believed that he went to the Town of Guerneville about daylight next morning.

2.

About one year after above robbery, July 25th, 1878, the Stage from Quincy to Oroville was stopped by one man, and W., F. & Co's box robbed of $379, coin, one Diamond Ring, (said to be worth $200) one Silver Watch, valued at $25. The Mail was also robbed. In the box, when found next day, was the following, (*fac simile*):—

*here I lay me down to sleep
to wait the coming morrow
perhaps success perhaps defeat
and everlasting sorrow
I've labored long and hard for bread
for honor and for riches
But on my corns too long yove tred
You fine haired sons of bitches
let come what will I'll try it on
My condition can't be worse
and if there's money in that Box
Tis munny in my purse
Black Bart
the Po 8*

■ Black Bart, the polite stagecoach bandit who left poems signed "Black Bart," was traced through a laundry mark on a dropped handkerchief.

water, are being cleared out for use. The present drouth is unprecedented.

Three Cow-Boys Bite the Dust.

SAN FRANCISCO, October 27.—A Tombstone dispatch says four cow-boys—Ike and Billy Clanton and Frank and Tom McLowery—have been parading the town for several days, drinking heavily and making themselves generally obnoxious. The city marshal arrested Ike Clanton. Soon after his release the four met the marshal and his brothers. The marshal ordered them to give up their weapons, when a fight commenced. About thirty shots were fired rapidly. Both the McLowery boys were killed. Billy Clanton was mortally wounded, dying soon after. Ike was slightly wounded in the shoulder. The officers were, with one slight exception, unhurt.

■ "Three Cow-Boys Bite the Dust" gives an account of the gunfight at the OK Corral as reported in San Francisco on October 27, 1881.

■ The gentlemanly bandit Black Bart.

■ This subpoena was signed by Wyatt Earp as constable and is dated June 25, 1870.

■ John Wesley Hardin was an outlaw known to have killed at least 44 men before a sheriff shot him dead in 1895.

■ Bat Masterson was a legendary gunfighter and sheriff of Dodge City. His signature, "W.B. Masterson," is shown here on a document that originated in Dodge City in 1885.

■ Roy Bean was a justice of the peace and saloonkeeper who styled himself the "law west of the Pecos." This affidavit for warrant of arrest was signed in Val Verde county, Texas, on October 15, 1887.

THE SENSATIONAL WESTERN LIFE DRAMA
JESSE JAMES
THE MISSOURI OUTLAW.

JESSE JAMES

EDITH FORREST

■ Jesse James's exploits were fodder for popular entertainment, including multiple movies.

■ Popularizers of outlaws and gunfighters, dime novels bore little relationship to reality.

CHAPTER 18

COWBOYS

No area of Western history represents as many American dreams and has been as romanticized as the cowboy. Owen Wister's novel *The Virginian*, first published in 1902, played a major part in creating this image, as did dime novels, Wild West shows, and, of course, cowboy movies and television shows. The sense of freedom, independence, and excitement was undoubtedly as real among cowboys of the 19th century as it is for the cowboys of today. It was extremely hard work, but it was an adventure in the expanses of the West, capped off with celebrating in the cattle towns at the end of long cattle drives.

$30	Monthly pay of a cowboy
$40	Price of a steer delivered to Chicago,1871
322,000	Number of Texas Longhorns driven north on cattle drives to Kansas
5,500,000	Number of cattle delivered to railheads, 1867–1885
5,000,000	Number of Longhorns in Texas
23,000,000	Number of cattle in the West in 1873

■ The cowboy's equipment: Colt single action .45 caliber Frontier six shooter, woolly chaps, bullwhip, lariat, saddle, knives, branding irons, and Winchester rifles.

■ An exceptionally fine pair of spurs.

FOR THE
COLLECTOR
AND HISTORIAN

Cowboy memorabilia is very popular with collectors; 19th-century artifacts are rare, but early 20th-century material can be easily collected.

■ The personal travel case of "Nellie," apparently a saloon entertainer, contains a crucifix—and a small pistol.

■ Cowboy and artist Charles M. Russell writes to announce that he's sending a horse, steer, and longhorn. "If you don't like the hackamore [bridle]," he writes, "take it of[f]. Im no fancy straw man."

HANDS UP!

■ *Hands Up!* appeared in Charles M. Russell's *Studies of Western Life,* 1890, the first of Russell's many books on the West.

The cattle business began in Texas in the 1860s. After the Civil War, demand for beef by the Northeastern states increased dramatically, and the advance of the railroads to trail heads like Kansas City, Abilene, and Dodge City made the transport of cattle to the east possible. The great era of the cowboys began to decline by the mid-1880s. The invention of barbed wire in 1874 meant the beginning of the end of the open range, the extension of the railroads ended the long cattle drives, and finally a devastating winter in 1886 and 1887 killed vast numbers of cattle, as well as ranchers and cowboys. It had become inefficient to have large herds, and ranches did not rebuild after the blizzards. The 25-year heyday of the cowboys still lives on 115 years later, however, in popular entertainment and people's minds.

Leonard Suett was a cowboy on the BQ Ranch in Iowa, and in June 1883 he wrote to his mother:

Will Mackey our cook and I have built a bed in the top of two little elm trees about 8 ft. above the ground. I have stretched my canvas over it to protect it from sun and rain. . . . I just returned today from a "side camp" on the western edge of our range where there is no fence [and] two men stay there and ride twice a day along the exposed side to keep the cattle in. This camp is about 10 miles from here. I spent two days and three nights there. The first day I rode "the line" with the men, the second our ranger was rounded up, and men from all the neighboring ranches came here to cut out their strays. It was quite an event. I spent the day in helping drive the cattle together and holding the bunches, while the strays were "cut out". . . . There are about 4000 cattle on this ranch and when all together they make a very imposing sight. Tomorrow I am going to take a span of mules and wagon and move the side-camp to a little spring we have just discovered (it is about three miles from where the camp is now located) as the water is not good where the camp now is.

One of the iconic images of the cowboy is *The Broncho Buster* by Frederic Remington, the artist's first bronze and his most popular. This example was cast during his lifetime (1861–1909) and is number 78. Michael Greenbaum in *Icons of the West: Frederic Remington's Sculpture* notes,

It was the rugged frontier character who possessed an "unearthly wildness," yet a "distinct moral fiber," that Remington depicted in his first bronze subject, *The Broncho Buster.* Copyrighted October 1, 1895, the twenty-four-inch statuette of a cowboy "breaking in a wild horse" was the first western action bronze of its kind, a frozen moment of nineteenth-century peril and drama. Remington supplied his poignant "wild rider" with a whip, sharp spurs and an air of confidence.

When completed *The Broncho Buster* was a technical triumph. The Henry-Bonnard Bronze Co. of New York produced the fine, smooth castings and the work was an immediate success with the public—a quintessential western image. *Harper's Weekly*, the magazine that regularly published Remington's illustrations and stories, ran a photograph and a favorable review on October 19, 1895. "Remington has stampeded, as it were, to . . . greater possibilities," wrote Arthur Hoeber. "He has struck his gait." *The Broncho Buster* quickly propelled the artist toward fame and the cowboy to the status of folk hero. The *New York*

■ *The Broncho Buster,* by Frederic Remington.

■ Winchester model 94 caliber 30/30 saddle ring carbine.

Times printed the following: "In point of fact, however, it is an initial effort, and certainly shows genuine taste and talent in that direction. Mr. Remington has long been known as a popular illustrator, whose work in the publications of the day has put him well in the front rank of the men who draw in pen and ink, and in this peculiar field he has been almost without a rival. Now that he has started in another direction, and begun so promisingly, his career will be remarked with still greater interest and subsequent work of this kind will be watched eagerly."

■ Artist Frederic Remington wrote this letter to his publisher in 1892: "I sent some little sketches for the 'Model' article and today ship another—on 'Camping Out' with some sketches. I will do you one more article before I go."

■ Frederic Remington's *Pony Tracks*, published in 1895, was his first book with a substantial text; it recounts his adventures in the West, often with the United States Cavalry.

CHAPTER 19

THE INDIAN WARS

The Indian Wars is a period of time that is difficult to define because the European settlers were at war with the Indians in one way or another virtually as soon as they arrived on the Atlantic shores. If the Indians didn't cooperate, in the settlers' eyes it was the Indians who were at fault. They were seen as barbarians. The tensions caused by two hundred years of the Indians' being seen as savages who needed to be "saved" by Christian missionaries finally came to a head when there was no place left to drive the Indians, and open warfare began in the West.

This was in 1854 in Wyoming, and the inciting event became known as the Grattan Massacre. In 1862, the Homestead Act fueled settlement and created more Indian problems. The Fetterman Massacre in 1866 was perhaps more a result of the arrogance of army officers than a result of Indian planning. Civil War veterans like Captain William Fetterman were looking for something to use their military talents on, and the Indians in the West were the most convenient target.

The following year, the Federal Peace commission found that most violence was caused by whites, not Indians, but despite the implementation of the commission's recommendations (closing various forts and closing the Bozeman Trail), before long the tide of settlement—or in the case of the Black Hills in South Dakota, the discovery of gold in 1875 and 1867—pushed the Indians off lands just "given" them by the government. In South Dakota this resulted in the Sioux War and the Custer Massacre.

A settler in Fort Stanton, New Mexico, C. L. Spring, writing to his sister in 1867 expressed the views of most, if not virtually all, settlers:

> Indians are very quiet. . . . [N]ot but I expect they will start out on their stealing expeditions this fall and winter. They are the greatest set of thieves you ever saw. These are the Apachae Indians. At fort summer there is 7000 Navayoe Indians which the Government are a trying to civilize. You would like to see some of the articles that the Squaw make such as dresses blankets

Wollen. They sell Blankets for 100 dollars. I intend to get some of the their things if I can. We captured, a wild squaw and her pappous this Summer in the Mountains, Killed her Husband. Well this is all about Indians.

FOR THE COLLECTOR AND HISTORIAN

This chapter of history is of interest to many collectors, reflecting, in part, the general interest in the plight of the Indians. Signatures of Geronimo and Sitting Bull occasionally come on the market at significant prices; forgeries are a serious consideration. Letters of army officers, except for General George Custer, are not very expensive. Unless associated with a major figure, guns and other artifacts are neither expensive nor hard to find.

■ This photograph of the famous chief Geronimo bears his drawn signature in pencil.

■ This circa-1886 photograph by C.S. Fly shows Geronimo and Apache chief Natches (in hat) mounted; at Geronimo's side stands his son. The photograph was taken in Tombstone, Arizona Territory.

■ "Scene in Geronimo's camp, the Apache outlaw and murderer" was photographed circa 1886 in Tombstone, Arizona Territory.

■ At the council between Geronimo and General Crook, depicted here, Geronimo agreed to surrender but fled that same night; as a result, Crook was replaced by Nelson Miles. The photograph was taken by C.S. Fly in Tombstone, Arizona Territory, circa 1886.

■ In another 1886 Fly photograph from Geronimo's Tombstone camp, the "Captive White Boy Santiago McKinn" is shown.

■ This "true Photo and Autograph of 'Sitting Bull,' the Sioux Chief at the Custer Massacre," was taken in 1882.

TATON KAIYOTONKA, *Sitting Bull*

The above is a true Photo and Autograph of "Sitting Bull," the Sioux Chief at the Custer Massacre.

Copyrighted, 1882, by Bailey, Dix & Mead.

Sitting Bull

■ George A. Custer signed this document while serving in the Civil War; it is dated July 10, 1863.

■ This Plains rifle by Joseph Golcher belonged to Sitting Bull. It has a .42 caliber, 36-inch octagonal barrel, as sold to the U.S. Cartridge Company Collection. The auction catalog entry states, "This rifle was purchased of a trader, who traded a breech loading rifle for it with Sitting Bull." It was loaned to the Smithsonian in 1906 and returned to the company in 1931. It was sold at auction in 1942.

■ This Winchester model 1876 was used by Indians, who wrapped the barrel with rawhide to keep the gun from losing parts, which were very difficult to obtain.

■ Winchester 1873 carbine featuring Indian tacks and decoration.

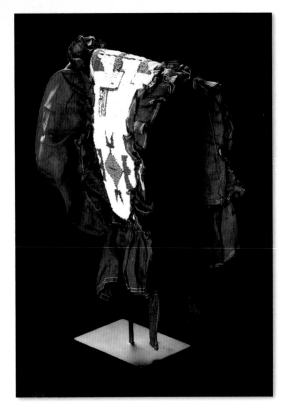

■ This Sioux woman's bonnet from the late 19th century features beadwork incorporating an American flag.

■ The Winchester 1873 saddle ring carbine, .44 caliber.

■ Medal awarded by the U.S. Army for service in the Indian wars.

■ The Remington New Model Army revolver .44 caliber saw extensive use in the Civil War and as a percussion revolver until 1872.

■ Beaded pouch autographed by Geronimo in ink.

■ The Smith & Wesson no. 3 "American" revolver incorporated several innovations, but army field tests in 1871 found it too complex for army use.

■ The Colt 1860 Army revolver with the First Model Richards Conversion. In 1870 this invention simplified converting the percussion revolver to the new .44 cartridges. In late 1871, 1,200 were issued to cavalry units.

■ Chief Joseph of the Nez Perce tribe was photographed by Edward Curtis in 1908. This photogravure was included in Curtis's monumental work, *The North American Indian Portfolio,* published between 1907 and 1930. In 1877, Chief Joseph led a long and dramatic struggle after the Nez Perce were driven from their homeland. Chief Joseph almost made it to Canada but was forced into surrender by United States troops. His surrender statement was as eloquent as his situation was tragic—and as the federal government's policy was disgraceful: "Our chiefs are killed. . . . The old men are all dead. . . . It is cold and we have no blankets, no food. . . . Hear me, my chiefs. I am tired; my heart is sick and sad. From where the sun now stands, I will fight no more forever."

■ Portrait of a "Zuni governor" taken by Curtis in 1908.

CHAPTER 20

THE KLONDIKE AND ALASKA: THE LAST FRONTIERS

The Last Frontier—Alaska's self-description—is most appropriate. Up until 1986, Alaska still had homesteading, offering 160 acres free to anyone who made the farming improvements and built a dwelling. In 1967, I drove to Alaska from Boston through the Yukon, and there could not have been a better time capsule of the American West. It was all there: people everywhere (excluding Fairbanks and Anchorage) were homesteaders and lived off the land—hunting, fishing, farming, trapping, and even sluicing for gold. It was as far west as you could go in pursuing the American Dream.

1896	Gold is discovered in the Klondike in the Yukon.
1897	40,000 people are in the Klondike.
1 ton	Weight of supplies, half food, required by Canadian authorities to enter the Yukon.
390 tons	Amount of gold taken out of the Klondike between 1896 and 1904.
-81 degrees Fahrenheit	Coldest temperature recorded in the Yukon.
30/30/30 rule	At -30 degrees with a 30 mile-an-hour wind, flesh freezes solid in 30 seconds.

■ John Heid was an early miner and attorney. He wrote his sister from Juneau in 1887: "The ships were loaded with excursionists & emigrants to Alaska. There must be at least 50 white women now in Juneau. The town is growing very rapidly and many are making money." The above photograph was with his letters.

The Yukon gold rush started when gold was discovered outside of Dawson City on the Yukon River in 1896. It was a second chance to strike it rich for everybody who had missed the California gold rush—but getting there was far more difficult than people realized, and the winters were unimaginably harsh.

The pictures of gold seekers carrying their loads up Chilkoot Pass in the Yukon cannot convey the difficulty of the route from the seaport of Skagway, Alaska, to Lake Bennett, where boats were built from available materials to head down the Yukon River to the Klondike. Even in 1967, when I hiked this route, equipment discarded by these dreamers was everywhere. The Oregon Trail was like this in the 1860s. I'm glad I had the chance to experience the Chilkoot Trail before the artifacts and the trail were absorbed by nature.

One early gold seeker was Archie Hoover, who left his home in Payola, Kansas, in the spring of 1898 to head for the Klondike gold fields. His diaries are very detailed and give a good sense of how the people providing supplies for those pursuing the dream of gold were very successful. His initial description of Skagway suggests he was somewhat overwhelmed by the number of restaurants, saloons, and bakeries. There was no shortage of businesses to supply those headed to the Klondike. He had an early indication in the spring of 1898, as the hordes from the south began to arrive in the Yukon, that it was already late in the game. He writes, "Skagway is very quiet now, the rush seems to be about over. It will start up again though as soon as the ice gets off the harbor."

Hoover and his companions camped just outside the town and then began to explore the road to White Pass. The original trail had deteriorated to the point that it was unusable, but there was an alternative: "This road is a new wagon road built by Brackett. The old trail is impassable now and Brackett Road is the only practical one from Skagway so he has a monopoly and charges cent and a half per pound toll accordingly. . . . We are dickering with a man named McConnell to haul our outfit to the snowline, from there we will sled it to Lake Bennet, if possible, if not we will pack it over."

On May 2, McConnell carted 900 pounds up the pass while Hoover and his partner carried packs of 60 to 75 pounds each. Along the trail they "noticed a bright rosy-cheeked boy." Hoover continues, "In coming closer I was surprised to find the boy was a girl. This was the first specimen of the emancipated Klondike Miss that I had seen."

Despite hiring a cart to move the bulk of their supplies, they had a very difficult time getting over the pass. "I was awfully tired and thought I had never passed a worse day but it was until the next one. We were about ten hours in making eleven miles"—and this was before they hit the snowline.

FOR THE
COLLECTOR
AND HISTORIAN

There has been very little collector interest in this area, and when series of letters or diaries come on the market they are inexpensive. Guidebooks for gold seekers are particularly inexpensive.

■ The *Klondike Nugget* was a "pioneer newspaper," providing news to the many prospectors who had come to the region in search of gold or a new start.

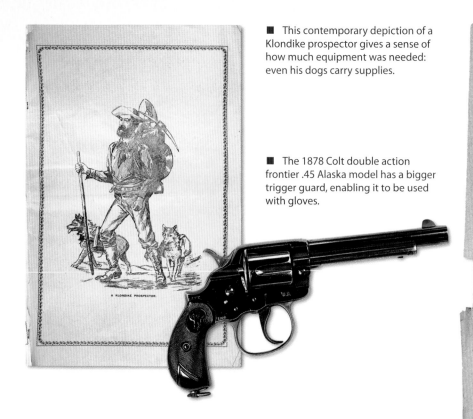

■ This contemporary depiction of a Klondike prospector gives a sense of how much equipment was needed: even his dogs carry supplies.

■ The 1878 Colt double action frontier .45 Alaska model has a bigger trigger guard, enabling it to be used with gloves.

■ The first issue of the *Klondike Gazoot*, the Dawson City, Yukon, newspaper, was published on April 2, 1897.

The melting snow caused them to sink into the thawing ground. Hoover describes a scene of chaos as new shiploads of gold seekers continued to start on the trail to go over White Pass. But Hoover and the other gold seekers had to go on.

The *Official Guide to Klondike Country and Gold Fields of Alaska*, published in 1897, provides a vivid picture of then-current events in the Klondike.

"Klondike or bust!" This country has been seized with the gold fever. . . . Men and even women talk of little else. In nearly every city parties are being organized to invade the Klondike district. Experienced miners who have spent years in Alaska advised them that the road would be set with hardships . . . but this friendly counsel has no effect stemming the rush. . . . Corroborative evidence of the richness of the new fields was received in Seattle in the shape of two million dollars worth of gold dust and now the cry . . . is raised in all parts of the land. There is nothing like the site of gold to insight a desire for possession of it.

A paragraph entitled "Richest the World Has Known" states, "Today the eyes of the world have turned toward our frozen acquisition in the north for within its borders has been discovered an El Dorado . . . [a] gold bearing district . . . richer . . . than any the world has know with the possible exception of California."

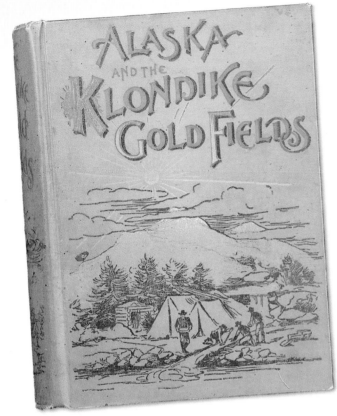

■ Robert Service, the most famous author of the Klondike, writes in this 1938 letter (right) about the origin of one of his most famous poems, "The Cremation of Sam McGee," and reminisces about the Klondike: "I was always a lone wolf in the Yukon and made few friends. . . . I still think of these great guys who made the Yukon what it was, even if it was tough."

■ *Alaska and the Klondike Gold Fields* was a standard guide, published in 1897, containing material on the history of the Klondike gold fields; routes and modes of transportation used to reach them; life in Dawson City; resources of Alaska; and how to find gold.

Subsequent sections include "Poor Man's Mines" and "Tender Feet Are Winners." The latter notes that "the big strikes were made by tender feet. . . . [F]ortune seemed to smile on the inexperienced men who went into the mining districts late last year as nearly all of them were the most fortunate. . . . Single individuals have taken out in two and a half months gold to the value of over $150,000."

The next section, entitled "Made a Thousand Dollars a Day," is followed by "Big Wages for Laborers," which declares, "If a man is strong healthy and wants to work he can find employment at good wages. Several men worked on an interest . . . and during the winter realized from $5,000–$10,000 each." The guide continues with additional sections that include "Has All the Gold He Wants."

■ Three prospectors from Quebec stand in front of their cabin, which bears a "Welcome to Camp Montauban" sign.

CHAPTER 21
THE WEST OF THE 20TH CENTURY

The turn of the 20th century saw the West being romanticized in magazines, in books, and particularly in Buffalo Bill's Wild West Show and Congress of Rough Riders. The American dreams of preceding generations became the fantasy dreams of the 20th century. The art of Charles M. Russell and Frederick Remington did much to preserve the image of the cowboy in the popular imagination, while Edward Curtis spent most of his life preserving the images of the Indians and their way of life in photographs. In *Taos Pueblo*, Ansel Adams's first book of photographs, Adams established the style that he would use for decades in portraying the West.

Edward Curtis began his monumental survey of Native American life in 1907. It was funded by the financier J. Pierpont Morgan and enthusiastically supported by President Theodore Roosevelt. Today, Curtis is widely recognized and admired for these striking early photographic images. *The North American Indian Portfolio* is remarkable for its melding of aesthetic considerations and ethnographic information.

Popular entertainment, including movies and television, created a very unrealistic view of the West until recently, when films such as *McCabe and Mrs. Miller* and, more recently, *Unforgiven* attempted to show what life in the West was really like: hard, sometimes dangerous and sometimes exciting, but always offering the opportunity for the pursuit of the American Dream.

■ *The North American Indian Portfolio* includes "Canon de Chelley," by Edward Curtis, as well as the following four portraits.

FOR THE
COLLECTOR
AND HISTORIAN

Photographs by Edward Curtis are frequently available, and prices reflect their importance and quality. Original works by Remington and Russell are very expensive. Letters by Buffalo Bill Cody, frequently about the running of his Wild West Show, are somewhat common, but pieces bearing the autograph of Annie Oakley are rare.

■ "Wolf—Apsaroke."

■ "Medicine Crow—Apsaroke."

■ "Horse Capture—Atsina."

"White Shield—Arikara."

■ Buffalo Bill (William F. Cody) was the greatest showman to bring the highly romanticized West to the rest of the world.

Classic Hollywood movies like *Stagecoach* (starring a young John Wayne) and *Santa Fe Trail* (costarring a young Ronald Reagan) contributed to the romanticized image of the old West.

The sharpshooter Annie Oakley was the most popular member of Buffalo Bill's Wild West Show.

A cowboy hat from the Hollywood film premiere of the Civil War Western *Virginia City*, signed by many members of the cast and attendees of the premiere, including Errol Flynn, Alan Hale, Ronald Reagan, Fred Astaire, and Mary Astor.

AFTERWORD

WESTERN HISTORY AND MY PURSUIT OF THE AMERICAN DREAM

My fascination with the American West has a very simple origin. The Boston neighborhood where I grew up was a cramped and confining place of two- and three-family houses, tiny yards, and a suffocating Irish-Catholic atmosphere. My family spent summers north of the city in a lakeside cabin without plumbing or electricity—and I loved every minute of my life there.

This was during the late 1940s, when movies and radio shows, and eventually television programs, abounded with stories about the American West. My vision of the West during those early years must have been highly romanticized, but that image didn't last long. I'd soon read enough history to realize that the West of Roy Rogers, Gene Autry, and Hopalong Cassidy was a fantasy world with no relation to reality except for the scenery. In fact, it wasn't this fantasy world that captured and held my attention, but rather the beauty and openness of the landscape and, most important, the dream of freedom and opportunity that inspired me with a sense of adventure not unlike the spirit of the first pioneers. While I never longed to be a cowboy or a gunfighter, I did yearn to escape from my neighborhood to the wide-open spaces of the West, where a man could be whatever he could do. I always liked Thoreau's words—"Eastward I go only by force, but westward I go free."

In 1961 I drove through the West, camping out along the way, but my first direct encounter with the "real" West—the untamed frontier that so intrigued me—was in 1967, when I drove to Alaska and the Yukon. During a month-long stay on a homestead in Northern British Columbia, I met a pair of true modern-day pioneers and observed the challenges they faced. Morley and Grace Clark lived a self-sufficient and very tough life. Morley hunted, fished, farmed, raised horses, and in the winter set trap lines and traveled by dogsled. His wife cooked, scrubbed, and laid up provisions without any of the conveniences we take for granted. My acquaintance with them was as close as I could come to a firsthand experience of the 19th-century American West.

I continued my pursuit of the West on subsequent summer vacations, exploring the Oregon Trail and then the Santa Fe Trail. My western travels reached a pinnacle when Steve Ambrose and I, my wife, and twelve other friends hiked, canoed, rode on horseback, and drove across Montana. Our journey followed the route forged by Lewis and Clark and included readings of the explorers' journal notations on the topography, the weather, the flora and fauna, and other details of the spots where we stopped along the way. It was the ultimate Lewis and Clark experience.

The steps in my Western journey seemed to evolve naturally, as my reflections on past trips inspired new adventures. I once spent a week exploring the original railroad tunnels in Donner Pass. When I shared my recollections of this trip with Steve Ambrose during a conversation about a book he was planning on the transcontinental railroad, we decided to find a way to travel over the Sierra Nevadas from Sacramento to Reno in a diesel locomotive. Much of our route was identical to the original one carved from the mountains with pickaxes and explosives by Chinese immigrants in the 1860s. As we drove the locomotive up to the Donner Pass, each of us took a turn as the engineer—but coming down the mountain was another matter. For that, we had to turn the controls over to a Union Pacific engineer.

The Sierra Nevada trip, in turn, gave rise to the railroad trip of a lifetime. Steve, his wife Moira, and I traveled from Council Bluffs, Iowa, to Cheyenne, Wyoming, in the private railway car of 19th-century railway magnate Edward Harriman. From Cheyenne, where two Union Pacific steam locomotives were brought out, we continued along the original route to Sacramento. To ride in the cab of a steam locomotive with one foot on the platform and the other on the tender (full of oil rather than wood, as it once would have been) and to watch the unfolding of a landscape almost unchanged since the building of the railroad was incredible. As I imagined the first transcontinental railway passengers looking out their window at these same prairies and mountains on their way to new lives and opportunities on the American frontier, I felt intimately connected to their ventures into the West. It was out of this experience that was born the idea of a book that would tell the story of the Old West through the words and artifacts of the explorers, travelers, and settlers who followed their dreams there.

All the illustrations and quotations in this book are taken from the collection of letters, diaries, books, and artifacts I've collected over the course of 55 years. In addition to books that inspired these pioneers to go west and letters about their dreams, plans, and experiences, I've collected examples of the things they used, both in their everyday lives and for special purposes, to provide a close-up glimpse of their world through their own eyes. These remnants of the past express—as no historian can—the realities, anxieties, and above all the hope of a new life that the West represented not only to the people who actually went there, but also to those who were sustained by fantasizing about escaping to the frontier.

Acquiring my collection has provided me with over a half-century of adventure, as well as a continual source of pleasure and inspiration. I hope this book enables you to share my adventures.

ABOUT THE AUTHOR

Kenneth W. Rendell has been a dealer since 1959 in historical letters and documents dating from the Renaissance to the present time. His business, with offices in Boston and a gallery in New York City, encompasses politics, the law, art, literature, music, science, the military, and other areas. He has authored the standard reference books in the field, including *History Comes to Life*.

Forgeries and journalistic hoaxes are among Rendell's many interests. He debunked the infamous "Hitler diaries" on behalf of *Newsweek Magazine* in 1983, and then headed the investigation for *Stern Magazine* into how the hoax had been perpetrated. For Time Warner he proved the diary of Jack the Ripper was a hoax, and he has been involved in every major forgery case in recent decades. He is the author of *Forging History*, the standard reference on the subject.

As an expert witness Rendell has offered his testimony in criminal trials including that of the Mormon "white salamander" murders. He received the Justice Department's Distinguished Service Award for his work leading to convictions for thefts from the National Archives and the Library of Congress.

Rendell is the founder and director of the Museum of World War II, which has been described as having no equal. His best-selling book *World War II: Saving the Reality* has won praise from historians and the American public.

The foundation for the present book is Rendell's extensive collection of Western American memorabilia. The *New York Times* has said that Rendell's collection "succeeds in giving a sense of the struggle to tame the gorgeous wilderness that stretched beyond the tidy civilizations of the east. . . . It's worth spending time with."